W9-AHK-754

Raising Money Smart
Kids

Raising Money Smart Kids

WHAT THEY NEED TO KNOW ABOUT MONEY —AND HOW TO TELL THEM

Janet Bodnar

Deputy Editor, *Kiplinger's Personal Finance*

KAPLAN) PUBLISHING

This publication is designed to provide accurate and authoritative information in regard to the subject matter covered. It is sold with the understanding that the publisher is not engaged in rendering legal, accounting, or other professional service. If legal advice or other expert assistance is required, the services of a competent professional person should be sought.

President, Dearborn Publishing: Roy Lipner
Vice President and Publisher: Cynthia A. Zigmund
Senior Acquisitions Editor: Mary B. Good
Cover Design: Design Solutions
Typesetting: the dotted i

© 2005 by Janet Bodnar

Published by Kaplan Publishing,
a division of Kaplan, Inc.

All rights reserved. The text of this publication, or any part thereof, may not be reproduced in any manner whatsoever without written permission from the publisher.

Printed in the United States of America

07 08   10 9 8 7 6 5 4

Library of Congress Cataloging-in-Publication Data

Bodnar, Janet, 1949-
    Raising money smart kids : what they need to know about money—and how to tell them / Janet Bodnar.
        p.   cm.
    Rev. ed. of: Dollars & sense for kids. ©1999.
    Includes index.
    ISBN 1-4195-0516-5 (7.25x9 pbk.)
    1. Children—Finance, Personal.   2. Saving and investment.   3. Finance, Personal.
I. Title.
HG179.B5669 2005
332.024′0083—dc22

                                                                        2005005376

Kaplan Publishing books are available at special quantity discounts to use for sales promotions, employee premiums, or educational purposes. Please call our Special Sales Department to order or for more information at 800-621-9621, ext. 4444, e-mail kaplanpubsales@kaplan.com, or write to Kaplan Publishing, 30 South Wacker Drive, Suite 2500, Chicago, IL 60606-7481.

Praise for *Raising Money Smart Kids*

"Janet Bodnar writes with the experience of a financial advisor and the common sense of a mom, offering advice—not edicts—that any family can use. *Raising Money Smart Kids* is a must-read for all parents and a good bet for teachers, youth workers, grandparents, and anyone with young people in their lives."

> Laura Levine, Executive Director, Jump$tart Coalition for Personal Financial Literacy

"If parents follow Janet Bodnar's advice, they won't just be *Raising Money Smart Kids,* they'll become money smart adults themselves! I can't imagine a parent who wouldn't benefit from *Raising Money Smart Kids.* This book is the financial version of Dr. Spock!"

> Suzanne Boas, President, Consumer Credit Counseling Service of Greater Atlanta

"If you have a child, and you know that at some point that child is going to ask, beg, or whine for you to buy something, then you need to read *Raising Money Smart Kids.* Being a money smart parent means learning the tools and, yes, the tricks of raising financially responsible children. This book will help you do just that."

> Michelle Singletary, Nationally Syndicated Columnist, *Washington Post*

"Janet Bodnar has created the best resource for parents trying to raise kids with the ability to cope financially and succeed in our society. A previous generation trusted Dr. Spock. Today's parents need Janet Bodnar!"

> Terry Savage, Nationally Syndicated Columnist, *Chicago Sun-Times,* and Author, *The Savage Truth on Money*

"Janet Bodnar has given us an awesome roadmap and directions to help our children, and ourselves, navigate the winding road to personal financial security. From adolescence to young adulthood and beyond, she provides families with a strong foundation to learn and practice the skills necessary for earning, spending, saving, and investing."

> Don Blandin, President and CEO, Investor Protection Trust

"Janet Bodnar has uncommonly good common sense and dispenses it in a way that both parents and kids can easily understand. Her book could help any parent raise kids with healthy money habits."

Kathy Kristof, Nationally Syndicated Columnist,
Los Angeles Times

"When Janet Bodnar offers advice, take it! *Raising Money Smart Kids* is great if you want to help your child become an adult who understands the real value of money. Janet's commonsense tips can help you sort it all out. *Raising Money Smart Kids* is the book both parent and child will use as a resource for years to come. Take my advice—get it!"

Andrea Roane, News Anchor, WUSA-TV, Washington, D.C.

"Janet Bodnar writes in a way that any parent can easily understand. Through anecdotes, quizzes, and real-life scenarios from her column, Janet provides invaluable teaching tools. She succeeds in making parents feel at ease talking to their children about money."

Dara Duguay, Director, Citigroup Office of Financial Education

"Janet Bodnar has done it again. *Raising Money Smart Kids* is the best book ever written on helping parents navigate touchy financial issues with their children. A must-read for every parent."

Olivia Mellan, Psychotherapist Specializing in Money Conflicts and Author, *Your Money Style*

"In an age when young people rarely see cash transactions, *Raising Money Smart Kids* fills the void by providing concrete and realistic suggestions parents and teachers can use to nurture sound financial habits."

Ronni K. Cohen, Executive Director, Delaware Financial Literacy Institute and Delaware Money School

"Janet Bodnar has once again delivered useful tools to help teach children of all ages that being money smart will be a key ingredient of future success."

Daniel Hebert, President, New Hampshire Jump$tart Coalition

Acknowledgments

When I first started writing about children and money more than a dozen years ago, I knew a fair amount about money, but I was still learning about kids. Since then, my children have taught me a lot, and in this book they have pride of place.

First and foremost then, I'd like to thank John, Claire, and Peter, my long-suffering money smart kids, for giving me the best financial advice and letting me share it with the world.

I'd also like to thank:

- My husband, John, for cooking me dinner
- My mother, Renie Bodnar, and my sister, Priscilla Jackman, for always getting me over the rough spots
- Cindy Greene, for tracking down the facts with good humor and good grace
- All the family members, friends, coworkers, casual acquaintances, and Money Smart Kids correspondents, whose anecdotes enliven these pages

Contents

In all of history, no children have had more money of their own, have had more pressure to spend it, and have needed more guidance on how to do it than the kids of America in the early years of the 21st century.

"Today, more than ever, children must learn about money, for it is both a source of confusion and an indispensable tool they must learn to use." Those words made a lot of sense back in 1950, in a *Kiplinger's* magazine article entitled "Will Your Child Know the Value of a Dollar?" And they're even truer today.

Decades ago, it was a lot easier to raise children as responsible money managers. When young people worked for pay, they typically contributed most of their earnings to the family kitty to help make ends meet. Consumer credit was not widely available, so people saved up for major purchases. Before TV, kids could covet only what they saw at their friends' homes or in a magazine.

Today, money is more abstract—plastic credit cards, electronic transfers, cash spewing from an ATM slot. Many teens work not to help support their family or save for college but purely to fund their own discretionary purchases. Some develop an appetite for clothes, entertainment, and consumer goods that they will have difficulty affording when, as young householders, they will have to pay for their own rent, food, car, insurance, and other basics of life.

The challenge for parents today is to teach restraint and responsibility in a society that doesn't put much value on those traits. This new book, Janet Bodnar's *Raising Money Smart Kids*, can be a big help.

As the mother of three, Janet has lots of experience in handling real-life money issues. She began offering kids-and-money advice in 1992 in the pages of *Kiplinger's Personal Finance* magazine, of which she is deputy editor. There followed a bestselling book, a Web column (http://www.kiplinger.com) syndicated by The New York Times Syndicate, and countless appearances on national TV and radio programs. In a few short years, Janet has become the Dr. Spock of money smart childrearing.

Her new book offers astute, practical advice for parents of children ranging in age from preschool through college and beyond: Advice on allowances and family chores. Advice on teen employment. Ideas on how kids can get started as savvy savers and stock market investors. Tips, too, on how parents and grandparents should make gifts to their young ones.

In all of this good counsel, one theme keeps recurring: the importance of communication. Effective parents include the kids in discussions and solicit their ideas, even though the parents make the final decision. And they try to set a good example in their own money management, because children learn more from our deeds than our words.

If all goes well, your kids will grow up with a healthy attitude toward money and the ability to manage it. They will become fulfilled, competent, and financially secure young adults. And they won't land back on your doorstep after you thought the nest was empty.

Knight A. Kiplinger
Editor, *The Kiplinger Letters*
Editor in Chief, *Kiplinger's Personal Finance*

Test Your Money Smarts

Warm up your parental reflexes with these 20 kids-and-money situations—common experiences, at least in principle, for most parents. Once you've identified your level of parental agility and authority, read on; you'll find plenty of my strategies and ideas for teaching your kids the value of a dollar. Remember, raising money smart kids starts with you.

1. Your 7-year-old daughter loses the $5 she got for her birthday from her Aunt Mary. You:

a. ask Aunt Mary to send another $5.

b. tell your child she should have put the money in the bank.

c. let her do chores to make up the $5.

d. tell your child she should have been more careful.

2. Your 14-year-old son has been saving half of his allowance and money earned from neighborhood jobs. Now he wants to use the money to buy an expensive iPod. You:

a. allow him to buy it.

b. offer him your old turntable instead.

c. tell him there's no way he can touch his savings.

d. buy it for him as a birthday gift.

3. Your daughter has mowed your lawn since she was 12. Now 14, she wants to make money by mowing neighbors' lawns. She also wants to be paid to do your lawn. You:

a. say, "Okay, and go ahead and use our mower and gas."

b. hire a neighbor's kid to do your lawn.

c. tell her to forget it because mowing your lawn is her job.

d. say, "Use our mower and pay for the gas you use. We'll pay you half of what you charge neighbors."

4. You usually pay $50 for your son's sneakers. Now he wants a pair of $150 NBA specials. You:

a. chip in the $50 and let your child come up with the balance.

b. say, "I'll buy a $50 pair, or you can still wear your old ones."

c. buy them, because "everyone else has them."

d. buy yourself a pair too (everyone else has them!).

5. Your 15-year-old daughter gets an allowance for which she is expected to help out around the house. She has ceased to help. You:

a. hire a neighbor's kid to help clean the house.

b. stop the allowance altogether.

c. continue to pay until the child turns 18.

d. tie the allowance to financial responsibilities and make chores a separate issue.

6. You're trying to teach your 16-year-old about the stock market. She invests her own money in a stock you selected. It loses money. You:

a. make up the loss.

b. hire a neighbor's kid to make future stock picks.

c. say, "That's how the market works. Too bad."

d. share the loss with her, and help her figure out what to do with the remaining stock.

7. Your son is getting his driver's license, which means that your insurance will go up. You:

a. sell your car and buy bicycles for the entire family.

b. pay the increased premium—he is part of the family after all.

c. make him get a job and split the increase.

d. pay the increase but make him pay for his own gas.

8. You finally allow your daughter to shop for her own school clothes. She comes home with the ugliest wardrobe you ever saw. You:

a. let her keep the clothes but have a discussion about buying clothes that suit her and will last.

b. grin and bear it, because at least she likes the clothes—and bought them on sale!

c. say, "I knew I couldn't trust you with that much money."

d. make her return the clothes—with you in tow.

9. Your 10-year-old took on a paper route to earn money but is getting lazy. He's in danger of getting fired. You:

a. hire the neighbor's kid to help him out.

b. tell him to do the job right or not at all.

c. pick up the slack by getting up early to help him deliver papers and collect fees.

d. warn him that he's likely to lose his job and income, and then allow him to do so.

10. You're standing in a toy store, and your son is insisting that he needs a $60 video game. You:

a. fork over the cash to avoid a scene.

b. fork over the cash, but tell him next time he'll have to pay part of the bill.

c. don't fork over the cash and otherwise proceed as in step b.

d. proceed as in c, and suggest that he try the game over at the neighbor's to see if he really likes it before he buys it.

11. After telling your children that they absolutely, positively cannot have a new video game system, their doting Auntie Mame arrives and presents them with one. You:

a. tell Auntie Mame that the kids can't accept the gift.

b. grit your teeth and accept the gift.

c. sit down and start playing.

d. thank Auntie Mame for the gift, and at a later date ask her to consult with you before purchasing expensive gifts for the kids.

12. Your daughter receives a $20 birthday check in the mail from her grandparents. You:

a. let her spend it as she wants—it's a gift.

b. deposit the check in the bank for your daughter.

c. tell your daughter to save $5 and let her spend the rest.

d. call Grandma and tell her $20 doesn't buy much nowadays.

13. You bought your 16-year-old a car on the condition that he not leave the school grounds during lunch hour. He does, and totals the car. You:

a. tell him to get his bicycle tuned up.

b. ground him for a month and limit him to using the family car at your discretion, provided he pays for his gas.

c. buy him another car.

d. would never be in this predicament, because you'd never buy a 16-year-old a car in the first place.

14. Your son is on his way out the door for a date when he casually asks for $20. You:

a. tell him you didn't know he had a date, and ask him where he's going.

b. give it to him plus an extra $10 for gas.

c. tell him that date and gas money come out of his allowance, as previously agreed.

d. give him $10 for gas.

15. It's your preschooler's birthday, and he gets so many presents from family members that he quickly gets bored and toddles off to play. You:

a. give the remaining gifts to the neighbor's kid.

b. put the gifts away to open another time.

c. proceed as in b, and determine that you will set up a college fund for your child and ask relatives for contributions in lieu of gifts.

d. open the rest of the presents yourself.

16. Your 17-year-old works three nights a week and weekends, and his grades have dropped significantly. You:

a. hire the neighbor's kid to do the homework.

b. make him quit the job.

c. don't do anything; he's almost an adult, and his grades are his responsibility.

d. tell him to pull up the grades and consider cutting back on hours or face quitting altogether.

17. Your 5-year-old wants everything in sight when you go to the supermarket. He begins to make a scene when you say no. You:

a. wear ear plugs and let him scream his little lungs out.

b. leave him home from now on.

c. buy him what he wants.

d. let him choose one item.

18. Your son is heading for college in the fall and will need spending money. You:

a. tell him that if he stays in his room and studies, he won't need spending money.

b. agree to send a weekly allowance.

c. tell him to get a summer job.

d. discuss his needs, see what he has available from jobs and savings, and agree to supplement that with an appropriate allowance.

19. Your 22-year-old son quit his first post-college job and has moved home "temporarily." You:

a. agree on a combination of chores and a contribution to household expenses, and mutually set the date by which he will move out on his own.

b. tell him that he's an adult now and has one week to get his act together and leave.

c. give up your home office temporarily so he can have his room back.

d. ask him to do some chores around the house.

20. Your kids, 6 and 8 years old, ask you what would happen if you died: Where would they live, who would take care of them? You:

a. tell them you aren't going to die and there's no need to discuss it.

b. ask them if they would like to live with Uncle Eddie (as your will currently specifies).

c. tell them that they would probably go to live with Uncle Eddie and his family (but you don't have a will and haven't discussed it with Uncle Eddie).

d. proceed as in b, and take the opportunity to write a letter to Uncle Eddie outlining how you would like the kids raised in your absence.

Answer Key
Add up the point values of your answers to get a sense of where you stand.

1. a. 0, **b.** 1, **c.** 2, **d.** 3   **11. a.** 1, **b.** 2, **c.** 0, **d.** 3
2. a. 3, **b.** 0, **c.** 2, **d.** 1   **12. a.** 3, **b.** 1, **c.** 2, **d.** 0
3. a. 2, **b.** 0, **c.** 1, **d.** 3   **13. a.** 1, **b.** 2, **c.** 0, **d.** 3
4. a. 3, **b.** 2, **c.** 0, **d.** 0   **14. a.** 1, **b.** 0, **c.** 3, **d.** 0
5. a. 0, **b.** 0, **c.** 0, **d.** 3   **15. a.** 0, **b.** 2, **c.** 3, **d.** 1
6. a. 1, **b.** 0, **c.** 3, **d.** 2   **16. a.** 0, **b.** 2, **c.** 0, **d.** 3
7. a. 0, **b.** 1, **c.** 2, **d.** 3   **17. a.** 2, **b.** 1, **c.** 0, **d.** 3
8. a. 3, **b.** 2, **c.** 0, **d.** 1   **18. a.** 0, **b.** 1, **c.** 2, **d.** 3
9. a. 0, **b.** 2, **c.** 1, **d.** 3   **19. a.** 3, **b.** 0, **c.** 1, **d.** 2
10. a. 0, **b.** 1, **c.** 2, **d.** 3   **20. a.** 0, **b.** 2, **c.** 1, **d.** 3

SUMMARY

0–10 Either you should adopt the neighbor's kid or you just like taking tests.

11–29 Keep this up and your kids will still be living at home when they're 30.

30–49 You're on the right track, but you're not there yet.

50–60 You and your kids are well on the way to being money smart. This book will help you fine-tune your approach.

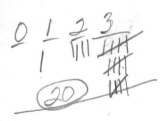

The Perils of Being an Expert

One morning, a few years ago, I left a note at my son John's place at the breakfast table reminding him to write thank-you cards for his birthday gifts.

I left the note in February. His birthday was in November.

Although John's younger brother and sister, whose birthdays are also in the fall, had faithfully written their notes, John's had somehow been neglected in the holiday hustle. But because I've gone on record about the importance of kids' sending acknowledgments when they receive gifts, I was determined that John would get his out, even if it was three months after the fact.

I have been dispensing advice on how to teach kids the value, and the values, of money for more than a decade. What started as a humorous, but helpful, story in *Kiplinger's Personal Finance* magazine has taken on a life of its own. In addition to my regular "Money Smart Kids" column in *Kiplinger's,* I write a weekly column on kids and money that appears at http://www.kiplinger.com, and is syndicated nationally by The New York Times Syndicate. And I've written four previous books on the subject of children's finances.

But the trouble with advising other parents on how to raise money smart kids is that I feel a responsibility to do the same for my own three children. And a heavy burden it is. People often assume I have a magic system for calculating just the right amount of allowance (I don't), or that my own kids never spend a penny (they do).

Actually, I tell people that all the advice I give has been used successfully by some parent—though not necessarily by me. Writing about children and money has made me more conscious of the subject, but, like any family, we've had our successes and failures.

One of those successes occurred when my son Peter, then 9 years old, had to wrestle with the moral challenge of "finders keepers." One day Peter spotted a $20 bill in the street near the curb. While he waited for traffic to pass so he could pick up the money, a woman jumped out of a car and grabbed the bill. "Is this yours?" she asked. "No," he replied. She pocketed the money and sped away.

At an amusement park a week or so later, Peter walked onto a ride and found $23 on the floor. "Is this yours?" he asked the child who had just vacated the spot. "Sure," said the kid, and pocketed the cash.

Several rides later, Peter clambered into a bumper car—and found $4 on the seat. With no obvious owner in sight, he turned the money in to the ride operator—only to be hooted down by his cousins, who speculated on how the operator would spend his windfall.

"Losing" $47 within a week would be a blow to any 9-year-old with millionaire aspirations. But though his shoulders were slumped, I told Peter he could hold his head high because his honesty was unsullied and his pride intact. To make the point, I gave him a $4 reward—and his shoulders snapped squarely back into place.

Another of our family's success stories is our $50 sneaker rule. I've never paid more than $50 toward a pair of sneakers. If the kids want something more expensive, they make up the difference.

As a result, they have rarely paid more than $70 or $80 for a pair of shoes—not cheap, granted, but not extravagant by today's standards. And they don't turn up their noses at buying last year's styles on sale.

To avoid the grocery store "gimmies" when my children were preschoolers, I told them they could choose one treat, and one treat only, on our shopping expeditions. Even as they got older, the kids always played by the rule. Sometimes they found it tough to choose between a soft drink and a package of cookies (they fervently hoped I'd give in and let them get both). But I have never had to deal with a tantrum in the candy aisle.

Getting Organized

On the other hand, one of my most glaring failures was my total inability to remember to give my kids their weekly allowance on time. I always ended up handing over two or three weeks' worth at once, which was a pain in the neck for us to keep track of. Also, the kids could go for years without getting a raise because I would forget to give them one. When John headed off to high school, with all the new expenses that entailed, it seemed an appropriate time to rethink our system.

After considering the alternatives, I decided to go with a kit called ParentBanc. The kit provided children with their own checkbook, in which they could credit deposits (allowance, gifts, earnings) and then write checks when they wanted to make withdrawals (payable by Mom or Dad). It was the kids' job to keep the check register up-to-date. (I bought the kits at a toy store, but you can create a similar system on your own with leftover checks and a ledger.). I liked the idea behind ParentBanc because it relieved me of having to remember to fork over money each week. Because my children were a little older when I started the system (15, 13, and 9), I felt I could get away with crediting an allowance monthly rather than weekly, and I wanted the children to learn how to write a check and balance a checkbook. I started by limiting the account to

---

DEAR JANET

Q. Every week I take my daughter out for lunch at a restaurant. I limit how much she can spend, but sometimes I worry that I'm spoiling her.
A. I have a confession to make: When my three children attended the same grade school, I took them out to lunch every Friday. We picked a fast-food place, so the tab was usually reasonable. And if anyone was spoiled, I was, because I got to spend time with my kids.

We took our time eating and caught up on the week's news. When each child headed off to high school, he (and she) left our group and was missed. The kids' presence was worth more than the price of an Extra Value Meal.

Treating your children is part of the fun of being a parent. As long as your daughter doesn't expect to feast on filet mignon, don't feel guilty. Enjoy your time together, and bon appétit.

allowance only, but later I included gift money and earnings for convenience.

Once we decided on a system, the kids and I had to negotiate how much each of them would get and what their financial responsibilities would be. We had already agreed they were due for a raise. But how big a raise?

As a starting point, we used average allowances as reported by the Yankelovich Youth Monitor survey. At the time, the average for 14- and 15-year-olds was roughly $9 per week, and I thought that made sense for John.

But my daughter Claire balked at the $7 figure for kids her age. Because there's only a two-year age difference between her and her big brother, they had always gotten the same allowance and had similar expenses. We compromised on $8.

The average for 9-year-olds was about $4 a week. Peter immediately protested that he was making less than half as much as his older brother and wanted to know if he would have to pay for less than half as much stuff. We compromised on $4.50.

With this significant increase in their income came a significant increase in their financial responsibilities. I spent several days writing down a list of expenses appropriate for kids their age: for example, movie tickets (and popcorn), rounds of miniature golf, after-school snacks, and extra caps and goggles during the swim season (they belonged to a swim team). The older two would have to buy birthday gifts for their friends, as well as tickets to school football games and dances. If they ran short of cash, they could always earn additional money by doing extra chores.

I didn't require them to give a certain percentage to charity, but I strongly recommended they contribute to church every Sunday. If they had money left in their account at the end of the month, I agreed to pay interest.

determine how much & what it pays for

What We Had Wrought

It only took a month or so for our new system to yield results—though not necessarily the ones I had expected. My kids became amazingly, incredibly cheap. Perhaps because they could see their account balances shrinking before their very eyes, they became reluctant to spend money.

They used to beg to go to the 7-Eleven after school for a soft drink; now that the drinks were on their dime, they decided they weren't so thirsty. Movies on Friday night? There just didn't seem to be anything they wanted to see.

All of the children had money left at the end of the month, so I credited the promised interest.

John spent more than half of his 36-dollar allowance, an amount that seemed in line with his expenses as a high school freshman. Claire spent a smaller percentage of her money but ended up buying more holiday gifts for friends, so it evened out.

And Peter, usually the first to part with his cash, carefully parceled out money he had received for his birthday so he could put off tapping his account.

Six months into the system, John had figured out how to use it to his advantage. Even when he needed cash at the end of a month, he held off on writing a check until after the interest had been credited.

After depleting her account buying holiday gifts, Claire slowly built it back up again by taking on babysitting gigs and carefully managing her cash. She hated to spend money (both hers and mine) on herself and was willing to wait patiently until her birthday or Christmas to get something she wanted.

Peter, meanwhile, needed help with both writing checks and balancing the account. If he weren't a typical younger sibling, always wanting to imitate his older brother and sister, I probably would have kept him on a weekly cash allowance (which he would have preferred).

We continued the system throughout the children's high school years. The kids' friends sometimes thought it a little weird when our kids whipped out their checkbooks to get cash before heading to the movies or the mall, but our children never complained when they dutifully made the subtractions in their check registers. I asked the kids to give me a little notice before they wrote a check so I could have cash on hand, and I tried to keep small bills—ones, fives, and tens—in my wallet.

As for my own faulty memory—I still forgot to credit the children's allowance on the first of the month. They teased me, but my memory lapses weren't so big a bone of contention because the kids usually didn't run out of money. And I always had a written record of when I last paid them.

As John and Claire got older, they took on the task of catching up on the bookkeeping when I fell into arrears. When they headed off to college, I wrote each of them a real check for the balance in their accounts, and we closed out the system. Peter is still in high school, and his account remains open—with a balance of $249.54 as I write this.

New Challenges

One of my biggest challenges was making spur-of-the moment decisions about who should pay for what—and how much.

For example, when John got his driver's license, should he pay for part of the $1,600 a year he added to our insurance bill?

Did it qualify as a "family movie night"—with admissions paid by Mom and Dad—if Mom went but not Dad?

Should we pay for John to go on a training trip with his high school swim team over winter break or require him to use his own money?

Some decisions were easy. For instance, because the school trip was an optional extracurricular activity, John paid for it out of his summer earnings. We decided that both parents would have to be present for an official family movie night (but I treated when I dragged my kids along to a show I wanted to see).

We didn't require John to pay for car insurance because he didn't have a regular paying job. But he did pay for his own gasoline (and parking tickets) and took his turn driving his younger siblings in the family car pool.

I always advise parents to take stock of their children, no matter what their ages, and picture them going off to college and managing a semester's worth of money on their own. If you think they'll be able to handle it when the time comes, you're on the right track. If the prospect gives you cold chills, some financial first aid is in order. Despite my own family's rough spots and false starts, our college-age kids don't overdraw their checking accounts, and they don't have credit-card debt. In my book, that is a pretty good definition of a money smart kid.

By the way, John eventually got around to sending those thank-you notes.

A Game Plan for Parents

So what does all this mean for you? It means you should take heart. Even in this age of consuming passion, you can still teach your kids to be savvy shoppers, supersavers, and cautious users of credit. Parents have power. They just need to find a successful strategy and the time to use it.

Of course, what works for you won't necessarily work for your neighbor. Your family values and financial circumstances, as well as the personality traits of your children, may be quite different. But there is a common theme in how you should teach your kids about money: Be candid, be consistent, and use your own good common sense.

Beyond those general guidelines, this book can help you fill in the particulars. Within it you'll find suggested solutions to the problems that plague parents: how to cure a case of the gimmies, set up a workable allowance plan, and cultivate the savings habit. And you will see how you can do it with a minimum of time and effort—for example, by turning everyday encounters with cash machines into minilessons on money management.

You'll also find guidance for helping your children cope with the economy at large by holding down a job or starting a business of their own. You'll hear from the people who study kids and money, as well as the real experts out there in the trenches—parents and children themselves. You'll find answers to financial questions of interest to kids—when they must pay taxes, how to set up an investment account, how babysitting money can be turned into a retirement fund. As frazzled parents, you're likely to feel overwhelmed by the task of turning your children into financial whiz kids. But the job is a lot more manageable if you forget about raising a future Peter Lynch, Sam Walton, or Bill Gates. Instead, focus on your top priority, whether it's encouraging your kids to give to charity or standing firm on not buying what everyone else has. You're the parent; that's your job. You're in charge, and if you set the tone in even one area, it will echo throughout your child's life.

That's often difficult to remember nowadays, when changing mores and increasing affluence undermine parents' confidence and weaken their willpower. It's easier to buy kids the stuff they want—and buy into the consumer culture as well.

I don't pretend to have all the answers. The advice dispensed here can't create more money in households where there's simply not enough. The prescribed strat-

DEAR JANET

Q. I was just reading one of your articles and am inquiring about your background. As a teenager, did you amass a fortune in the stock market? Did you take the initiative to go to a local broker and use your savings to invest? What experience did you have as a teen that makes you qualified to dispense information about and for teens of today?

A. Hmm, I sense a challenge here, but I'm happy to take you up on it. As a teenager, I did not amass a fortune and use my savings to invest. In fact, I didn't know what a stockbroker was, and I had no savings to speak of.

It's the experience I've had since I was a teenager, both as a financial writer and a parent, that I think qualifies me to dispense information for teens of today and their parents. I know how to steer people in the right direction and give them choices so they can make their own decisions.

Teens of today are still teens. They may hate to admit it, but they need all kinds of guidance from parents—not just in learning the financial facts of life but in using that knowledge as part of a value system. And parents are looking for advice on how to get their kids off on the right foot financially. I'm happy to do what I can to give everyone a push in the right direction.

egies won't work unless parents are willing to talk with each other and with their children. And some problems are beyond the scope of this book. If you suspect that a child is using his allowance to buy drugs, for example, how much of an allowance to give is the least of your worries. Cut off all funds and get professional help.

But after fielding hundreds of questions from parents in my columns and speaking to dozens of parent groups, I know what's on parents' minds when it comes to teaching kids financial values. And I've collected dozens of valuable strategies that have worked successfully for families (even mine!). Feel free to choose the ones that make sense for you. In this book, my aim is to offer reasonable solutions in a readable form that real people will find useful—and even entertaining.

Why You Need a Snappy Comeback

Sprinkled throughout each chapter in this book you'll find a selection of questions from both parents and youngsters. Over the years I've learned that when it comes to money, kids ask the darnedest things. Parents on the receiving end find their children's queries:

- **Exasperating:** "Mom, can I have that?"
- **Amusing:** "How much will I get from the tooth fairy?"
- **Puzzling:** "Why is a nickel bigger than a dime?"
- **Awkward:** "How much money do you make?"
- **Embarrassing:** "How come you two are always fighting about money?"

It's from family discussions about subjects like these that children will learn their most lasting lessons about the value—and the values—of money.

Unfortunately, kids and their questions can't be scripted. On the contrary, you can count on their catching you off guard, when you're least prepared to answer. Ill at ease or in a hurry, we've all given our children the bum's rush at one time or another, with an abbreviated, even abrupt, response—usually along the lines of "Yes," "No," or "Maybe."

Yes, No, Maybe

In the "yes" group are parents who take the path of least resistance—or maybe they just like to spend money. "Since she's been born, I've hardly bought myself anything. I'd rather spend on her," one parent told *Forbes* magazine in an article titled "Babies As Dolls" about the booming market for infant clothing and equipment. Said another parent, "My kids have tons of stuff, but if they want something, I just don't know how to say no." And these kids are barely old enough to ask a question. Imagine the scene when they really turn up the heat at age 8 or 13—or 21 or 35.

At the other extreme are parents who respond with a knee-jerk "no" that's commendable but ineffective. Their strong stand is undermined by a shaky foundation, because they don't bother to explain why they're denying whatever it is their kids want.

In the vast middle—and we've all been there—are the wafflers, who, when put on the spot, respond with a resounding "maybe" in any of its forms: "We'll see." "I don't know." "Go ask your mother/father." "Do you think I'm made of money?" For lack of a great comeback, we take refuge in the flip response, the old cliché, the evasive answer—anything to avoid the question. And we miss a golden opportunity to teach a minilesson in money values. Besides, kids are people too, and they deserve to have their questions taken seriously and answered thoughtfully.

So at the end of many chapters you'll find questions that, in one form or another, your kids are bound to ask you at some time. For each question, I'll offer you a response that will get you out of a jam, fill a void, smooth over an awkward moment, satisfy your children's curiosity, and leave them with something to think about so they're less likely to bring up the subject again.

Postscript

After writing a "Money Smart Kids" column about my trials, errors, successes, and failures with my own children, I received the following response from a reader whose experiences were heartwarming, humorous—and oh, so typical:

"I really got a chuckle (or two or three) out of your column. Like you, I have a $50 limit on what I will pay for a pair of sneakers. I have had it for years and find that it works like a charm. Both my children (9 and 12 years old) know the rule: If they really want it, they have to pony up the difference. So far they have never had to pay because they have always chosen to stay within the limit.

"I, too, have a terrible time remembering to give my children their allowance. I tried paying them a 'late penalty' as a way of helping me remember to pay, but it never worked. I could never remember what the penalty was, and the concept seemed lost on them.

"Worse, there are times when I'm not certain that I have paid their allowances, only to have them insist I did not. At these times, they attack my memory ('Mom, you know you always forget things'). If I can't reconstruct in detail when, where, or how I paid them, I usually end up anteing up again.

"I like your checkbook idea—the allowance is either written down and therefore paid or not—and I will broach it with my children. They like to count their money—something about the smell, touch, etc.—so I'm not sure how receptive they will be.

"Thanks for a great column. I look forward to reading it."

A Kid's Eye View of Money

With all the other demands on your time, teaching your children about money has all the allure of cleaning out the basement: You know you should do it, but you just keep putting it off.

And time isn't the only factor. Money is one of the last great taboos; nowadays, parents may find it easier to talk to their kids about sex and drugs than to tell them how much money they make. To complicate things even further, money matters can't always be reduced to a "common cents" discussion. Within a family, parents can wield money as a weapon, flaunt it as a symbol of power, or use it as a stand-in for love. And looking at how you manage money can reveal things about your own personality that you'd rather not face. If you're an unreformed shopaholic, for example, you may feel understandably ambivalent about urging your teens to stay within a clothing budget. And so, like the basement, you leave it for another day.

Even if you're willing to take on the task, you face the same problems you do when trying to discuss sex: How much do your kids already know? Not nearly as much as they should, according to a slew of studies that measure the financial savvy of young people. In a recent test of high school seniors conducted by the Jump$tart Coalition for Personal Financial Literacy (a group of government, educational, and financial organizations), the average score was 52.3 percent—less than a passing grade.

Other studies show that kids are particularly weak when it comes to understanding investing, saving for the future—including college—and credit. In a survey by Northwestern Mutual on how parents teach their children about money, less than 40 percent of parents said they discuss credit cards and loans with their kids. Parents, by the way, were also understandably reluctant to discuss individual family finances because "children have no business knowing this." In this book, you'll find easy—and nonthreatening—ways to address all these topics and many more. But for now, let me give you an insight into a kid's eye view of personal finance.

I Take a Field Trip

As part of my own field research, I once spent a day having a wide-ranging discussion with a group of middle school students. We talked about how they spend money and how they save; what they want to be when they grow up and how much they think they'll earn; which commercials they like and whether they actually buy the products. My sample wasn't scientifically selected, but it did represent an ethnically and economically diverse group of kids in a major urban area. And early teens have certain advantages as subjects: They're old enough to know something about money but not so old that they think they know everything.

On most of the topics we chatted about (the stock market being the notable exception), the youngsters had a good grasp of basic money management skills—up to a point. For example, they knew enough to be wary of credit cards but were a little fuzzy about what evil fate would befall them if they neglected to pay their bill in full each month.

The good news for parents and educators is that it wouldn't take much to fill the gaps in kids' knowledge. For example, the children knew they would be paid interest on a savings account, but they had never heard of dividends paid to shareholders, so a few simple definitions would help. Using examples to illustrate how fast money grows or how long it takes to pay off debt will hold their interest longer than a lecture on the evils of borrowing or the virtues of thrift. Many youngsters admitted that they took buying cues from their peers but were open to a discussion on how to resist peer pressure.

But let's listen to the kids (with asides from me).

ON SPENDING. If there's anything kids like to spend money on, it's clothes—often expensive articles of clothing bearing names other than their own. Bridget said her glittery silver sneakers cost $95, "but if they were a bigger size they'd probably be $120."

The students were blunt about what clinches the sale. "Most people consider you cool if you wear the right clothes," said Safiya. Added Abdul, "I just buy what everybody else wears."

But it was encouraging to know that they didn't always feel obliged to go along with the crowd: "What you wear doesn't determine who you are," insisted Mia.

DEAR JANET

Q. I'll bet there are lots of parents who would like to teach their children how to manage money but are embarrassed to bring up the subject because they're not very good at managing money themselves. And what if kids ask questions we don't know how to answer?

A. Relax. Most of the questions your kids ask about money aren't going to be complicated. The subjects that come up most frequently with children involve everyday events: comparing prices at a store, asking for something they see on TV, negotiating an allowance, opening a savings account at a bank. All of these are topics you should be able to handle (especially after you read this book).

But let's suppose your kids do put you on the spot. Maybe you feel sheepish about encouraging them to save money because you don't have a regular savings program. And how can you warn them about the pitfalls of credit when you're charged to the max on all your cards?

Instead of ducking those issues, use your children's questions as an opportunity to get your own financial house in order. For example, if you join your employer's 401(k) or other retirement plan, you can honestly answer yes when your kids ask if you save money. If your credit card bills are out of control, see a credit counselor if necessary and come up with a plan for paying them off. And thank your children for helping you become a money smart parent.

So don't hesitate to sell your children on daring to be different. They'll be willing to listen (and buy cheaper clothes as a result). "I don't think you should spend $17 on a red T-shirt with someone's name on it when you can get a red shirt for $4 or $5," said Kendra.

If kids must look like everyone else, at least once in a while, there are less expensive ways to do it. "You can buy a designer sweater for $75 or a fake one for $10, and nobody can tell the difference if you cut out the tag," advised Ashley.

A sure way to help kids kick the brand-name habit is to make them kick in for their clothes. Would Bridget have bought a pair of $95 shoes if she had had to spend her own money? "No way (giggle)."

ON MARKETING. When it came to spending money, the kids showed healthy signs of growing into skeptical consumers, wary of being talked into buying things they didn't want or need.

Take commercials, for example. All of the children had a favorite, often because it made them laugh. But did it also persuade them to buy the product? Not necessarily. "I buy something because I like it," said Mia. "Sometimes I can't even remember what the commercial was selling."

A couple of children did admit having been victims of marketing ploys—but sometimes they were willing victims. For instance, John let himself be talked into paying 50¢ extra for a superlarge drink at the movies, only to find that "it wouldn't even fit in the drink holder."

So was it a bad deal, especially because he could have gotten free refills on a smaller drink? Maybe not, said John. "You'd have to leave the movie to get the refill, and you'd probably miss one of the good parts."

And Maureen thought that an extra 50¢ was a small price to pay: "You can never have too much soda at the movies," she reasoned.

ON CREDIT CARDS. None of the students had actually used a credit card, and they disagreed about whether they'd want to. Eric, for one, was reluctant: "I like to spend, so I'd probably max it out." Anna, on the other hand, was willing to take a chance because "I think I'm pretty good with money."

Although the kids had a general grasp of the perils of credit, they weren't quite clear on the fine points—for example, what happens if you don't pay your bill in full each month. "You have to take stuff back," said Eric. "They take your limit down a little," said Chris. "The repo man comes," said Abdul.

Only one of the children knew that you're charged interest on any unpaid balance, and none knew what that interest rate might be. The consensus guess: 10 to 15 percent.

ON BANKS. Nearly all of the youngsters had savings accounts, but they didn't always know what their balances were or how much interest they were being paid—or that banks would also charge interest (at a higher rate) if you took out a loan. And the only CDs they'd ever heard of were the ones that play music or computer games.

A few kids knew, at least in theory, how a checking account works. "You can't spend more money than you have in your account," said Allison, "and every time you write a check, you subtract it." But at their age, none of them had any real-life experience writing a check, and they didn't know what would happen if you overdrew your account.

When it comes to money, never assume that children will pick up even the most basic facts on their own. It's up to you to tell them exactly how much interest banks pay on a savings account, how much they charge for a loan, and how much you'll pay if you bounce a check. As kids get older, knowing that a bank CD pays a higher interest rate than a regular savings account should be music to their ears.

ON THE STOCK MARKET. When I asked the students what it means to own a share of stock, few would even hazard a guess. Andrea had the right idea, but an exaggerated order of magnitude: "If you buy a share of stock in McDonald's, you say to the company, 'If you earn a million dollars, I want to get at least one-third of that or one-half.'" None of the students could define the word *dividend*.

You wouldn't expect most youngsters this age to know much about the stock market—not because it's too complicated for them to understand, but because adults *think* it's too complicated and don't bother to discuss it. I've found that kids who do follow the market are an enthusiastic minority, often inheriting their interest from parents and grandparents. If you own stocks, don't sell your children (or grandchildren) short. Encourage them to pick a company or two and follow the stock price in the newspaper or online. Better yet, buy them shares of their own.

ON JOBS. Several of the children were already in the labor force, and a couple of them were *entrepreneurs* (a word that Eddie could even define). Stephen offered a pet-sitting service for his neighbors but was timid about setting a price for his services. "They just offer me money," he said.

Once they were old enough to get a part-time job, the kids guesstimated that they would earn anywhere from $3 to $8 an hour, but they weren't sure about taxes. "I don't think children would have to pay taxes like adults, because adults have to take on more responsibilities," said Andrea. (Working-age kids should know that the federal minimum wage is $5.15 an hour but that if they work ten hours, they won't actually take home $51.50. Sorry, Andrea, the IRS doesn't let kids off the hook.)

These children knew what they'd like to be when they grow up: lawyer, pediatrician, engineer. But they were a little shaky on how much they could earn: "$35,000 a case"; "I don't know"; "at least $1,000 a year."

They didn't think it fair that some athletes are paid more than others—"They play in the NBA, they play on the same team, they should all get the same amount of money," said Nick—or that athletes in general are paid more than teachers. But they had a glimmer of understanding about why that is: "Entertainment," said Andrea.

ON RELATIVES. When the kids want something that they can't afford and their parents won't spring for it, they have no qualms about appealing to other family members. Grandparents are considered a particularly soft touch.

"I'm into really baggy pants, but my dad doesn't like them because he says I look like a thug, even though I don't mean to," said Eric. "So I ask my grandparents, and they'll go out and buy them because grandparents spoil you to death."

Grandma, you've been warned.

Teaching Financial Literacy

Studies about kids and money consistently show that young people overwhelmingly depend on their parents as their primary source of financial information. Surveys also show that parents would like schools to help teach financial literacy.

So I was taken aback when two reporters working on a story about financial education in public schools called to tell me that a number of parents had expressed reservations about the idea. "I'm very leery of someone else coming in and teaching my children about that," said one mother. "It's kind of like sex education," said a dad. "It's a loaded gun." What did I think about those responses, the reporters wanted to know.

After I got over my initial surprise, I had to admit I could understand the parents' concern. Money *is* a loaded issue, and parents may question whether teachers will emphasize what they consider to be appropriate values.

But I could also reassure parents that they needn't worry. As I learned on my middle school field trip, kids have so many gaps in their knowledge that small lessons from both teachers and parents can yield a big payoff. And both schools and parents share an interest in teaching kids about deferred gratification, planning for the future, and responsible spending. Financial facts kids learn in school need to go hand in hand with a healthy attitude and open communication about financial matters at home.

For their part, schools have the advantage of being able to use a classroom situation to explain such concepts as compound interest or to play a computer-based stock market game. Any interactive tool scores points with kids. A friend of mine had great success teaching high school students about the cost of living by letting the kids compare how much they'd have to earn in different cities to maintain the same lifestyle (see the salary calculator at Homefair.com).

RESOURCES FOR TEACHERS (AND OTHERS)

Sometimes all you have to do to teach kids about finance is use your head. One teacher uses a 1986 vintage photo of herself sporting a pink Mohawk hairstyle to explain the time value of money to her high school classes. She shows students how much she could have earned had she invested the $84 a month it cost to maintain her "do."

There's no shortage of more traditional curriculum materials for students of all ages. The Jump$tart Coalition for Personal Financial Literacy maintains a clearinghouse of course materials at http://www.jumpstart.org.

After observing financial education classes over the years, I've learned that what successful classes have in common are teachers who get excited about money matters and have a knack for illuminating them. I once had the pleasure of watching ninth-grade English teacher Kathryn Robinson use Homer's *Odyssey* to teach her students at Chaffin Junior High in Fort Smith, Arkansas, a basic principle of economics: Meeting goals means making choices, and each choice has a cost.

In Virginia, teachers Susan Hynes and Amy Kelly took a routine civics unit on careers and turned it into "Budget Bash," a game of life for their eighth-grade students at Rachel Carson Middle School in Herndon. The kids used the Internet to research careers, buy a car, and get a mortgage. Their goals were to cover their virtual living expenses out of their salaries and save as much as possible during the month-long game.

Hynes and Kelly adapted an exercise called "The Real Game," substituting Virginia salaries and adding their own "chance" cards ("Spend $200 on a 25th anniversary gift"). Hynes's mother, an accountant, came in to talk about taxes, and one parent showed her daughter how to compute Virginia's car tax.

"Our biggest challenge was keeping the students realistic," Hynes told me. To squirrel away as much as they could, the kids did things they couldn't get away with in real life. For example, some eliminated long-distance phone service because "our parents will call us." To cut costs, one "married" couple deleted one of their children.

Although it wasn't possible to duplicate the real world exactly, the game gave students a big jump on other children—and even adults. They became whizzes at using online mortgage calculators and navigating sites to shop for cars and insurance. And some took away a lesson many people never learn: "We had to compromise on just about every decision."

Six Skills Kids Need to Know

Even though classrooms are the perfect setting for role-playing, parents have an edge when it comes to teaching their children real-life money management skills and focusing on their own family's values—whether that means investing in the stock market or giving to charity. Parents should take the lead in helping kids learn the six money management skills I think every child needs to know before leaving home:

1. **How to manage a cash allowance.** No school lecture and no computer program will teach kids how to set priorities and make spending decisions better than by having them get along on ten bucks a week.
2. **How to manage a checking account** (and an ATM or debit card). Every teenager should have an account

and know how to balance it—preferably as soon as he or she gets a part-time job. (Cosign or open a custodial account if your child is under 18, and the bank requires an adult signature.)

3. **How to save for a goal.** Nobody can be thrifty just because it's the virtuous thing to do. Kids need a reason not to spend, whether it's saving up to buy an action figure or a car. Consider matching all or part of what they put aside.

4. **How to figure the time value of money.** That's a fancy way of saying that small amounts saved when you're young will eventually grow into big piles of money. To show kids how rich they can be, let them plug numbers into a compounding calculator (like the one at Kiplinger.com/tools or the Saving Rocks page at OrangeKids.com).

5. **How to get out of debt (or not).** Instead of delivering a lecture, use this eye-opening example to illustrate the pitfalls of credit: Say you put $50 a month toward a $2,000 balance on a credit card that charges 18 percent interest. It will take you 62 months to pay off the balance—and cost you $1,077 in interest (use the calculators at Kiplinger.com/tools to try out different number combinations).

6. **How to compare prices.** Start with unit pricing at the grocery store and build up to Abercrombie versus Old Navy (which will help kids parcel out their clothing allowance).

And there's one more thing kids need to know that only Mom and Dad can teach: They won't get everything they ask for.

The Adman Cometh

Now you have a rough idea what your children know—or think they know—about money. And you're willing to take on the task of filling in the gaps in their knowledge because you know that what you don't teach them, their peers—and the media—will. And what an education it will be: that clothes make the woman and sneakers the man, that video games and cable TV are their birthright, that credit cards will satisfy every need and gratify every wish. They will learn, in short, that money really does grow on trees. So let's take a look at their financial reality—their income, their spending patterns, and the influence they have on how you spend your money.

Money Really Does Grow on Trees

You can't blame kids for buying into that myth when they're buying so much else these days. James McNeal, an expert on marketing to children, has estimated that by 2006 children between the ages of 4 and 12 will spend more than $50 billion a year. McNeal's studies show that parents are totally in charge of their kids' purchases only up to about age 3; after that, children are given choices—what kind of beverages to drink, ice cream to eat, toys to play with. At about age 2, many kids begin asking for things on their own, either because they've seen them in the store or on TV. From that point on, children are a recognized consumer force. By age 3½ kids are selecting the things they want and watching their parents buy them (typically cereal, toys, and snacks, in that order); by 5½ the kids are making the purchases (toys, snacks, and gifts for others), and the parents are watching. By age 8 children make independent (unassisted) purchases while shopping with their parents.

In one poll by KidzEyes.com, more than one-third of 6- to14-year-olds reported buying something for themselves once or twice a month. And income isn't a factor. Kids in households earning less than $35,000 a year and more than $100,000 are equally likely to be frequent shoppers, making purchases several times a week.

What do they buy? Snacks (including sweets and beverages) and toys top the list, with clothes gaining. Boys are more likely than girls to buy computer software or games, electronic equipment, and videos or DVDs. Girls shop for jeans, T-shirts, shoes, and music. Toys are more popular among kids in the younger half of that age group. Sadly (in my opinion), the older half—the so-called tween market—is outgrowing traditional kid things, such as toys and children's entertainment, at an earlier age. They're rushing (or being rushed) into teen interests, such as music and brand-name clothes.

For the most part, kids are doing all this consuming with their parents' blessing. Children are getting more money at a younger age than was the case in the past, and letting them make purchase decisions is seen as a way of teaching them to be self-reliant. That's also a big help to frazzled moms and dads, many of whom are single parents or part of a dual-earner household. So it's not surprising that in addition to the money children spend directly, they have an enormous impact on what their parents buy. McNeal estimates that children between the ages of 4 and 12 influence adult purchases to the tune of nearly $700 billion a year—a figure he believes is growing at a rate of 20 percent annually—in dozens of product categories, from food and clothing to sports and recreation equipment.

The more expensive the purchase and the more adult in nature, the less influence children have. But nowadays kids even have a say when it comes to buying cars. One mom I know said she and her husband sold their minivan after just two years because it didn't have two-zone air-conditioning and "the kids were miserable."

Teenagers are spending about $98 a week of their own and their parents' money, according to Teenage Research Unlimited in Northbrook, Illinois; that's $169 billion coming out of the pockets of 12- to 19-year-olds. Boys spend $59 of their own money and $29 in family money; for girls, the figures are $51 and $43. As they have for generations, teens are buying clothes, cosmetics, snack foods, and movie tickets. What's different today is that they're spending more on electronic gear and other big-ticket items. In addition, more than half of the girls and more than a third of the boys do some grocery shopping every week to help out those frazzled moms and dads.

An Advertiser's Dream

That kind of buying power is simply too tantalizing for advertisers to ignore, and increasingly they're bypassing parents and making their pitch directly to children. Retailers of all kinds are targeting kids directly year-round, not just at the holidays or back-to-school time. In particular, they have set their sights on Generation Y, today's 4- to 21-year-olds, who will eventually replace the baby boomers as the financial and cultural powerhouse generation.

In an effort to capture the brand loyalty of budding households, retailers are stretching the definition of school supplies to pitch sofas, chairs, and other housewares to college kids. At the younger end, some clothing chains are growing as fast as their prime customers—girls aged 7 to 14.

One study by Harris Interactive showed that youth marketers think it's okay to start advertising to children at age 7, even though they don't believe children are able to view advertising critically until age 9 (or make intelligent consumer choices until nearly age 12).

Among the marketers interviewed, 91 percent said young people are being marketed to in ways they don't even notice; 72 percent believe most companies put pressure on children to grow up faster than they should; 61 percent said advertising to children begins at too young an age; and 58 percent believe too much advertising is directed toward children.

"Kids enjoy new things and they aren't set in their ways, so they're an ideal target," said Irma Zandl, who heads the Zandl Group, a New York City research firm that studies the youth market.

Over the years, the list of products that have owed their success to children has been long and varied: string cheese and individually wrapped cheese slices; fruit snacks; Old Navy clothes; Sony PlayStation. After Jolly Rancher candy repositioned itself to appeal to the tween, or preteen, market (kids from about 9 to 12), it became a hit with an age group that craved its

---

TEN RULES TO LIVE BY TO TEACH YOUR KIDS FINANCIAL VALUES

1. Don't be afraid to talk about money with your children. They need to learn that money is simply a useful tool of everyday living, not something to be coveted, feared, hoarded, hidden, or ashamed of. It can't buy happiness, but it can create choices.

2. Don't indulge your kids. Love does not equal stuff.

3. Don't send mixed messages, delivering a lecture on the wastefulness of a new videogame system while treating yourself to a big-screen TV.

4. Don't be inconsistent. If you've made it a rule not to lend your kids money, don't waffle the first time they ask for a loan.

5. Don't quit before you start. Children will accept any rules you set and any system of managing money so long as you stick with it.

6. Don't fall back on platitudes. You can't expect your kids to "understand the value of a dollar" unless you teach them.

7. Don't brush off your children. If they ask you a money-related question, give them an answer that's honest and age appropriate.

8. Don't relive your childhood. Be realistic about how far a dollar will stretch nowadays.

9. Don't overload your kids with information. They don't really want to know how much money you make; they just want reassurance that you're doing okay.

10. Don't gripe too much about your job. You don't want to turn your children into cynics about the world of work.

superfruity flavor. Kids wield such clout that 1- to 3-year-olds are now a market segment. "It's staggering to see how brand aware 2-year-olds are," said one ad agency executive. "The marketer who gets there first and best gets there to stay."

Although adults might be health or price conscious, that kind of appeal won't work with children. Advertisers have to be careful not to offend parents, who are still, after all, the biggest spenders in the house and the ones who ultimately make most purchase decisions. But advertisers' main goal is to hit kids where they live: sports, music, and an overwhelming desire to be cool and fit in.

How Kids Trick Their Parents

If youngsters are tempted to consume conspicuously, indulging their wants as never before, advertising isn't totally to blame. Advertisers may be pulling children, but parents are pushing them simply by making so much money available and giving them so much leeway to spend it.

At a conference I attended on marketing to kids, one highlight was a panel discussion with mothers and their children. Marketing professionals in the audience were interested in how to get the kids to pay attention to their products yet still get past Mom, who remains the gatekeeper. As a parent and an adviser to parents on how to resist sales pressure from their kids, I found that my own loyalties were divided. When, for example, one woman complained that her son will eat only one kind of sandwich— Louis Rich plain oven-roasted turkey on white bread—and confessed that she no longer tries anything else, as a parent I had to agree it would be pointless to waste money on food that wouldn't be eaten.

But when a young man confided that his strategy for getting the things he wants is to trick his parents by promising to pay them back and then hope they forget about the debt, I wanted to stand up and shout, "That's why you should never advance your children money to buy something—or if you do, at least hang on to the item until they come across with the cash."

The kids candidly revealed other tricks: "I beg," said one forthright youngster. "I tell her I'm not going to move till I get it," said another. "I go to my Daddy," confessed a third.

And the moms admitted that those tactics often work: "Older kids have a lot more influence because they're louder and in my face more," said one. "I can spend twice as much money because of what my daughter sees on TV," said another. "I've lost control," admitted a third.

The parents were surprisingly willing to give their children a say in spending decisions that ranged from vacations to home decor. ("I'm glad my daughter is out of her green phase," said one mom.) But parents weren't pushovers, and they had their own strategies for negotiating with their kids: "When we disagree about a purchase, we have a cooling-off period and wait for a day." "I give them choices that I can live with." "I won't buy Lunchables."

Marketers attending the conference were as fascinated as I was by the interaction between generations as they peppered the panel with questions. "How do you decide which restaurants to eat at?" someone asked. "Mom makes us agree on one," answered one boy. "We rotate around," offered another youngster. But one ad agency executive stressed that marketers "have to take a responsible view of nurturing and protecting kids" even while selling to them.

Most heartening to me, however, were the results of an industry survey of what's on the minds of children 10 to 14. They were interested in making and saving money, but they also expressed old-fashioned concerns about family issues, such as wanting to get along better with their siblings and worrying about the health of their grandparents. And Mom and Dad are still the biggest heroes in their children's eyes.

After the parent-child panel, I asked the "no-Lunchables" lady how she makes her rule stick. "We just don't buy them," she said. And are her kids willing to go along with that? "If you put your foot down, they are. You just can't do it all the time. You have to pick your battles." That's worth shouting about.

Are Kids Savvy Shoppers?

Today's children may be sophisticated consumers, but they themselves confess to sometimes being naive and even gullible shoppers. *Zillions,* a lively consumer magazine for children that is no longer published, used to run a fascinating feature in which it asked a group of kids to recite their worst "buying blunders." In one issue, for example, Maggie said she had plunked down $20 for a board game that looked exciting in TV ads but turned out to be boring; Jonathan handed over big bucks for sneakers that didn't help him improve his basketball game; Becky bought a shirt at one store and later saw it at another store for half the price; Theresa bought a cheap squirt gun that broke the first time she used it.

But thanks to the efforts of the Jump$tart Coalition and lots of others in the financial literacy movement, the number of school-based and independent programs to teach children about money is growing. Look around the country, and you'll see that where kids are given the incentive and opportunity to learn, they're catching on quickly:

- **At Young Americans Bank in Denver,** whose customers are all younger than 22 and come from all 50 states, the average loan customer is 17 and has borrowed an average of $2,000 to buy something like a car or a musical instrument. Kids may not understand the term *annual percentage rate,* but somewhere along the line they've picked up the notion that it's a good idea to repay a loan. (For more on Young Americans Bank, see Chapter 9.)
- **In a class on economics,** fourth-graders in Wilmington, Delaware, rattle off such terms as *market clearing price, factors of production,* and *opportunity cost* as they

discuss marketing strategies for the new products they have cooked up: the "super-duper spaghetti scooper" and other gizmos for making it easier to eat spaghetti (see Chapter 11).

- **In a discussion about money with a third-grade class** in Maryland, kids want to talk about everything from collectibles to currency exchange rates to the Great Depression.
- **Despite their reputation as yuppie puppies,** school children around the country socked away more than $125 million in 25 years as part of Save for America, a reincarnation of the old school saving program (see Chapter 9).
- **Each year, teams of high school students** come to the Federal Reserve Board in Washington, D.C., to argue their case for which direction the Fed should take in setting monetary policy. Winners of the Fed Challenge receive thousands of dollars in scholarship money.

Marketing expert James McNeal has observed that most college students would be hard-pressed to figure out the unit price of a six-pack of beer. But he also maintains that, overall, children "manage to spend

---

DEAR JANET

Q. To keep my 7-year-old daughter from spending all her money every time she goes into a store, I gave her some advice that works for me. I told her that whenever she's deciding whether to buy something, she should say, "If in doubt, don't buy." Now when she goes to a store and looks at all the items she "really wants," she often walks out without buying anything. At first she was kind of disappointed, but then I pointed out that when she really wanted something, she'd have more money and no doubts.

A. There's no doubt parents and children can learn a lot from your experience. First, you had a sound money management tip. Second, you took the trouble to communicate it to your daughter. Third, she listened to you. Fourth, it worked. Fifth, you followed up, so the point will probably stick. Sixth, it didn't take a lot of time. Lots of similarly frustrated parents would have lectured, yelled, or thrown up their hands and watched their kids fritter away their money. You've shown there are simple yet effective alternatives.

and understand money and the marketplace system reasonably well." Even the kids in the *Zillions* article learned some valuable lessons: Maggie tries out a new board game at a friend's house before springing for it herself; Theresa took back her broken water pistol and got a refund; Becky looks around for bargains instead of buying something at the first place she shops; and Jonathan is practicing harder to improve his game. (Note: You can find an archive of past *Zillions* articles at http://www.zillions.org.)

A Different Kind of Peter Principle

My own optimism about children's ability to catch on is based on the counsel of my most trusted financial advisor: my youngest child, Peter. Mind you, he's not the most frugal kid. But you won't find a more reliable guide to what's on a youngster's mind when it comes to money.

As he has grown, I have always relied on him to test a financial game, review a book, or watch a video. Now as a teenager, he has his finger on the pulse of the teen market. When his eyes widen, I get a clear view of which ads and products capture a kid's fancy (he's even lobbying his father and me to buy a Nissan Altima when we replace our old Ford Taurus station wagon. "It's a sweet car," says he.)

But it is Peter's spontaneity that I have always valued most. Once, when he was younger and trying to decide which pair of sunglasses to buy, he looked at me and wailed, "You write books about this. Tell me what to do." On another occasion, he suddenly blurted out that when he makes his first million dollars, he couldn't possibly spend it all in one day. Tops on his wish list was a $300 baseball bat (to help him hit higher and farther), but he would also buy "a lot of stock in things that have gone down because they have to go up again."

After picking up one of the kids-and-money videos I periodically review and popping it into the

VCR, Peter pronounced it "pretty good" but noted a flaw or two: "They showed 17-year-olds who didn't know that you have to pay bills or that taxes are taken out of your paycheck. When you're 17, you should know that."

How Does It All Translate to Your Kids?

So faced with a marketing blitz, what are parents to do?

First off, recognize that we parents are part of the problem. How can we complain about marketing to kids when we rush out to clothe them in designer outfits—creating a generation of little "mini-mes"? How can we complain about pushing them to grow up too fast when we're hiring tutors to teach preschoolers to read or buying 2-year-olds television sets for their bedrooms? If we shower our kids with money and the freedom to spend it without limits or responsibilities, we're failing in our role as protectors of our children and becoming enablers.

An interesting survey by the Center for a New American Dream attempted to quantify what parents know from long-suffering experience: Children will nag as often as they can to get something they want. How often is that? Nine times, on average, according to the 12- to 17-year-olds surveyed. Kids aged 12 and 13 are a particularly pesky bunch; 11 percent admit asking their parents more than 50 times for products they've seen advertised.

Now, I'm a little skeptical about polls like this. Why nine nags? Why not a round ten? And why stop at 50? Do teenagers really keep count? Be that as it may, other research shows that 70 percent of parents are receptive to their kids' begging (I'm surprised it isn't higher). The "Nag Factor" study even breaks down parents into groups. For example, the group dubbed "indulgers" is made up of "pushover" parents who buy on impulse. In another group are "kid pals"— "childlike" parents who enjoy interacting with their

---

DEAR JANET

Q. It's bad enough that kids' birthdays have become a big deal, but now other holidays are turning into a marketing extravaganza. Valentine's Day used to be a card, a box of candy, or flowers. Now it's lingerie, jewelry, and cars. Retail marketing is trying to lay on the guilt trip that if we do something less than is suggested, we just don't care. And kids are being caught up in it.

A. Retail marketing is trying to do what it has always done—sell us stuff. One of my husband's favorite movie lines comes from the 1947 classic *Miracle on 34th Street.* Commiserating with Kris Kringle about the commercialization of Christmas, young Alfred, a fellow Macy's employee, tells Kris (in his best Brooklynese), "There are a lot of bad 'isms' floating around this woild, but one of the woist is commercialism."

We're a wealthier country than we were back in 1947, so today's retailers want to sell us fancier, more expensive stuff. That's not all bad. We're fortunate to live in a prosperous society that offers so many choices. As far as the big-picture economy is concerned, whatever we buy, whether cards or cars, helps the rest of the world become more prosperous too.

From a household perspective, however, it's not always easy for parents to raise kids with a sense of proportion amid so much plenty. The challenge is to strike a balance, making the most of our consumer society without being consumed by it.

And I get enough positive feedback from parents and children to remain optimistic. We survived commercialism back in 1947, and we'll do it again.

---

children. Meanwhile, "conflicted" parents dislike kid advertising but find it hard to resist their children's requests.

Perhaps parental resistance would be stronger if we could all band together in a kind of PAC—Parents Against Conspicuous Consumption. Unfortunately, being a parent is often a lone-wolf operation.

But moral support is at hand from an unlikely source—children themselves. Surveys indicate they're not necessarily suckers for every sweet-talking marketing campaign that sashays into the mall.

I've seen studies in which a majority of teenagers questioned agreed "there is too much pressure to wear the 'right' clothing." Teenagers have been known to show a healthy tendency toward thrift, shopping at stores that specialize in cheap chic and used clothing (my kids love to pick up 50¢ shirts at Goodwill). And boys and girls continue to look up to their parents, using them as role models. "I think Mom has combined work and family very well," said Betsy, 12. "She takes her job seriously, but she always has the time to be with me and my sisters."

And kids will listen—even if you say no. Once when I was being interviewed on the radio, a young woman called in to say that when she was a child, her parents had a rule about holiday gifts: she wasn't allowed to ask for anything she had seen advertised on TV. I asked her if she had been willing to accept that rule. Not only did she accept it, but she and her older brother also were happy to pass it along to their younger siblings (perhaps because misery loves company).

The lesson here, parents, is that despite the marketing blitz, you still have influence over your kids. Don't be afraid to use it.

The Apple Doesn't Fall Far from the Tree

Author Suze Orman has brought personal finance to the masses by milking our psychological hang-ups about money. Those hang-ups, Orman insists, have their roots in our "early formative experiences" with money, memories of which are "riddled with self-doubt, unworthiness, insecurity, and fear."

Whew! I'm not willing to admit that an adult's feelings of inadequacy can be traced to not getting a raise in her allowance. But if early money experiences don't scar you for life, they do leave their mark. A friend of mine named Kim has never forgotten that when she was a kid, her father made her account for every penny of her allowance in a ledger (which she still has). She found the exercise so tedious that when she got older, she vowed never to keep such close tabs on her finances.

With my own children, I sometimes goof by not following my own advice. I have preached ardently and often that because children take you literally, parents should never respond to their kids' comments about money with a glib answer that can be misunderstood. Yet when my daughter, Claire, and I once chatted about how much she had spent on books for school, I commented (jokingly, or so I thought) that she was sending us to the poorhouse. Claire blanched. "That's not true, is it?" she asked. When I assured her it wasn't, she responded, "Don't ever say that to a kid." And she's right.

The message to parents is to be careful what you say to—and in front of—your children when you're discussing money with them or with your spouse. Kids take you literally, reacting in ways you hadn't bargained for and may not be aware of until years later. Even if you never sit your children at your knee and lecture them on the birds and bees of finance, they'll get an education just by watching and listening to you.

Do you scold your spouse for spending too much money—and are you chided in return for being too stingy? Within your family, do you talk freely about money, or are you secretive? Is money a lightning rod for emotional as well as financial tensions? Parents can wield money as a weapon, as in the case of the higher-paid breadwinner who metes out financial crumbs to other family members to keep everyone in line. Parents can flaunt money as a symbol of power—as do the Joneses, with whom everyone is always trying to keep up. Or they can use it as a stand-in for love by substituting presents for their presence.

Your children's attitudes toward money will be shaped by nature—what they inherit from you—and nurture—what they pick up along the way. Despite the heavy influence of their peers, it's likely they'll end up much like you. So have a go at picturing yourself as they see you and tune in to the message you're sending.

Careful, the Kids Are Watching (and Listening)

Parents who grew up during the Great Depression spent a lifetime trying to teach a new generation of children what it was like to have to save coffee grounds. Wealthy families with mixed feelings about their money often overemphasize the virtue of not having any. The self-made man, on the other hand, sometimes insists that his children follow his example. Because circumstances can't be duplicated, those are often unrealistic expectations. Yet they can't help but have an effect on you, even if, as in Kim's case, the effect is precisely the opposite of what your parents intended. You're likely to return to your roots eventually, however, even if you feel inclined to stray in between. Although she no longer keeps a written record of her expenses, Kim admits that when she got older, those early ledgers helped her keep mental track of where her money was going, and she's a smarter money manager as a result.

When I was a child, I didn't get an allowance. Instead, my parents gave me money when I needed it. A sure prescription for creating a spoiled brat? On the contrary. One reason I didn't get an allowance was that we didn't have a lot of money. I didn't have an outside job, but I was responsible for doing much of the housework while my mother worked. Today I'm much more comfortable financially, but I still spend carefully and save a lot. By not giving me an allowance or making me get a paying job, my parents probably broke some rules about teaching me money management (and I certainly could have used more experience handling cash). But it was the atmosphere at home that counted most in shaping my restrained money habits as an adult.

DEAR JANET

Q. My kids are growing up on the opposite "side of the tracks" from where I was raised. They experience more, have access to more, and want for less than I ever did. Without a doubt, my greatest challenge as a parent will be to instill the same work ethic, ambitious drive, and there-is-no-safety-net attitude that I had, which enabled me to be where I am today. I've actually considered liquidating all of my assets, moving back to where I came from, and reliving a lifestyle similar to that which I grew up with, simply to increase the probability of those same values being adopted by my children.

A. That's not a bad idea. Unfortunately, it's probably not realistic for many families. So the challenge is to re-create the conditions of your youth in your new situation. That's tough but not impossible. For example, in a survey of the top 1 percent of the wealthiest Americans, most of those wealthy parents said they expect their children to contribute to the cost of their college education by getting a job. (For other strategies you can use to pass on fundamental values, see this chapter.) There are no guarantees, but parents who feel as deeply as you do can't help but make a positive impression on their children.

Your Money Profile

Your basic money personality is key to determining your attitude toward money. See if you recognize yourself in the following portraits.

The Accountant. You keep your checkbook balanced, and one of your greatest thrills is watching your savings account grow. You blanch when your spouse spends impulsively on a piece of furniture or a set of golf clubs. You can be a downer to live with, but you'll never be broke. For you, money means security.

The Social Worker. You regard money as filthy lucre, and the quicker you wash your hands of it the better. You are, however, willing to spend it on the people and causes you love. You volunteer to host the family dinner every Thanksgiving, and you probably have a "Save the Whales" bumper sticker on your car. For you, money means affection.

The CEO. You own a BMW and a Mercedes, live in a house you can't afford, and are planning to remodel the kitchen with your next bonus. When your kids bring home a good report card, you write them a check. Your motto is "The one with the most toys wins." For you, money means success.

The Entertainer. Every Friday afternoon you have a couple of drinks with the gang from the office, and you pick up the tab. Every Saturday night you go out to dinner with the neighbors, and you pick up the tab. You never balance your checkbook and can't be bothered saving receipts. You drive your accountant spouse crazy, but your neighbors and coworkers love you. For you, money means esteem.

You can probably place yourself and your spouse in one of these four broad categories but not necessarily in the same one. Show me a couple who don't fight about money, goes the old one-liner, and I'll show you a couple on the way to their wedding. Once any two people get together, financial squabbles are all but guaranteed. Disputes about money are among the leading causes of divorce in the United States.

Olivia Mellan, a Washington, D.C., psychotherapist who specializes in trying to resolve conflicts about money, breaks down money personalities further into types that are polar opposites:

Hoarders versus Spenders. Hoarders find it difficult to spend money; Spenders can't seem to hang on to it. A subspecies is the person who goes on spending binges, saving up pennies only to blow them all at once.

Money Monks versus Money Amassers. Monks feel anxious when they have too much money; Amassers feel anxious when they don't have enough.

Money Worriers versus Money Avoiders. Worriers balance their checkbook over and over and finish their taxes in January; Avoiders ignore the checkbook and can usually be found licking the stamp on April 14.

Risk Takers versus Risk Avoiders. Takers relish gambling on the stock market and even more exotic investments; Avoiders are reluctant to venture forth from the security of bank certificates of deposit.

Even if you and your spouse are similar, one of you will tend to take on the role of foil. In a family of hoarders, for example, someone has to spring for living room furniture and clothes for the kids. If you're both spenders, one of you will feel the need to play guardian of the checkbook. Either way, some conflict

---

DEAR JANET

Q. One of our kids is conscientious about saving and budgeting, but the other can't seem to save anything. What are we doing wrong?

A. The only thing you're guilty of is having children.

To a great extent, a child's attitude toward money is shaped by his or her own personality. And as every parent knows, kids within the same family can have very different personalities. The shy, serious older child may be diligent about saving, whereas the carefree, gregarious little brother spends every cent he gets his hands on.

You can't change your kids' birth order or personalities, but you may be able to modify their behavior. By requiring them both to save part of their allowance, you can guarantee that each has at least some money put aside.

Right now your words may seem to be falling on one pair of deaf ears, but youngsters do remember what they've been taught. Sometimes it just takes a while for the lesson to sink in.

is certain, and your children are bound to pick up on it. In extreme cases, children may take the side of the preferred parent, choose the position that will win them the most affection, or simply leave the field altogether and refuse to have anything to do with money.

A financial psychologist who deals with such problems recalls a poignant personal experience. After he and his wife divorced, he took his then 10-year-old daughter to a fair. While they were strolling through the booths, she suddenly realized that she had forgotten to bring her own money to spend—and worried that her father didn't have any. "She had picked up my stress and was hoarding her cash to take care of Dad," said her father. "So we worked on convincing her that I was all right, and that she should keep her money and learn to spend and enjoy it."

Ways to Meet Each Other Halfway

None of the money personalities described above is necessarily bad; all have their good points. In fact, your spendthrift spouse probably secretly admires your self-discipline, and you probably admire his or her ability to have fun with money. What you need to do is avoid getting too far out of balance. The key to defusing potentially tense situations is to know what makes your spouse crazy, and to resolve, if not to change your ways completely, at least to meet your partner halfway.

In her book *Money Harmony* (Walker, 1995), Mellan recommends a series of weekly exercises in role reversal, or practicing behavior that's out of character for you. For example, in the case of a money monk married to a money amasser, the monk should try splurging on something that he or she would otherwise consider selfish or indulgent, whereas the amasser sets aside a day on which he or she doesn't spend, save, invest, or deal with money at all. They write down their feelings and reactions, give themselves a reward for their efforts, and continue the exercise for several weeks—long enough, ideally, for it to make a permanent difference in their behavior or for them to at least appreciate one another's position.

Does This Sound Familiar?

Here's a look at some other key flash points guaranteed to ignite financial fireworks in a marriage, with suggestions on how to defuse them.

He: "You're always spending money we don't have."
She: "You're so tightfisted we never have any fun."

Try shock therapy. Present the spender with your paychecks and your bills and let him or her handle the budgeting. For cases in which spending has gotten seriously out of control, you may have to get a neutral third party, such as an accountant, to take over the family books or consult an organization such as the National Foundation for Credit Counseling (8611 Second Avenue, Suite 100, Silver Spring, MD 20910; 800-388-2227) or Debtors Anonymous (General Service Office, Box 92088, Needham, MA 02492-0009; 781-453-2743).

Remember, though, that the spender isn't necessarily the one who is at fault here. Sometimes the sober half of this duo is simply afraid to part with money. When that's the case, it might help to lay out your financial goals—retirement, children's education, a major vacation—to see whether you're on track toward achieving them. Once you see where you stand in dollars and cents, one spouse may be convinced that you need to spend less, or the other might feel more comfortable about spending more. "People are willing to change their behavior as long as they don't feel like they're being blamed," said one family counselor.

This kind of exercise can be invaluable for kids too. One reason they seem to think money grows on trees is that they have no experience in setting goals and making choices. They just don't understand why they can't have everything they want when they want it. It helps them to hear that you're holding off on buying the new car because the house needs painting or forgoing dinners out to help pay for your vacation at the beach.

One mother recalls the day her 12-year-old son announced that he wanted to play lacrosse and presented her with a list of equipment adding up to more than $200. She told him she didn't think lacrosse was in the cards, and she told him why: He had never played before, and it seemed like a lot of money to spend on something he wasn't sure he'd stick with. He ended up agreeing, mainly because "he heard me say what I was thinking and not just 'we can't afford it,' " said his mom.

She: "Our money's just sitting in the bank. We ought to invest."

GOLDEN RULES FOR FENDING OFF FIGHTS

For richer or poorer, in good times and bad, it's possible for spouses to avoid, or at least defuse, many of the most common disputes about money by adding the following resolutions to their marriage vows:

- **Talk about money openly** and matter-of-factly. Silence is not golden and could lead to unpleasant surprises later.
- **Settle the issue** of joint versus separate checking accounts. Either system will work if you both accept it. Or both of you could chip in to fund a third kitty for household expenses.
- **Designate which spouse will pay bills,** balance the checkbook, or handle investments. Whether you pool your money or keep separate accounts, someone has to do the financial housekeeping.
- **Know where your money is.** Even if your spouse is the numbers whiz, you can't afford to tune out. Touch base periodically so you know how much you owe

on your credit cards and how much is in your retirement accounts.
- **Don't begrudge your spouse** small indulgences. Each of you should have some money to spend with no explanations needed.
- **Consult with each other** on purchases of, say, $500 or more. That counts as a big indulgence, and your partner deserves a say.
- **Don't criticize your spouse** about money in front of others. Talk openly, but talk privately.
- **Coordinate your responses** when your children ask for something, so they don't play one parent against the other. If Mom says no, Dad says no.
- **Discuss your goals regularly,** preferably at a time when you're not under the gun to solve a money problem. Even when you keep separate accounts, you need to coordinate financial plans—if you hope to retire together someday.

He: "Yeah? You want to end up like Charlie, who lost his shirt in the market?"

The ticklish problem of different tolerances for risk can be easily resolved if you both realize you don't have to commit to all or nothing. If one of you must take risks, do it with 10 percent of your assets instead of 100 percent. If you're reluctant to move beyond the safety of a bank, take it one step at a time by investing in a relatively safe utility stock or blue chip company instead of an emerging-market mutual fund. If each of you has your own IRA or 401(k) tax-favored retirement plan, each of you can decide how to invest the money.

If you still can't reach an amicable agreement, you might seek help from a neutral third party, such as a financial planner, who can recommend investments and act as a buffer to absorb some of the worry (and the blame).

He: "How can I balance the checkbook when you can't even hold on to an ATM receipt?"
She: "I've got more important things to think about."

Whip the disorganized spouse into shape by starting small: Get him or her at least to toss receipts into a spiffy-looking storage bin—or a garden-variety shoebox. Move on to assigning specific tasks—who's going to balance the checkbook, who's going to monitor credit card charges so you don't use up your credit line. Set aside one day a month to talk about family finances. Then switch bill-paying responsibilities every six months.

If all else fails (and it just might), be prepared to go it alone. One couple settled their squabbling when the wife officially hired her husband to be her bookkeeper. Now that they've made it a business arrangement, she takes their finances more seriously and he's less resentful.

If you're the one who's stuck with keeping the books and the very word *budget* sets your teeth on edge, make it easy on yourself. As long as you're meeting your savings goal, you probably don't need to fiddle with a budget at all. If you aren't, you don't have to keep track of every nickel and dime. Instead, make a guess about what your expenditures are and then compare your estimates with the bills as they come in. That will show you where your spending is out of line, and you can focus on those areas where you want to cut back.

She: "Your kids are already costing us a bundle in child support. Why do you have to spend so much on them when they come to visit?"
He: "They're my kids—I'll spend as much as I want."

Court-ordered child support is one thing, but what often rankles a new spouse is unanticipated demands on the noncustodial parent's pocketbook. One solution is to set aside a certain amount for extra child-related expenses. But money may not always be the problem. The new spouse may simply want reassurance that he or she is top priority, and you may get better results by expending a little extra time and attention rather than cash. Kids and money are often at the center of other prickly problems involving divorce and remarriage. "Whatever money means to you and your spouse will be magnified if you go through a divorce," said one psychologist. (For a more extensive discussion of some of the problems and solutions, see Chapter 16).

He: "You spent $120 on a pair of sneakers for Johnny? You're spoiling that kid rotten."
She: "I'm only buying him what the other kids have."

It's the sociological phenomenon of our time: love equals stuff. The more stuff our children have, the more we must love them—and the better parents we must be. It's exacerbated by parental guilt about not being around more and by the very natural desire for our kids to fit in.

The solution is both breathtakingly simple and excruciatingly difficult: Just say no. That applies equally to both parents, because it's critical that you put up a united front. Your kids will still love you in spite of your refusal to gratify their every wish (or perhaps because of it). If you think those $120 sneakers are an outrageous purchase, put your foot down and tell your son that they don't fit into your budget. If you're inclined to compromise, tell him how much your budget does allow and let him make up the difference.

Use the same strategy even when you can afford the shoes (or the MP3 player or any other item your kids covet), and it's the principle, not the cash, that is at stake. Never lie to your children and tell them you can't afford something when you can. Be honest and tell them why you choose not to buy it or why you'd prefer to spend your money on something else.

One child psychologist tells the story of well-to-do parents who had given their teenage son a car, with the understanding that he not use it to leave school at lunchtime. Sure enough, the son flouted the rule and smashed up the car to boot. His father's immediate response was to buy him another one, thereby teaching his son a lesson that would "damage his perception of money for the rest of his life," said the psychologist.

The Wealth Effect

I once received this e-mail from a young man in his 30s: "I was raised in a very privileged household, with my father owning a very successful company. I enjoyed many lavish vacations and cruises, 'off-the-chart' Christmases, private schools, etc. Sadly, I never learned very much financial responsibility. Subsequently, after I inherited my father's estate, I was clueless about how to control these investments and ignorant about just how quickly one can go from black to red. I was always used to a certain standard of living and made every attempt to continue it. The only problem was, I did not have the income that my father had to support my 'needs.'"

Certainly this young man's "privileged" childhood is far from typical. Nevertheless, one of the biggest challenges in our affluent society is saying no when so often we are able to buy our kids what they want. "Parents want to know if there's a certain level at which money becomes toxic," one estate-planning lawyer told me. In fact, any amount of money can be toxic if you lavish too much of it on your kids.

A few years ago, I did a special report for *Kiplinger's* magazine about how wealthy parents maintain family values when the value of the family soars. What I found is that the rich aren't so different from the rest of us in their goals for their children: They want them to have a sense of struggle and accomplishment, an appreciation for what money can and can't buy, and, eventually, financial independence. To these families, I would recommend the same strategies for teaching financial values that I would recommend to those of us who are not quite so fortunate. But the richer you are, the tougher it is, and the rest of us can learn from their success stories.

It's always important to talk to your kids about money and answer their questions in a forthright and age-appropriate way, without telling them more than they need (or want) to know. But it's especially important to offer some explanation when, for example, you move from a tract house to a custom-built home after your business is sold, and your daughter's friends tease her about living in a mansion. Faced with that situation, one mother told her daughter that "it was our dream house, and we had been planning and saving for it for years. Plus her father could do a lot of the work himself." Having a response to give to her friends "made our daughter more comfortable."

When children are overcome with a case of the gimmies, wealthy parents are deprived of the convenient fallback, "We can't afford it." But I found that the families who are most successful in teaching kids financial values are those that found other ways of setting limits. "I probably say no more than most parents," one mother told me. When her seven-year-old daughter saw a doll she wanted, Mom told the child that it was "a little expensive" and suggested that she put it on her birthday wish list—there to fade from her daughter's memory. One young teenager I interviewed didn't get a new car when he turned 16. Instead, he inherited the family's old minivan and got a job scooping ice cream.

Even in wealthy families, "most of the people I talk to have pockets of money," said one financial adviser. "There's a pocket for living expenses, a pocket for philanthropy, a pocket for investing. That way, parents can honestly say to their kids, 'We have a ceiling on spending.'"

In my opinion, the most effective way for any family to teach children about limits is to give them an allowance: a fixed amount of money they receive regularly to cover agreed-on expenses. In Chapter 8, I outline my allowance philosophy in more detail—and tell you how to set up a system that works.

One of the toughest challenges for successful parents is to enjoy their wealth without giving their children a sense of entitlement (see the Q&A on page 50). No matter what your income, your children will learn their most fundamental lessons about money from the example you set. Even though you certainly have a right to enjoy the fruits of your labor, don't go overboard. Nouveau millionaires often hope that their middle-class roots will keep their kids well grounded. "We live in the same house and have the same cars," said one father who had sold his steel-fabricating business for several million dollars. "Our big splurge was a vacation to Europe."

Many wealthy families use philanthropy to send children the message that their success was a result of both hard work and good fortune, and that it comes with the responsibility to give back. One mom and dad set up their own foundation and required their four children, ages 6 to 17, to make recommendations on how foundation funds should be distributed.

In the end, the best antidote to the toxic shock of great wealth—as well as garden-variety American affluence—is to be a hands-on parent with a firm value system that you consistently communicate to your children.

Mistakes to Avoid

You probably won't be able to change your money personality. The idea is to reach a happy medium or at least be aware of, and honest about, your shortcomings. If you have a tendency to pinch pennies, let your kids in on the secret and tell them why you consider it a good—or bad—trait. If you're a shopaholic, tell them you're not the world's greatest authority on budgeting. They'll appreciate your candor and learn from your experience.

In talking to your children about money, follow these three other golden rules:

1. Don't Duck the Issue

Whether they're pressed for time or just reluctant to bring it up, parents often give the subject short shrift. But children do think about money, and sometimes they get some cockeyed notions about it. One woman recalls that when she was in elementary school, she wanted more than anything to take an after-school class in horseback riding, which cost $80 at the time. Her middle-class parents could probably have afforded the lessons, but she didn't dare ask for them. "It sounded to me like $80 would plunge the family into poverty . . . like it was the end of the world," she recalls.

Another woman remembers that when she was in second grade, she was "overwhelmed by the abundance of crayons, stars, paper, and pencils in my teacher's supply cabinet. I couldn't imagine that my parents could ever afford to buy me those kinds of things, so I stole a bunch of them." Her parents, of course, made her return them and 'fess up.

When kids raise some issue involving finances, even if the connection seems tenuous to you, don't ignore them or give them a curt response. Take the opportunity to teach a lesson—or correct a misconception—that they'll thank you for years later.

2. Be Consistent

If you've decided to give your children an allowance and you've made a "no advances" rule, don't waffle—

standing firm one week and handing over extra money the next. Your child will never learn the discipline of living within a budget if you keep expanding the limits. Today she's getting an advance on her allowance, tomorrow she'll be using one credit card to pay off the balance on another.

Repeat the following sentence ten times: "I will never tell my children, by word or example, to do as I say and not as I do." Your lecture on the wastefulness of scrapping a perfectly good video game system just to get the latest model will fall on deaf ears if you regularly trade in a perfectly good car just to get a new one with the latest bells and whistles.

3. Don't Be a Cynic

Adults routinely complain about their jobs and criticize their bosses as a way of releasing tension. After venting their spleen, they usually go back to work and forget about the incident. But for youngsters who witness the outburst, the memory can linger. In one nationwide survey, 69 percent of mothers and 60 percent of fathers said they like their jobs a lot. But among third- through twelfth-graders interviewed, only 42 percent said their moms like their jobs a lot, and only 41 percent thought their dads were content.

For children, that perception can have destructive consequences. One psychologist who counsels underachieving teenagers encounters many 17- and 18-year-olds who have become "incredibly cynical" about the working world, because they have been exposed too early to a negative attitude instead of to the enthusiasm and inner satisfaction they need to see. If your kids ask whether you make as much money as your boss, don't answer, "I wish," as if you're somehow being shortchanged. Better to respond, "No, but someday *you* will."

Kids also need to start learning, by word and example, how much things cost as well as how to use money, earn it, save it, and keep it in perspective. The following chapters give you ideas on how to tackle that task with kids of different ages.

Turn page for Kids' Questions→

KIDS' QUESTIONS

Q. "Dad, can I have $15 for a new CD? Mom says no, but all the other kids have it."
A. Tell your child that if Mom (or Dad) says no, the answer is no. There are lots of other issues here—whether you can afford the $15, whether you should cave in to your child's peer pressure, whether your child should be buying the CD with his or her own money (all of which are covered elsewhere in this book). But in a situation like this, your most important consideration is to stand by your spouse. If you do, chances are you won't hear this question again. If you crack, your action (and your child) will come back to haunt you.

If you really disagree with your spouse or if your child is exploiting a sore spot between the two of you, you and your spouse should talk it over afterward to agree on a response. But this is one discussion that doesn't have to take place in front of the children.

Q. "Why do you two always fight about money?"
A. You may not always fight about money, but your children are obviously getting a different impression.

Don't overreact or go on the defensive. Instead, ask your children to describe a time when you and your spouse argued about money. What they define as "fighting" might simply be a run-of-the-mill parental discussion about whether to get the car fixed or buy a new one. If that's the case, you can reassure your kids by bringing them in on the discussion, which is critical anyway if they're ever to learn how to make such decisions themselves. If they're old enough to eavesdrop, they're old enough to participate.

If your kids were right on target and you *are* always fighting about money, you may have to seek outside help from a marriage mediator (contact the Association for Conflict Resolution, 1015 18th Street, N.W., Suite 1150, Washington, DC 20036; 202-464-9700). "Fighting in front of the kids isn't bad as long as the kids see you finding a solution," said one mediator.

Q. "How come you and Dad went out to dinner and a show but you won't buy me rock concert tickets?"
A. Go ahead and tell it like it is: You earned the money and you can spend it any way you want.

Kids shouldn't be so selfish as to presume that they always get first dibs on the family's resources. You don't need to justify your actions to your children, but it doesn't hurt to remind them that your family's income has to be divided among lots of different expenditures, one of which is R&R for Mom and Dad. You might also remind the child that although you may not choose to buy concert tickets, you did spring for an electric guitar (or whatever) on his birthday. Then go off for your night on the town.

In the future, you can head off this question by making concert tickets and other expenses part of your children's budget to be paid for out of their own allowance or earnings.

Q. "How come you bought David a new jacket and you didn't buy one for me?"
A. What parent hasn't been tempted to retort, "because we like David better than we like you." Actually, that's not a bad comeback—assuming it's not true and you're smiling

while you say it. Meeting your child's unspoken criticism head-on with a little humor can ease the tension and give you a chance to explain that you intend to buy your whole family new Jackets eventually, but you Just happened to find one in David's size that was on sale.

Children are sensitive to what they perceive to be favoritism, whether real or imagined (and let's hope it's usually imagined). To the extent it's possible, follow the one-for-all rule: When you buy something for one of your children, buy one for all of them. That's easy enough to do with small items—books from the bookstore, treats at the dollar store, even souvenirs if you go on a business trip (save the bags of peanuts from the plane or the goodnight mints on the pillow in your hotel room). A little extra money buys a lot of goodwill.

If you're going to be shopping for back-to-school clothes and you don't want to take all the kids along at once, let them know that they'll each have a turn. If you're buying a new ball for your young basketball player, it isn't unreasonable to consider a new glove for your baseball player. Of course, if she doesn't need a new glove, there's no reason to spend the money. But as long as you've created an overall atmosphere of fairness, she won't feel slighted.

Q. "Kids cost too much. I'm not going to have any when I grow up."

A. This isn't exactly a question, but it does demand a response. Somewhere along the line, your kids got the idea (incorrect, I hope) that they're undesirable. Tell them that the rewards of having children far outweigh the expense.

Remember that talking to your children about money will set them straight about what it can and can't buy, but talking about money over their heads as if they weren't there is simply asking for trouble. It may seem that all your children want to do is spend your money, but often they do worry about whether your family has enough:

- Watching her mother write a $65 check for a month's worth of piano lessons, ten-year-old Michele looked soberly at her mom and asked, "Can we afford this?"
- A fifth-grade teacher arranged a special field trip for her class to a nearby aquarium. When she told her students that it would cost $12 each, several of them came up to her and told her that the trip was too expensive and they probably wouldn't be able to go.

It's true that money is tight in many households. But in these cases it's likely that the kids' fears were out of proportion to the costs involved. That's not unusual, as children aren't always clear on the difference between $65, $650, or $6,500. Kids need to develop a sense of relative costs and values so that they know which expenses might be expected to fit into your budget and which would be a stretch. In the case of the piano lessons, for example, the mom could have explained that music lessons are a worthwhile expense and $65 a reasonable cost. But if the child also wanted to take dancing lessons for $65 a month, she might have to choose between the two.

Youngsters also need to know that they're not a burden but a responsibility that parents (presumably) have taken on willingly.

Government statisticians routinely calculate the cost of raising a child from birth to age 18. Parents often read the number, shake their heads and sigh, "If only I had known. . . ." But even if you had known, you probably would have gone ahead and done it anyway.

Q. "Who will take care of us if you die?"
A. There's nothing wrong with reassuring your children that they shouldn't worry because "that's all been arranged"—assuming it's true. But it would be even better if you could tell your kids who you have named as their guardians should anything happen to you. And if you haven't named any guardians, your child's question should be the encouragement you need.

Many parents rely on informal arrangements—"My wife's sister has agreed to take care of our children in case my wife and I aren't here." But if both you and your spouse should pass away before your children are grown without formally naming a guardian, the courts will decide who's going to bring up your kids. And you can't count on your wishes being honored.

A judge who doesn't know your children and family could choose the one relative you wouldn't want.

In fact, for parents of minor children the single most important reason for making a will is to name a guardian for the kids. Many parents put off writing a will because they see it as a downer—a way to dispose of their assets after death. Think of it instead as a way to protect your most precious assets.

Q. "How much money do you make?"
A. Instead of dismissing the question with an abrupt, "That's none of your business," go with an answer that's vague but more polite, such as "more than some families but not as much as others." That's a nicer way of not answering the question, which you shouldn't feel obliged to do. When it comes to teaching children about money, parents have lots of responsibilities. Telling your kids how much you make isn't necessarily one of them.

For one thing, no matter how much you make, whether it's $40,000 or $140,000, grade school kids (and even high schoolers) will have trouble putting it in perspective. It will sound like an enormous sum to your children—certainly more than enough to buy the $100 bicycle or $200 video game system they want. For another thing, you have a right to your privacy. Even though it's certainly desirable to talk with your children about money (that is, after all, what this book is about), you can't be blamed for not wanting your affairs blabbed around the neighborhood—which your kids will almost certainly do, if only in innocent conversation.

Besides, when young children ask this question, chances are they don't care about the numbers anyway. They're just trying to get an idea of your relative wealth and where you stand vis-à-vis other families. They'd also be relieved if you assured them that you're not at risk of being turned out into the street. As your kids get older, you may choose to be more forthright about how much you earn. But it will make more sense to your children, and be more comfortable for you, if you put your income in the context of your expenses. Children need to know, for example, that after taxes your take-home pay is a lot less than your actual salary. They need to know that you can't spend money on just anything because you have to cover certain fixed expenses first, such as the mortgage and car insurance. One dad gave his teens a crash course in household finances by converting his pay into cash, stacking the money on the table, and inviting his kids to watch the pile dwindle as he paid the monthly bills.

Some parents have even turned over the bill-paying chores to their kids. "For several years, since Mary was 12, I have given her the bills and the checkbook, and she does the rest," one mother wrote to me. "I just do a quick review and sign the checks." What many adults would find tedious Mary finds fascinating, said her mom. "From this experience she not only acquires the skill of managing a checkbook but also gains a real sense of what it costs to run a household on a month-by-month basis."

Q. "Are we poor?"

(Often preceded by "You never buy me anything.")
A. It's easy enough to snap, "We would be if I bought you everything you asked for," but that's probably not the case. Typical middle-class families aren't poor (even though it sometimes feels that way), and it would be misleading and unfair to let your children think you are, even unintentionally.

But your funds are limited, and kids don't understand the concept of limits, especially as it applies to them. Explain that watching where your money goes doesn't mean you're poor. It just means you have to parcel out your income to cover lots of different expenses.

A variation of this question is, "Why are you so cheap?" Assuming that your child is being serious and not merely fresh, explain that shopping for the best price or deciding not to buy something doesn't mean you're cheap, just that you want to make your money go as far as it can.

It might help to give your kids more hands-on experience in the art of managing money. The next time you buy their back-to-school clothes, for example, tell them in advance how much you can afford to spend, and then let them have a hand in choosing the wardrobe without busting the budget.

If your children do have a misconception about your financial status, it's healthier for

them to think you're poor and cheap rather than rich and extravagant!

Q. "Are we rich?"

A. If the first thing that pops out of your mouth is "Whatever gave you that idea?" think for a minute. *You* may have given your kids that idea. Even if you don't feel rich, you probably live comfortably enough that your children think you are. Or maybe their curiosity was piqued by a specific event—you bought a new car, for example, remodeled your house, or got a job promotion.

In any event, answering the question with one of your own isn't such a bad idea. It gives you a chance to find out what's on a child's mind and gives you a few seconds to get your thoughts together. "Are we rich?" is similar to "How much do you make?" in that it demands a diplomatic answer that will still satisfy children. One mom didn't miss a beat when her six-year-old put her on the spot. "We're not rich," she replied, "but we have enough money to buy the things we need and some left over to share."

Now, if your name happens to be Rockefeller, you'll eventually have to tell your kids that you are, in fact, rich. But the rest of the advice in this book should be as helpful to you as to any other parent.

Q. "How come we don't have a big-screen TV like the Joneses?"

A. On hearing that one, many parents would be inclined to offer to let their disgruntled offspring move in with the Joneses. Unless you really expect that to happen (and a big-screen TV can be very tempting), stick to answering the question, whatever the answer may be: "Because we can't afford a big-screen TV," or "Because we're saving our money for a trip to

Disney World next spring," or "Because we think a big-screen TV is a waste of money." Kids are willing to accept the truth when it's offered.

Sometimes a question like this is just an attempt by your children to make you feel guilty. But sometimes kids are genuinely curious about where you fit in on the scale of wealth compared with other families. In that case, take the opportunity to explain that different occupations pay different salaries. That in turn can kick off a discussion of jobs and careers, such as why basketball players are paid more than teachers, why someone might want to be a writer rather than a doctor even though doctors earn more, or why being your own boss might be attractive.

Explain that some people might choose a lower-paying job because it suits their talents or gives them more satisfaction—or be forced into one because they don't have the skills or training for anything better. Now is a good time to make your pitch about getting a good education if your kids want to be able to afford a big-screen TV or a trip to Disney World when they grow up.

Q. "Why do you have to go to work every day?"
A. Don't respond with a flip but familiar remark about "putting bread on the table for you." A response like this makes it sound as if you're literally a step away from starvation—and it's all your kids' fault.

Tell your children instead that you work to earn money to pay for all the things your whole family needs and wants. Tell them you work to earn money to save for the future—to pay for next year's vacation or a new car. Tell them you work because you're good at what you do. Tell them you work because you enjoy it.

Children don't always hear a dispassionate discussion of adult jobs. They're more likely to overhear your grousing about the boss or yearning for early retirement.

It's healthier for all of you to get your children involved with what you do. Take them to work on a regular workday so they know where you go every day. Talk about the people you work with and what your job involves.

You may spend more of your waking hours on the job than with your children. So anything you can do to make your kids feel more a part of your mysterious outside life is bound to bring you closer together, make you less resentful of the time you spend apart, and make your children less fearful of the day when they'll have to go to work to put bread on the table.

You can also have a big influence on their career choices. One study of children from kindergarten to sixth grade showed that more of them wanted to follow in Mom's footsteps than in Dad's. Among fifth-graders, 33 percent of the girls—and 30 percent of the boys—said they wanted to have the same job as their mother. Only 11 percent of the girls and 13 percent of the boys cited their father's job. The study concluded that the kids chose Mom's field more often because women tell their children more about their jobs and are more likely to take their children to the place they work.

One woman who runs a business out of her home even took her two children on a tour of her home office and carefully explained that that's where she goes to do her job and earn money. Several weeks later she mentioned that she was short on cash and would have to make a trip to the bank, when her son piped up, "Mommy, you can just go into your office and make some."

Q. "Why do you have to get a new job so far away and make us move? I don't want to leave my friends."

A. Instead of setting yourself up as the bad guy, emphasize that you're all in this together. Acknowledge that the move will be an adjustment for you, too, and even a little scary. But your new job will make it easier for your family to buy the things they need (including, presumably, things the kids want). If you've been out of work prior to the move, your children have probably sensed your tension and felt the financial pinch, and may actually be as relieved as you are that you have found work.

It's true, though, that long-distance moves get more difficult as your kids get older. "The ultimate nightmare is to take a teenager away before senior year," said one child psychologist. If you're in that situation, try to defuse possible conflicts by letting your kids know as early as possible that a move is in the works and bringing them in on discussions about buying houses and choosing schools. You might even consider taking them with you on a scouting expedition to your new home.

Q. "If you lose your job, how will we get money to buy food?"

A. You mean well, but if you say "Don't worry about it. That's my problem," you're actually being too reassuring. If your job's in jeopardy, of course your kids will worry. Even if they're not quite sure what it means to be unemployed, they can sense you're upset, and they're going to pick up on your cues. It's easy for them to imagine that things are worse than they are.

Be as straight with them as you can about how a job loss might affect your finances, but don't burden them with problems they can't handle. You can tell them, for example, that you'll get money from unemployment benefits without telling them that those benefits will eventually run out. Tell them that many people nowadays lose or change their jobs, and explain how you're going to go about looking for a new one. Tell them you'll have to cut back on spending for a while, and ask for their suggestions.

Whatever you do, don't try to shield the children by continuing to spend money you can no longer afford. Kids are surprisingly adaptable to economic circumstances. A survey by the American Board of Family Practice showed that to help their families through a financial crunch, a majority of teenagers were willing to get jobs, buy fewer clothes, and give up some of their allowance.

Small Change: The Preschool Years

Perhaps the shortest question I've ever been asked was this one-liner: "At what age do you start turning an ordinary little child into what you term a money smart kid?"

The one-line answer: at whatever age an ordinary little child starts showing an interest in, and asking questions about, money. I feel compelled to add, however, that far from pushing kids to grow up faster, I consider myself a pulling parent, keeping them young as long as possible. As I said at the beginning of this book, there's no point in trying to make your child into a little Peter Lynch or Bill Gates or running your family like an accounting firm. When it comes to financial issues, as in everything else you discuss with your kids, your role is to satisfy their curiosity in an honest and age-appropriate way.

Dealing with money is such a natural part of life that you don't even have to set aside extra time to talk about it. Instead, you can take advantage of situations that crop up every day. When your child begs to press the buttons on the ATM, use the opportunity to tell her how the money got there in the first place. Dragging your children to the supermarket becomes more pleasant for all of you if you keep them busy scouting out the best deals. A visit to your office opens the door to a discussion of where the money comes from to pay the household bills.

Your ultimate aim is to turn out independent adults who know how to manage money and have a healthy regard for what it can and can't buy. But with preschoolers you'll have to start with a less lofty goal—

for example, how to tell the difference between a penny, a nickel, and a dime.

Let 3-year-olds choose among those three coins, and they'll almost invariably choose the nickel because it's the biggest. Let them choose between a quarter and a dollar bill, and they'll take the quarter, which, after all, you can spin, flip, drop into a bank, and stack with other coins. Let them choose between a dollar bill and a $50 check and they'll take the dollar bill, which at least looks like money. Abstract concepts are beyond the grasp of most preschoolers. They focus on the concrete and so should you, showing them what coins look like and how they can be exchanged for other things.

Not that preschoolers aren't capable of some surprisingly sophisticated behavior. My friend Laurie was floored when her son, Jake, then 4½, announced that he was going to open a business selling lollipops—and save his profits to buy a car. Laurie operated her own home-based business selling children's clothing, and Jake had observed with more interest than his

---

DEAR JANET

Q. The other day I went to pick up my 5-year-old from school, and her teacher handed me $32. Apparently my daughter had taken $33 from my purse and spent $1 on candy before her teacher spotted what was happening and took the rest of the money. How should I handle this?

A. Keep calm. You're dealing with two situations here. The first is that your daughter took money from your purse; the second is that she took a lot of money from your purse.

In the first case, let's assume your daughter wasn't being sneaky but simply going straight to what she knows to be the source of cash. This is potentially the more serious problem, but it can be handled by telling your daughter that helping herself to money is a no-no. She has to ask.

As for the amount she took, children this age often don't understand the abstract value of money; three $10 bills are the same as three $1 bills. They'll know better once they learn about money in school. You can help things along by counting out exact change when your daughter handles money so she knows how much she needs to buy a candy bar.

With any luck, this will turn out to be an innocent—and isolated—incident.

mother realized. He began asking his mom's custom-ers to buy lollipops and eventually got his grandfather to build him a plywood stand from which he could conduct his business. Then he decided he wanted to expand into selling juice as well.

Of course, there were a few snags in the opera-tion. At first, Jake wanted to sell the lollipops for $14 each until he was talked down to 3¢. And his mother said it took him a while to grasp the concept of paying his supplier.

It wasn't surprising that Jake apparently pulled the $14 figure out of the air. One parent once told me that she was at her wit's end because despite her best efforts to teach her 5-year-old about money, the child thought everything cost $64. Where had she gone wrong, the mother wanted to know. She hadn't, of course. To her daughter the $64 figure was simply a tangible symbol of money—an idea she would grow out of as she got older and more sophisticated and learned more about money in school. Until then, you can take advantage of lots of everyday activities to fa-miliarize your preschoolers with family finances.

At the Grocery Store

Most children get their first look at the world from the seat of a shopping cart. So learn to make the most of the opportunity and avoid some nasty scenes as well. For example, present your children ahead of time with several coins (adding up to 50¢, $1, or whatever you deem appropriate) and tell them they can spend the money on something of their own choosing (for more tips on how to forestall a bad case of the gimmies, see the questions on page 67).

As you cruise the aisles, let the children toss your items into the cart and count them as they go in. Keep the children busy hunting for the brand of soup or crackers that you buy, or let them choose between two different kinds of cereal. If they decide to buy something from a vending machine, let them put in the coins and scoop out the change.

Watching Television

If your children spend part of Saturday morning in front of the television, make it a point to join them to see what kinds of commercials are being pitched their way. Preschoolers can't always tell when the television show ends and the ad begins. They need you to explain to them that when they hear the voice saying, "We'll be right back after these brief messages," they're about to hear a sales pitch for something you may not want them to have.

Play this little game with your kids to show them how to be a "TV star": Take three apples that look similar; then "dress up" one of them by sticking raisins or marshmallows into it, putting it into a colorful box, or shining a flashlight on it. Ask your children which one they'd be inclined to buy. If they choose the spiffed-up apple, have them take a bite out of each one. Does the "star" actually taste any better?

Don't be surprised if, despite your best efforts, your preschoolers still want it all. Don't panic either. At that age, it's natural for them to ask for everything they see—and promptly forget about it as long as you don't feel obliged to buy it for them. In fact, it's important for youngsters this age to get used to hearing you say no. Don't fall into the parent trap of giving in to your kids out of fear, guilt, or pure indulgence.

Sounds easy, but in today's world that often takes an iron will, a stiff backbone, and a tight fist. For instance, it seems that a growing number of parents think nothing of spending hundreds of dollars on a child's version of a couture jacket or skirt. Asked by a newspaper reporter how she came to fritter away $20,000 on a closetful of clothes that her 2-year-old rarely wore, one mother gave a response that was

---

FIVE THINGS 5-YEAR-OLDS NEED TO KNOW

1. A dime is worth more than a nickel, even though it's smaller.

2. Coins can be exchanged for other good stuff.

3. The toys they see on TV won't look as flashy, or work as well, at home.

4. Saving money can be fun when they can use it to buy something later.

5. They will not get everything they ask for.

enough to take your breath away: "I can afford it, so why not?"

After catching my breath, I can think of plenty of reasons why not—starting with the simple fact that no child needs a $250 Versace jacket. Period.

If this book came equipped with a sound card, you would hear bones rattling as I figuratively took the parents of America by their shoulders and gave them a good shake. Because that's not possible, here's a verbal shoulder-shaking should you ever be tempted to drop a bundle on designer duds (or their equivalent) for toddlers:

- **The only name** on kids' clothing labels should be their own.
- **Don't kid yourself** into thinking that you're buying this stuff for your children; you're buying it for yourself.
- **If you lead your children** to believe that spending money on expensive clothes buys happiness, they will end up broke and sad.
- **Parading kids around** in miniature versions of adult outfits is not cute. They grow up fast enough without being pushed.
- **Dressing for status** is a no-win game. Someone will always be able to go you one better.
- **Simply having money** at your disposal is never a good reason to buy something.
- **If you buy your 4-year-old** a $300 jacket and $99 jeans, he or she will never learn either the value, or the values, of money.
- **Every family needs** at least one adult, and that person should be you.

Far from doing your children a favor or helping them get on in the world, you're doing them a disservice by teaching them the shallowest of lessons: that clothes make the kid, that it's fine to cave in to peer pressure, and that you're willing to pay the price. You'll still be paying when your child is 44.

Lending a Hand

Children this age are old enough to pick up toys, put away clothes, or help make their bed. They probably won't do any of those things, of course, unless you make the demands manageable, stick to them, and give your kids a hand. For kids, chores become less work and more play if they're doing them with Mom or Dad. Settle on one chore a day and let them choose which one it will be. Present it as a privilege that they enjoy now that they're growing up.

Of course, you can offer a little incentive as well. It can be as simple as a chart showing the chores to be done and the days of the week. Each time a job is completed, your daughter gets to stick a star on the chart. Seven stars and you might buy her a small treat—an ice cream cone or a drink at the local convenience store. Think of it as a reward—positive rein-

DEAR JANET

Q. I've heard of a kids' piggy bank with separate compartments for things like spending, saving, and giving. Can you help me find one?

A. You can choose among several such banks, each with a unique twist. Here's a sampling:

- **Moonjar moneybox** (http://www.moonjar.com). These colorful, collapsible cardboard boxes come in three sections, one each for spending, saving, and sharing. Each kit includes a guide for using the boxes and a passbook for recording transactions.
- **Money Savvy Pig** (http://www.msgen.com). From Money Savvy Generation, this translucent polystyrene pig is available in six colors and has four compart-

ments: save, spend, donate, and invest. A coloring and activity book is also available.
- **My Giving Bank** (http://www.mmforkids.org). From the late Larry Burkett's Money Matters for Kids ministry, this clear plastic bank focuses on finances from a Christian perspective. The bank's three compartments, for saving, spending, and giving, are in the form of a bank, a store, and a church; includes Bible-based financial information for kids.
- **Money Mama Piggy Bank** (http://www.prosperity4kids.com). Money Mama comes attached to three little china piglets, one each for giving, saving, and investing. The rest goes into big mama for spending. Also available: *Money Mama & the Three Little Pigs,* a picture book.

forcement for doing something good—rather than a bribe, a payoff for not doing something bad. (For more on rewards and when to give them, see Chapter 8.)

Whiling Away a Rainy Afternoon

You have to figure out something to occupy the children's time anyway, so once in a while you might as well kill two birds with one coin by occupying your kids with money-related games and activities. There are, of course, old standbys such as playing store. I personally like the idea of letting children play with one of the nifty savings banks you can buy nowadays—everything from motorized coin sorters to talking ATMs. And if you're looking for an excuse to get out of the house, why not an excursion to a dollar store, where the price is always right for kids.

In her book *Moneyskills: 101 Activities to Teach Your Child About Money,* author Bonnie Drew offers lots of other ideas. Here are a few games from Drew's book that are appropriate for getting preschoolers used to handling coins. I chose these because they're manageable, short, and fun.

STORY TIME. Let your children handle a penny, a nickel, a dime, and a quarter. Show them the pictures on each coin and tell a story about each one. (Remember, it's Lincoln and the Lincoln Memorial on the penny, Jefferson and Monticello on the nickel, Franklin D. Roosevelt and the torch and olive branch on the dime, and Washington and the American eagle on the traditional quarter.) Then let them make impressions of the coins in clay. Hint: Kids especially like to save commemorative state quarters.

TREASURE HUNT. Fill a box or dishpan with sand, rice, beans, or packing peanuts, hide five pennies in it, and ask your children to dig for the "treasure." Have them count out the coins. You can add other coins later and ask the kids to sort them into groups.

HEADS UP. Start with five nickels and five pennies. Explain that the side of the coin with the man's head is called "heads" and the other side "tails." Show your children how to spin and roll each coin and ask them to guess which side will be showing when it lands, heads or tails. Have them balance a nickel on the tip of a finger and see how far they can walk across the room. When the coin falls, let them call heads or tails.

ANIMAL CRACKERS. Place five pennies and a nickel on a table and explain that five pennies are worth the same as one nickel. Then break out a box of animal crackers and let the children "buy" them for one cent per cracker; let them buy five crackers at once with the nickel. Pour a small cup of juice and pretend that it costs five cents. Let your children choose to buy the juice with either five pennies or one nickel. Then eat and drink up.

TOY STORY. Aside from homemade activities, there's an increasing number of financially oriented toys on the market these days—everything from old favorites

---

DEAR JANET

Q. We give our two daughters, ages 5 and 4, loose change and a dollar bill here or there, but they always play with it or lose it. I have helped them decorate their own money jars, hoping to inspire some saving habits. I have used charts and graphs to show them the amount of money saved and have encouraged them to save toward "something," but to no avail. They continue to play with their money.

A. It's normal for children that age to see money as something fun to play with.

Remember that any instruction you give children about money should be both engaging and suitable for their age. Decorating money jars is great for preschoolers. But charts and graphs—ugh!

Encouraging children to save toward "something" is too abstract. When your daughters mention a specific thing they would like to have, suggest that they save their money in their money jars, decorated with a picture of the coveted item. Make sure it's not too expensive, so it won't take long to meet the goal. When they have enough cash, take them to buy the item and enjoy their reward.

like Monopoly to solar-powered cash registers. Remember that infamous Barbie doll with her own credit card? Money-related toys can be great teaching tools for kids—if you choose them wisely.

For instance, some toys aimed at preschoolers, such as cash registers or supermarket shopping sets that come with scanners and groceries, generally teach positive lessons and are harmless enough. I do have a sneaking suspicion, however, that to a youngster this type of toy can be a bit like pleasant-tasting medicine: Parents give it and kids are willing to take it, but they don't necessarily ask for it on their own.

More controversial are such toys as that credit card–carrying Barbie, which teach lessons you may not want your kids to learn. At the very least, you'll have some explaining to do—and if you feel a toy is so objectionable that it requires a warning, why buy it in the first place?

My favorite money toys for children are board games. Even as I'm writing this, I'm looking at Monopoly, The Game of Life, and a stack of other games that my children and I have played, plus a few new ones we haven't gotten around to yet. One that's suitable for preschoolers is Shopping Spree (http://www.intplay.com), in which players age 4 and older move around the board to make purchases from different stores while preserving enough cash to pay for parking when they're finished shopping. Games bring family members together in a fun activity while giving children a painless lesson in personal finance (for a listing of other games, books, videos, and Web sites that help teach kids of all ages about money, see Chapter 6).

DEAR JANET

Q. I want to teach my 5-year-old and 2-year-old about money and saving. I would like to take them to the bank and open regular savings accounts for them with money from their piggy banks. Is this a good idea?

A. Opening savings accounts for your kids is a great idea, but I wouldn't empty their piggy banks to do it. Children this age are a little too young to understand how a real bank works; they'll just think their money has been swallowed up forever. Keep some cash in their piggy banks, where they can see it, touch it, and watch it grow.

What You Can Expect

You'll be surprised at how fast preschoolers catch on. It didn't take long for Jake, the lollipop tycoon, to figure out that there are five nickels in a quarter and four quarters in a dollar. At this age, if you've accomplished that much, you've accomplished a lot.

Don't be upset when your 4-year-old tears open birthday cards, shakes them to see if there's money inside, and immediately asks to be taken to the store to spend it. You're not raising a greedy little kid, just a normal one. For preschoolers, spending is more immediate than saving. If your child knows that money can be exchanged for things, you're off to a good start that you can build on.

KIDS' QUESTIONS

Q. "Can I have a cookie?"
(Your 4-year-old in the grocery cart)
A. Often, parents agree to such a request because it seems a small price to pay to head off a tantrum. But give in that easily, and in the next aisle your child will want a sweet cereal, in the next aisle a candy bar, and in the next aisle a frozen yogurt.

Next time, try leaving your child at home. Failing that, lay down the rules in advance. Tell your kids they may each choose one treat—either a cookie or a candy bar or a box of sweet cereal or whatever else is appropriate. If they settle on the first thing they see, remind them that they get only one choice, and they might want to think about other possibilities before making a final decision. That should keep them busy and get you off the hook. They'll be so eager to see what new goodies are waiting around the next corner that, with luck, you can hold off buying anything until your shopping trip is just about over. One mom actually puts a small carry basket underneath her grocery cart and tosses in items her kids say they want. When they get to the checkout counter, each child gets to keep one thing from the basket.

It isn't saying no that brings on a temper tantrum. It's saying no after a string of yeses that tempts your children to test your sincerity with a stream of tears. They'll soon tire of the tactic if they know the rules ahead of time and are convinced you'll stick to them. Setting limits early and often heads off bigger confrontations later.

Q. "Can I have one of those big cars that goes by itself so I can drive?
(Your 5-year-old watching a commercial for a battery-operated kiddie car)
A. This is a much bigger item, and a much bigger issue, than a cookie at the store. I personally think preschoolers shouldn't be cruising around in a vehicle that's powered by anything but their feet, so I'd answer this question with a simple no. But you can always improve on a negative response by telling your children why you're denying their request. If you think self-propelled vehicles are too dangerous, too expensive, or just plain too grown-up for kids who should be transporting themselves via pedal power, say so. Your kids will know you've given your response some serious thought and aren't just trying to put them off—and they won't harbor secret hopes of getting a convertible for their birthday or under the Christmas tree.

Q. "Can I use my money to buy a candy bar?"
(Your preschooler waving a $10 bill)
A. We both know that with that much money your child could buy ten candy bars, and you'll be tempted to say so. Don't be surprised if your child doesn't get it. Preschoolers don't think in abstract terms. To young children, all paper money is the same. Four quarters are preferable to a dollar bill because there are more of them (and they spin), and a nickel is better than a dime because it's bigger.

Simplify your tactics. Tell your kids that a $10 bill is much more than they need for one candy bar and that they should save it to buy other things. Then help them count out the exact change they'll need.

If the children are still fuzzy about how much things cost, don't worry. At least they understand that money can be exchanged for other things, which is about as much as you can hope for at this age. They'll pick up the more abstract concepts when they learn about money in school.

Surviving with Tweens

By second grade, children no longer prefer a nickel over a dime, and they can even make a stab at counting change. But they still have trouble taking in the big picture about money. My friend Bonnie, who specializes in teaching students about economics, learned a lesson or two from her own daughter, Morgan. When Morgan was 8 years old, her mom convinced her to put a $10 birthday gift in the bank by reminding her that she could draw it out again if she wanted to buy something. Would the bank give her the same $10 bill, Morgan wanted to know. Her mother explained that she would get a $10 bill but not the same one, because the bank had already used that one to lend to other people. Morgan was appalled. In her mind, the purpose of a bank was to keep her money on a shelf until she was ready to take it out.

Similarly, one TV producer I know recalls that when she was a child her grandparents gave her a collection of $2 bills. She decided to put them in the bank for safekeeping—and was devastated to find that the bank didn't keep the bills safe at all. Instead, they were put back into circulation, and her prized collection went kaput. "I don't think my parents realized what I was thinking at the time," she said. "At least, they didn't jump in and stop me from depositing the money."

Despite their misconceptions, children this age are eager to learn from you, so take advantage of the influence you still have. When one bargain-hunting mother noticed "spendthrift rumblings" in her 7-year-old daughter, Jamie, she began to take Jamie with her on her regular canvasses of yard sales. "It was a real eye-opener for Jamie to see that she could get the figurines she collected for 25¢ at a yard sale instead of $7 at a store," said Mom.

How to Spend a Buck

They're too big to sit in the shopping cart, and having them tag along grumpily behind you at the grocery store is like trying to shop with a ball and chain attached to each leg. But when you're at the supermarket there are ways to get rid of your kids—nicely—that will benefit both them and you:

1. **Send your children to the cereal aisle** with instructions to find a box of cereal that will be popular with your family, doesn't list sugar among its top ingredients, and costs less than, say, $4. Tell them they can pocket the difference between your price limit and the actual price of the cereal. To challenge older children, show them how to look for the lowest unit price instead of the lowest price per package.

2. **Have the kids choose three kinds of soft drinks** (or some other product): a big-selling national brand, a less popular national brand, and the store brand. Note the prices per package and the unit prices. When you get home, pour the soft drinks into three unmarked glasses, and try your own taste test. Which soft drink tastes best? Which is the best value?

3. **While you're making your shopping list, let your children plan a special lunch** for themselves and one or two of their friends. Have them stick to a budget—say, $10—and encourage them to use the newspaper food advertising supplement as an aid. Then, while you do your shopping, send them off to do theirs and see if they can beat the budget without having to modify the menu.

4. **Have your children help you clip grocery coupons** and then track down the items at the store. Offer to

LISTEN TO YOUR MOTHER

"How to count change" (from the question on page 88) was the first of what I had intended to be a list of ten tips for youngsters on how to feel comfortable about handling cash in public or buying something on their own. My idea was to ask grown-ups to contribute the best advice their own parents ever gave them on how to avoid losing their money or being cheated. But so many adults weighed in that the top 10 became the lucky 13. Here are the rest, with compliments to contributors and their parents:

2. Always stuff your dollar bills deep in your pocket so they don't fall out when you reach in for a coin or bus token. Better yet, stuff them into a wallet or change purse, which you're less likely to pull out by mistake.

3. When ordering at a fast-food restaurant, round off the menu prices to estimate your total. That way you'll know you've been overcharged in case the clerk goofs and hits the Big Mac key twice.

4. Don't break the big bills. If your purchase comes to $7, pay with two ones and a five instead of a $10 bill. Once big bills are broken, you have a tendency to spend the money.

5. Spend the old, wrinkled bills and save the good ones for vending machines.

6. Always pay the pennies. If the price comes to $3.63 and you have a $5 bill and a handful of change, pay the three cents so that you don't get more pennies in change.

7. Ditto above, but with paper money. Suppose your purchase comes to $11 and you have a $20 bill and several ones. Give the clerk $21 so that you get a $10 bill in change. It's less cumbersome, and follows Tip 4 to save the larger bill.

8. If you have to use a big bill to pay for a small purchase, say to the clerk, "Here's a twenty," so there's no confusion. A good salesclerk should keep the bill out of the cash register until you get your change.

9. Clean out your pockets or purse each day and toss the coins into a savings jar. One man still follows this rule as an adult, and his spare change adds up to $40 to $60 a month, which he deposits in the bank or uses to treat himself to a nice dinner at a restaurant.

10. Don't take all your money to the movies or the mall. Take along only as much as you need to make your purchase. That way you don't risk leaving your life savings in your seat or frittering it away at the candy counter.

11. Don't shove a pile of crumpled bills onto the counter and expect the salesclerk to sort them out. After the age of 6 or so, that stops being cute and starts becoming an annoyance to the clerk and the other people waiting in line—not to mention an invitation to be ripped off.

12. If you're out with your parents and want one of them to hold on to your money, make sure it's in a separate wallet. Loose bills and coins have a habit of getting mixed up with a parent's own funds, never to be sorted out.

13. Don't put money in your mouth; you never know where it's been. Actually, you do know where it's been, which is an even better reason not to put it in your mouth!

match any savings you realize and let the kids put the money into their savings accounts.

5. **Give the kids part of your list** with instructions on choosing the items you need. Your son takes frozen foods, your daughter takes dairy products, you take the middle of the store, and you rendezvous at the meat counter.

The result: The children learn valuable lessons in how to use a unit price tag, how to read ingredient labels, how to compare different brands, how to evaluate product advertising, and how to stay within a budget. And you get your shopping done in peace (in a fraction of the time).

Once they've absorbed the basics at the local market, you can branch out. When his two sons, Craig and Lyle, were in elementary school back in the '70s, my friend Ed gave them the responsibility of being "Dad for a day." The family lived in the New York City area, and the boys were always begging to be taken to an amusement park. So Ed would give the "designated Dad" a budget and make him responsible for planning a family outing to the park of his choice. The boys would be up at dawn to push their red wagon to

---

IT MAY LOOK YUMMY . . .

The next time you see a commercial for a big, juicy, fast-food burger, ask your kids how the picture stacks up against the real McCoy. Then share with them a few fun facts about food commercials. For example, those juicy burgers you see on TV are mostly raw, just seared for a few seconds on each side; the grill marks are added by hand, the sesame seeds are glued onto the bun one by one, and a piece of cardboard is slipped into the bun to keep it from getting soggy.

Other tricks of the food stylist's trade: Shortening, sugar, and food coloring make ice cream that doesn't melt; liquid school glue makes cereal milk that looks creamy; and dishwashing liquid makes hot chocolate that looks bubbly (the marshmallows are Styrofoam balls).

These and other behind-the-scenes glimpses into advertising aimed at children are included in *Buy Me That,* a half-hour video created by *Consumer Reports.* It's available from Ambrose Video (800-526-4663).

the icehouse around the corner and buy ice for the cooler. In the car the designated Dad would sit behind the driver and hand over the money at tollbooths. At the park the kids would haggle over whether to eat or ride. (Craig always wanted to splurge on french fries, whereas Lyle hoarded his pennies for an extra turn on the roller coaster.) The kids were required to hold enough in reserve to pay the tolls on the way home but "once their money was spent, that was it," said Ed. With Craig in charge, the day sometimes ended early, but Lyle often came home with money in his pocket, which he was allowed to keep.

Did the lessons stick? Lyle got his college degree in finance and works in the mortgage department of a commercial real estate firm. Craig produces music videos and picked up enough money sense along the way to run his own business.

Watching TV with a Critical Eye

By this age, kids are sophisticated enough to figure out when a commercial doesn't ring true in practice. When the oldest of my three children was 8, I took them all to McDonald's to sample Mighty Wings, spicy chicken wings that McDonald's had been trumpeting in an advertising blitz. The 8-year-old observed that the real wings weren't nearly as juicy-looking as the televised version and the hot sauce wasn't as thick.

But ultimately you want to help youngsters spot the hype before they're disappointed in a purchase.

DEAR JANET

Q. My 9-year-old daughter has trouble holding on to cash. Last week she was going to a movie with a friend after school, so I gave her a $10 bill. Apparently she accidentally pulled the money out of her pocket while she was at school and lost it, so her friend's mother had to pay for the movie. I paid her back, of course, but it was embarrassing. How can I make sure this doesn't happen again?

A. You probably can't. Your daughter is, after all, a kid, and kids are prone to bouts of carelessness and lapses in attention.

Your best bet to safeguard the money is to designate a special place for your daughter to keep cash and nothing else—one of those neat minipurses or a specific pocket in her backpack. That way she'll be less likely to pull it out when she reaches into her pocket for a tissue or a stick of gum.

In the future, consider having your daughter use her own allowance to pay for movies she sees with friends. Then if the money happens to disappear, it will be her loss and not yours.

When your children see a commercial showing kids whooshing by on a skateboard or guiding a remote control car around hairpin turns, ask them if they could do the same without practice. Kids naturally expect a toy to work exactly as they saw it perform on TV, so it's important to warn them that they may need to be patient and learn to master a skill.

Before you spring for a much-wanted toy, take your children to the store and have them look at the coveted item in its box, where it isn't surrounded by a glitzy TV background and special effects.

Instead of rushing to be the first one on the block to have a new toy, encourage your children to be patient and let someone else be the guinea pig. After your kids have had a crack at playing with the toy,

---

CHILD'S PLAY

Talking with your children about money needn't be a chore. On the contrary, you can make a game of it. Even in today's high-tech world, some of the best teaching tools available to parents are low-tech board games. Here's a selection of classics and promising newcomers, all kid-tested by my panel of experts.

- **The Game of Life** (Milton Bradley). A big hit among children of all ages because "it covers everything," in the words of one 11-year-old. "Everything" includes careers, college loans, mortgages, car insurance, dividends, and taxes—an entire course in money management. Younger children may need some help reading the words, but they don't seem to have much trouble grasping the concepts.
- **The Allowance Game** (Lakeshore Learning Materials; 800-421-5354; http://www.lakeshorelearning.com).

Easy for younger children to understand and appreciate. As they make a circuit of the board, players are instructed to do things "that kids really do," such as play a video game or forget their homework. And the money denominations are manageable: the first player to save $20 is the winner.

- **Monopoly** (Parker Brothers). Still popular, although from a child's standpoint, this game's slower pace and longer playing time (does it ever end?) is a drawback. And compared with the other games, "you only do one thing," says a 10-year-old—buy and sell property. Parents can pick up the pace and pique the interest of younger kids by making a slight change in the rules: Let players start building houses and hotels as soon as all the properties are purchased, even if they don't own a monopoly.

they may find they can live without it after all. One youthful reader once told *Zillions,* a consumer magazine for kids that's no longer published, about the dumbest purchase he had ever made: an expensive remote control car that wound up eating batteries. If only he had waited, he discovered, he could have gotten the next generation car with rechargeable battery packs.

Children this age are old enough to understand the difference between fact and opinion, and you can use this as a talking point when you watch a commercial on TV. The next time you and your kids see the latest NBA hero quaffing a cold drink, ask the kids why they think he has chosen that particular form of refreshment:

- **Pit** (Parker Brothers). Talk about classics. This card game about cornering the market on commodities (barley, corn, flax, hay, oats, rice, rye, or wheat) was introduced in 1904. The action is still frantic enough to please modern-day kids (and adults). And children will love ringing the opening bell.

- **Monopoly Junior** (Parker Brothers). A welcome alternative to the senior version for both children and adults, because you can actually finish a game in a reasonable amount of time. Instead of Boardwalk and Park Place, players buy Bumper Cars, Roller Coaster, and other attractions at an amusement park and charge each other admission instead of rent. The money denominations are smaller than in regular Monopoly, and the playing pieces are bigger—no little green houses to keep track of.

- **Presto Change-O** (Educational Insights, 800-933-3277; http://www.edin.com). At first blush the idea seems too simple: Follow the "Earn" and "Spend" directions on a circuit of the board and be the first to save $10. But there's a trick: Your stock of cash can never include more than one nickel, two dimes, three quarters, four $1 bills, or one $5 bill, so presto change-o, you're constantly rebalancing your accounts to make the right change. A 7-year-old found it "challenging"—and so did his mother.

- **Money Wise Kids** (Aristoplay; 800-634-7738; http://www.aristoplay.com). Players roll the dice, collect the appropriate amounts (a six counts as $6 and so on down to one, which counts as $10) and exchange smaller bills for larger ones. The first to get a $100 bill wins. It's fast-paced action for short attention spans, but only two at a time can play.

- **Is it because** that's the absolute best-tasting drink on the market?
- **Did the soft-drink company** pay him to do the commercial?
- **Why would an advertiser pick** a TV or sports star to pitch its product?
- **Would your kids buy the drink** on the strength of a basketball player's say-so?
- **Does the player actually like the drink**—or is it possible that he can't stand the taste of the stuff?

Studies show that simply talking to your kids about ads can make a difference in how they regard commercials and how much they ask for. Children this age can also detect hype; by this time, they've probably bought or received as a gift something that didn't measure up to its TV image. My own kids became particularly cynical about toys that came in deceptively large boxes and turned out to be tiny as well as toys that had to be assembled out of many (even tinier) parts. One of their biggest disappointments was racing-car sets that took hours to put together and then promptly broke when the cars skidded off the tracks, the batteries ran out, or the layout collapsed. I finally

---

DEAR JANET

Q. When my niece turned 13, I set aside a sum of money and took her shopping for the day, helping her make choices about what to buy so her money would last. Now her younger sister is turning 13, and I'd like to do the same thing. But this child is more into the greed factor, and she just wants the money. What can I do to make her not chase after money alone (and blow it in the first hour), and yet make her day unique?

A. How about giving her a lesson in deferred gratification? Take her shopping, but instead of buying stuff right away, keep a running tally of things she would like to buy and how much they cost. At the end of the day, you and she can sit down over dessert and go over her list together, making choices about how she wants to parcel out her cash. Then you can give her the money, and she can go back to make her purchases.

By the way, I hope your nieces appreciate your generosity—not just in giving the money but in sharing the lessons that go along with it.

told the kids not to bother asking for any more rac-ers, and they complied without a murmur of protest.

Children also need to know that kids have rights as consumers. If they buy an item that breaks, doesn't work or fit, or is otherwise unsatisfactory, take them to the store to return it and get their money back.

Tricks with Allowances

By this time, your children are old enough to get an allowance (much, much more on that subject in Chapter 8). If you give an allowance (and I recommend that you do), dole out a variety of small-denomination coins and bills. If the allowance is $2, for ex-ample, you might give a one-dol-lar bill and four quarters. This helps teach children money equivalents and also makes it eas-ier for them to set aside money for specific purposes, such as sav-ing or charitable giving.

Be on the lookout for "hot buttons"—unexpected openings to slip in a lesson that otherwise might fall on deaf ears. One fa-ther recalls his frustration in try-ing to get his son, Rolf, to save money, when Rolf was about 8 years old. Then Rolf saw the orig-inal *Star Wars* movie and was hooked; he voluntarily saved his money to join the official fan club and was determined to become a Jedi knight. Dad saw his chance and leaped. "We talked about how Jedis have to save money for college, and the next day Rolf put on his Jedi robe and opened a savings account." Years later, Dad observed with satisfaction that Rolf had several thousand dollars in the bank that otherwise wouldn't

DEAR JANET

Q. My friend's son, who is 10, is adamant about getting a cell phone. His parents are uncertain, whereas I contend that handing a kid a cell phone teaches fiscal irresponsibility. What is your opinion?

A. I'm with you—and not just because of fiscal responsibility. You have described a situation in which a 10-year-old is "adamant" and his par-ents "uncertain"—precisely the opposite of the way a parent-child relationship should work. Kids can have input, but parents should have the final say.

That applies to all kinds of parent-child is-sues, financial and otherwise. As for having a cell phone, a 10-year-old should never demand one and rarely needs one unless safety is an issue. For example, Mom and Dad may want to be able to contact their son after school to check on childcare arrangements. But that should be their decision, not his.

be there "just because we talked about the need for Jedi knights to go to college."

Rainy Day Perk-Ups

Nothing tops old standbys such as Monopoly or The Game of Life for teaching kids how to handle money. If Monopoly seems daunting for younger children, it's okay to bend the rules a bit to let players build houses and hotels even if they don't own all the properties of a single color. Or try Monopoly Junior, which older kids (and adults) will like too, because you can play an entire game in about 45 minutes. You'll find a selection of my family's favorites on pages 74–75.

Then again, you don't need to buy a board game just to play around with money:

■ **All those catalogs** cluttering your den are freebies just waiting to impart a lesson or two. Give your children an imaginary budget of say $250 or $300, and let them choose an entire winter or summer wardrobe.

DEAR JANET

Q. My dad lost his job. He has a part-time job, but money is very tight at my house. Now that I'm 11, I need a lot more things than I used to. I don't know what to do.

A. When money is tight, it's hard on everyone in a family, and you all need to pull together. Now isn't the time to ask for "a lot more things."

And be honest: Do you really "need" those things, or do you just "want" them? You may want a new pair of jeans because they look good, but you may not need them if your old ones still fit and aren't worn out. So you may have to wait until your parents feel they can spend the extra money.

One thing you can do right now is try to earn a little extra money on your own by doing chores for people in your neighborhood—such as babysitting, raking leaves, or running errands for older people.

Now that you're 11, you're old enough for someone like your mother or dad to show you how to shop for bargains. A new shirt may cost $20 at one store, but you may be able to pay a lot less for the same shirt or one just like it if you wait till it goes on sale, shop at a less expensive store, or poke around at yard sales. My kids pick up great shirts for 50¢ each at Goodwill thrift stores.

■ **If you decide** to order take-out food, make it your kids' responsibility. Present them with the menu, a price limit, and instructions to plan a meal that satisfies the whole family and doesn't bust the budget.

Facing Down Peer Pressure

As your children move through their tween years—roughly age 8 through 12—they'll be influenced more by their peers and their peers' possessions. Now you'll hear the plaintive wail that death is the only imaginable alternative if they don't get the designer jeans or the newest high-tech gadget or whatever the latest overpriced fad happens to be. Steel yourself. It doesn't hurt to give in on small things or even on a few big ones that are really important to your kids. But every family has its line in the sand, whether it's high-fat convenience foods, a new video game system, or a cell phone, and it's worth digging in your heels. In fact, it may be more important for you to give your kids the satisfaction of listening to their wishes than to satisfy them. "In past generations, nobody ever died from not getting a Betsy Wetsy," said Eda LeShan, author of *What Makes You So Special?*, which counsels kids on how to deal with peer pressure.

What does hurt is for kids to feel they have to be like others in order to be worthwhile. Sympathize with their desire to fit in, and meet them halfway, but emphasize that it's okay, even desirable, to be different. Kids who don't learn to buck the crowd when they're young will have trouble saying no when they're teens.

Remember that the choices you make regarding such things as where you live and where you send your children to school can make a big difference in the amount of peer pressure on your kids and in their, and

---

FIVE THINGS 10-YEAR-OLDS NEED TO KNOW

1. They will have to pay for their own trading cards, movie tickets, snacks, or other expenses out of their allowance.

2. They will not get an advance on their allowance.

3. They should be able to navigate a supermarket with a cart and a list, and bring home a bargain or two.

4. They should have a savings account in a real bank—and they should learn that although they can withdraw their money, it won't be the same cash and coins they put in.

5. They will not get everything they ask for.

FUN MONEY MATERIALS

Take advantage of rainy days and bedtime to slip your children some broccoli with their milk and cookies. Dozens of books, software programs, magazines, videos, and Web sites teach kids about money and economic concepts in the context of fun. Here's a sampling:

Books for Younger Kids

- *Alexander, Who Used to Be Rich Last Sunday,* by Judith Viorst (Aladdin Paperbacks, Simon & Schuster), about a boy whose money burns a hole in his pocket.
- *Arthur's Funny Money,* by Lillian Hoban (Harper Trophy), in which Arthur sets up a bike-washing business to earn money for a T-shirt.
- *The Berenstain Bears Get the Gimmies,* by Stan and Jan Berenstain (Random House), in which Brother and Sister Bear have the "galloping, greedy gimmies." Other money-oriented books in this series include *Trouble with Money, Mama's New Job, Meet Santa Bear.*
- *Eyewitness Books: Money,* by Joe Cribb (Dorling Kindersley); an encyclopedic history of money, foreign currency, and trading.
- *From Gold to Money,* by Ali Mitgutsch (Carolrhoda Books). Defines bartering, counterfeiting, minting, and earning money.
- *Freckle Juice,* by Judy Blume (Yearling Books), in which Andrew uses five whole weeks of allowance to buy a secret freckle recipe and learns some valuable consumer lessons as a result.
- *The Go-Around Dollar,* by Barbara Johnston Adams (Simon & Schuster), in which a dollar bill travels from person to person. The book also explains where and how money is made.

- *The Peanut Butter and Jelly Game,* by Adam Eisenson (Good Advice Press). Young people learn the consequences of spending all their money the moment they get it.
- *If You Made a Million,* by David M. Schwartz (Harper Trophy), in which Marvelosissimo the Mathematical Magician shows what money looks like and demonstrates the concept of a million dollars.
- *Money, Money, Money,* by Nancy Winslow Parker (HarperCollins). This brightly illustrated text explains the meaning of the art and symbols on U.S. paper currency.
- *The Monster Money Book,* by Loreen Leedy (Holiday House). Members of the Monster Club discuss money, managing and spending their dues, and how to be a smart shopper.
- *Tops and Bottoms,* by Janet Stevens (Harcourt Children's Books). Burned in a land deal with a wily rabbit, a lazy bear vows never again to be caught sleeping on the job.
- *Coin Count-y,* illustrated by Jim Talbot (Innovative Kids). This bank in a book features coin slots on each page so kids can keep track of how much they save while they follow the story to the Dollar Roundup.
- *Lucky the Golden Goose,* by John Wrenn (Red Truck Publishing). Lucky, a farm goose who's paid in pumpkin seeds for his down, teaches a lesson in planting your assets to make them grow.
- *My Dad's Job,* by Peter Glassman (Simon & Schuster). A young boy visits his father's office, where he encounters bulls, bears, hostile raiders, and other fun things.

- *It's a Habit, Sammy Rabbit!* by Sam X. Renick (http://www.itsahabit.com). The first in a series of adventures in which Sammy Rabbit learns the value of saving.
- *Tight Times,* by Barbara Shook Hazen (Picture Puffins), and *Ramona and Her Father,* by Beverly Cleary (Avon Camelot); both deal with parents who have lost their jobs.

Software for Younger Kids

- *The Coin Changer* (Heartsoft). Realistic graphics teach money counting and time skills.
- *Treasure MathStorm* (The Learning Company). Players learn math and time and money skills while they collect treasures, catch elves, and melt the ice kingdom.
- *Dollarville* (Waypoint). Children learn basic money skills by helping Dollarville's citizens with their money problems.

Books for Older Kids

- *All the Money in the World,* by Bill Brittain (Harper Collins Juvenile Books), in which a boy gets his wish for just that, with disastrous consequences.
- *Coping with Money,* by Richard S. and Mary Price Lee (The Rosen Publishing Group). Advice on allowances, budgeting, investing, and saving for college.
- *The Kid's Guide to Money,* by Steve Otfinoski (Scholastic). This illustrated guide discusses ways to earn, save, spend, share, and invest money.
- *Smart Spending: A Young Consumer's Guide,* by Lois Schmitt (Simon & Schuster). Explores budgeting, misleading advertising, consumer fraud, warranties, and consumer complaints.

- *Double Fudge,* by Judy Blume (Puffin Books, Digest Ed.). Five-year-old Fudge becomes obsessed with money, much to the disgust of older brother Peter.
- *The Everything Kids' Money Book,* by Diane Mayr (Adams Media). Packed with money trivia, games, and Web sites.
- *The Toothpaste Millionaire,* by Jean Merrill (Houghton Mifflin). Appalled by the price of toothpaste, Rufus Mayflower develops his own and plans to retire a millionaire by eighth grade.
- *Money Isn't Everything: Mama Had to Work on Christmas,* by Carolyn Marsden and Robert Casilla (Viking Books). Gloria is resentful when both of her parents must work on Christmas.
- *Money Sense for Kids!* By Hollis Page Harman (Barron's Educational Series). A reference book that covers minting, making, saving, and investing money.
- *The Money Book Store* catalog (Institute of Consumer Financial Education, http://www.icfe.com; 619-232-8811). Lists other financial games and books.

Software for Older Kids

- *Hot Dog Stand* (Sunburst Communications). Players manage money and run a business operating a hot dog stand at football games. Part of the Survival Math series.
- *The Oregon Trail* (Broderbund, 5th Ed.). Adventurers travel by covered wagon from Missouri to Oregon. They learn to purchase the supplies they need and make their money last the trip.
- *Roller-Coaster Tycoon* (Infogrames). Not only do players design their own theme park, but they must also make it profitable.

FUN MONEY MATERIALS *continued*

Videos

- *The Making of Money* (Bureau of Engraving and Printing; 202-874-3315). A history lesson on U.S. paper money and a fascinating look at how currency is engraved and printed.
- *Piggy Banks to Money Markets* (Kid Vidz; 800-840-8004). Told through the eyes of children who experience the pleasures and pitfalls of running their own business or otherwise earning money.
- *Money: Kids and Cash* (The Learning Channel & the American Bankers Association; 800-338-0626). A two-tape set that's organized in short segments: how prices are set, why people value gold, money in other countries.
- *Money: Bucks, Banks and Business.* (The Learning Channel & the American Bankers Association; 800-338-0626). A two-tape complement to *Money: Kids and Cash.*
- *Schoolhouse Rock: Money Rock* (Disney). Characters such as Lester the Investor and Tax Man Max teach money basics.
- *A High Price to Pay* (http://www.peterpan .com). Teddy assumes that rich kid Jeff gets all his neat stuff from his parents. Turns out Jeff earns money to buy his own stuff.

Magazines

- *Young Money* (http://www.youngmoney .com; 888-436-8714). Covers careers, investing, money management and entrepreneurship.
- *Y&E Magazine* (http://www.youngbiz .com). Focuses on budding capitalists.

Web Sites

- *Kidsbank.com.* Shows where money comes from and how a bank operates.
- *PBSKids.org.* Covers financial issues, such as making and budgeting money, in its "It's My Life" section.
- *Wise Pockets* (http://www.wisepockets .com). Designed for children in grades three to six, this site shows parents and teachers how to use popular children's books to teach kids about money.
- *Sense & Dollars* (http://www.mpt.org/ senseanddollars). A user-friendly blend of text and interactive games for middle and high school students.
- *Moneyopolis* (http://www.moneyopolis .org). Math skills solve real-life financial problems.
- *Consumer Jungle* (http://www .consumerjungle.org). For older teens, this site is loaded with detailed information on buying a car, deciphering credit card agreements, and renting an apartment.
- *Independent Means* (http://www .anincomeofherown.com). Focuses on encouraging girls and young women to be financially independent.
- *FirstGov for Kids* (http://www.kids.gov). Click on "Money" and be connected to links that will take you to more than 15 sites about money and finance.

your, ability to resist. Sending your kids to an expensive private school can end up costing far more than the tuition if you're constantly being pressured to keep up with the Jones kids' winter ski trips and summer camps.

DEAR JANET

Q. My daughter consistently misplaces her money. Most of the time she leaves it in pants pockets, and I find it when I do the laundry. I then tell her that it mustn't be that important to her, so it's no longer hers to spend. Is there a better way to teach her "fiscal responsibility"?

A. Instead of reacting to each incident, make sure your daughter knows up front what the rule is: Any money Mom finds out of place (in pants pockets, on the kitchen counter, under couch cushions), Mom keeps. If your daughter is forewarned,

she may be more inclined to keep track of her money.

Rest assured that this is a common problem, especially among younger children for whom money may not be that critical. As kids get older, with more maturity and bigger expenses, they're in greater need of the cash and tend to take better care of it.

Meanwhile, cut your daughter a little slack. I, too, find money in pockets while doing the laundry—and sometimes the pockets are mine!

The easiest way to deal with such influences is to avoid them altogether by not sending your children to the expensive private school in the first place.

Whatever lifestyle decisions you make, at some point you'll probably have to fight the battle of the latest fad. But if you've been talking to your children about money-related issues all along and are willing to keep talking, you won't have to relinquish the field to their friends. Kids can accept differences among families if they understand their own family's philosophy and financial circumstances and if they feel they're getting a fair hearing.

If you need encouragement, meet Trish and Steve, parents of eight children, seven of them girls. How do they handle the clamor for name-brand apparel? "The deal is, we'll keep the children fed and clothed and housed, but looking cool is up to them," said Trish, a dedicated bargain hunter. The kids analyze their closets for things that come close to the latest fad and use money they've earned to buy the rest—usually from sale racks. "They rarely ask for things other kids have," Trish told me. "They know we would rather have a lot of children instead."

**Turn page for
Kids' Questions→**

Q. "Can I have a new action figure?"
(Your 8-year-old in the toy store while you shop for another child's birthday gift)
A. When children are preschoolers and asking for small items such as a cookie at the grocery store, it's easy to keep the gimmies in check by granting them one request (see the preceding chapter). By the time they're 8 or 9 or 10, the stakes are higher and so, presumably, are their financial resources. Tell them you're going to the toy store to buy someone else a gift, and if they want to tag along in hopes of getting something for themselves, they should bring their own money.

Q. "Can I have [fill in the blank]?"
(Asked by any child of any age about anything when all you want to do is get through your errand list)
A. Sometimes a parent will agree to anything just to get out of a particular store or situation. No matter how flustered you are, "No" is always preferable to "Oh, all right" or even "We'll see." If your children detect any wavering at all, they will immediately assume it means yes. Tell your kids you are buying what's on your list and only what's on your list. If there's any reason at all why you shouldn't deny their request outright—maybe they've asked for a new folder for school or something similarly noble that they know you're a sucker for—at least be specific in telling them that "school supplies are for another trip," by which time their urge to buy may have passed.

Q. "Can I play ice hockey?"
(Or gymnastics, swimming, or any other sport that can't be conducted in your backyard and requires more than a ball and a pair of sneakers)

A. Put your children's latest requests in context with all the other things they do. Financial considerations aside, there's no reason to add yet another activity if their schedule is already fully booked. I propose a "rule of three": No more than three days a week per child of activities that require being chauffeured (so soccer practice twice a week counts as two, but piano lessons at school don't count). If there's no room in your kids' schedules for anything else, expensive or otherwise, the answer to their request should be obvious.

Suppose your child's request isn't out of the question—just expensive. Test her commitment by telling her she'll have to make choices: If she wants to swim two or three times a week, she'll have to give up gymnastics. If he really wants to try ice hockey, he'll start with used equipment.

Q. "Why do we have to buy my clothes at The Bargain Barrel? Why can't we shop at Chez Chic, where the other kids go?"
A. You can nip this classic confrontation in the bud if you're willing to make a deal with your children. If your conscience and your wallet allow, tell them you'll buy an item or two from this season's "name" store but not their whole wardrobe. So your son might choose the monogrammed shirt all the kids are wearing, but he'll have to wear it over standard-issue jeans. With a limited amount to spend at the store of choice, he'll be inspired to shop harder for bargains or clearance sales (guided by you, of course).

Your kids will learn how to look cool on a budget, and you'll still have your pocketbook and your principles intact.

Q. "Why won't you buy me a new video game system? All the other kids have one."

A. "If all the other kids jumped off the Empire State Building, would you jump too?" will no doubt leap to your lips. But don't try to be too clever or you'll end up outsmarting yourself. Kids won't necessarily make the connection between jumping off buildings and buying video games (or if they do, they'll probably choose to ignore it).

Say what you mean, which, I hope, is that "because everyone has it" is the last reason you'd consider buying something. It's critical that your children understand that your family's values may not be the same as the Jones family's. Maybe you can't afford to keep up. Maybe you feel your children's current video game system is in good enough shape and they don't need a new one (unless you're willing to let them buy it with their own money). Or maybe you just don't want to referee disputes between siblings about whose turn it is to play (in which case you might consider compromising on a couple of handheld game systems).

In any case, the decision is up to you, not the Joneses. And whatever you decide, your children will not be social outcasts, they will not die (you didn't when you were young and tried the same ploy), and they will not stop loving you or move out.

That doesn't mean you should never buy your kids something all the other kids have. It just means you shouldn't buy them *everything* all the other kids have. Be discriminating, choosing those things your kids want most and—if you've done your job—least expect. The element of surprise is more than half the fun for both of you.

Q. "How come you always take my money to pay the pizza man or the baby sitter?"

A. Okay, maybe you don't *always* take their money. But tell your children the truth: Parents often borrow spare change from their kids because their kids are the only ones who ever seem to have any. It goes with being part of a family. If parents can learn to put up with little annoyances like kids who leave wet towels on the bathroom floor, kids can learn to put up with parents who raid their cash stash.

However, children do have a right to be paid back in a timely fashion. Parents don't intentionally neglect to repay the money; it just slips their mind. Consider this a friendly reminder and an opportunity to clear your conscience. Before you go on to the next question, give your daughter the $5 you owe her.

Q. "[Insert name of brother or sister] always borrows money from me and never pays me back. What should I do?"

A. You could tell your child, "That'll teach you not to lend him (or her) money any more," but that's only part of the lesson to be learned. Brother or sister also needs to be taught the consequences of failing to repay a debt.

Try a little tough love by taking both siblings aside and laying down the house rules about borrowing, which might go something like this: Henceforth, any loan of petty cash is expected to be repaid by allowance day, at the latest. If that doesn't happen, you'll deduct the money from the borrower's next allowance—plus interest—give it to the sibling, and tell him or her not to advance any more cash.

This may sound a little drastic, but the idea is to get the delinquent sibling to shape up before he or she gets a reputation as a deadbeat. And you may never have to charge interest or cut off a kid's credit. When one parent outlined the house rules to his children, the $3 that big brother had borrowed weeks before mysteriously turned up on little sister's dresser.

I don't object in principle to siblings lending money to one another as long as neither the borrower nor the lender is being taken advantage of.

Q. "I lost the $20 you gave me to buy a DVD. Can I have more money?"

A. The lost money was your child's responsibility, and you're under no obligation to make up the loss.

Having said that, I'm willing to make an exception if your child is sufficiently chastened. I once heard from a young woman who vividly recalled an incident from her youth, in which she lost the money her mother had given her to go to the grocery store. "I felt awful, and just having to go home and confess was worse than any punishment my mother could have inflicted." If your child has scoured the store for the missing money and is obviously upset about the loss, go ahead and buy the DVD yourself. If a child loses money by accident rather than by habit, there's no need to rub salt in the wounds.

That's especially true if you're partly at fault. Parents shouldn't get into the habit of peeling off $20 bills to give their children. Young children especially feel uncomfortable about carrying that much cash. Not only do they worry about losing it, but they also worry about losing the change—or being cheated by a dishonest sales clerk because they're little kids. Give your child an amount of money that more closely matches the purchase price. If you don't have anything smaller than a $20 bill, pay for the DVD (or whatever) yourself.

Q. "I lost my library book and they're charging me $10. Will you pay it?"

A. In a situation as clear-cut as this one, not even your children should seriously expect you to come up with the cash. But make sure your kids understand that the fine won't go unpaid. If they don't have the money right away, they'll have to save it out of their allowance or do extra chores to earn it.

When children lose money, they feel the impact immediately. When they lose something other than money, the financial consequences aren't always as direct. It can take time as well as a little effort on your part to get the point across. A couple of other situations:

- Your son tries out for football but quits, carelessly leaving his uniform in his locker instead of turning it in. A month later you get a $150 bill for a lost uniform. Your son doesn't have $150, and it would take too long to work off a debt that size. The school wants its money now. Advance your son the cash but deduct $5 a week from his allowance until the loan is repaid (or let him do extra chores to work off the debt more quickly).
- For Christmas you bought your daughter the snazzy watch she'd had her eye on for months. By Easter the watch is history, and your daughter is pining for a replacement. Let her pine. If you're willing to consider buying a new watch (and there's no reason why you should), at least make her wait until her birthday. Absence may make the watch grow less attractive or your daughter more careful.

Q. "Why do you always make us turn off the lights when we leave the room?"

A. Even though it's true that you don't own the electric company (as many parents like to remind their children), kids, even teens, are often in the dark about household expenses.

Tell them you have to pay the power company for the electricity you use each month, just as you pay the gas company for heat, the telephone company, the cable TV company, the supermarket, and so on down the line. Because there's only so much money to go around, you don't want to pay anyone more than you have to. That way you'll have more money left for other things the kids might enjoy—like going out for pizza on Saturday night. Now you're speaking their language!

Q. "Can I give all my money away to poor people?"
A. Admirable though it may be, the impulse of some children to give away all their money is as unrealistic as wanting to spend it all on toys for themselves. And other children can take unfair advantage of their generosity. Caught without exact change, one mom and dad sent their 9-year-old to school with a $5 bill to pay for a $2 lunch. When the girl's friends asked her for money, she didn't have the heart to say no and ended up giving away all the change.

The trick is to bring kids down to earth without dashing their spirit. In the case above, Mom and Dad sat down with their daughter and explained that they needed the change from the $5 to help buy groceries for dinner, or pay for the next day's lunch, or buy school supplies—expenses that a 9-year-old could understand. A week or so later, they deliberately sent their daughter off to school with a $5 bill in her wallet and a reminder to bring home the change. She did. (If you fear that your children are a soft touch, don't give them any extra cash that could end up in some other child's pocket.)

In order to grow up with a healthy attitude toward money, kids need to learn that it's a tool with lots of uses. Just as overspenders need to be prodded into saving money, overgivers need to have their charitable instincts channeled. Help them focus on a favorite cause that appeals to them, preferably one that's in

your community so the kids can take their money there themselves or donate their outgrown toys and clothing.

Q. "There's a contest on TV, and the prize is a trip to Disney World. Can I enter so we can go?"
A. Your children will likely not win the contest, but hope springs eternal. Explain to them that with a limited number of prizes and lots of entrants, the odds are against them. But let them enter anyway. Losing is a fact of life best learned by experience (and your kids will be less inclined to buy lottery tickets when they grow up).

One woman recalls her own childhood experience with games of chance. "One day my dad decided he would teach me to play poker. Once I had mastered the game, he suggested that we play for pennies. With the innocence of youth (and, I must confess, a touch of greed), I quickly agreed. Dad proceeded to clean me out. I was shocked. He later gave me back the coins, along with a lecture on get-rich-quick schemes and the risks of gambling. But what I remember most vividly was the feeling in my stomach when Dad won all my pennies."

Some contests are more child friendly than others. The best of them should be easy to enter, have decent odds, and award lots of prizes instead of one big one. Kids should be able to write in for a list of winners. For many children, losing isn't as much of a disappointment as not knowing who won. Here's an excerpt from a letter written to a children's TV show by one disappointed 10-year-old: "I entered your sweepstakes last year. After I sent it in I never heard from you again. I wasn't sure when you were going to pick the winners and I was upset." In this case, the letter writer was at least rewarded with a personal response if not the grand prize.

If the contest requires your children to write or draw something, or otherwise expend some constructive effort, entering could be a worthwhile experience regardless of the outcome.

Q. "When I pay for something, how do I know they won't cheat me just 'cause I'm a kid?"
A. Although it may make sense to respond "Always count your change," don't assume that children know how to do so. They may be frantically trying to subtract numbers in their head, unaware that there's a much easier way.

If they buy something that costs $3.63, for example, and they hand the clerk a $5 bill, tell them to count the change from the smallest denomination to the largest: two pennies to make 65¢ , then a dime to make 75¢ , a quarter to make $4, and a dollar bill to make $5.

This system isn't intuitive. One woman sheepishly confesses that she didn't figure it out until she was a teenager and got her first job working the cash register at a bakery. (For more tips on how to handle cash, see the list on page 71.)

Q. "The antenna on my new remote control car is broken. What should I do?"
A. Now is not the time to say "I told you that car wouldn't last." If a toy has broken through no fault of theirs, children should do the same things you would do if you bought something that didn't work: Call the manufacturer's 800 number if one is available, or take the item back (even if it means an extra trip to the store on your part).

Kids are consumers, too, and are entitled to the same remedies as grown-ups if they're dissatisfied with a product. But they don't know the ropes and often feel at the mercy of adults. So you'll have to give them some basic tips—for example, always save the sales receipt—and go with them to return the item until they build more confidence.

Q. "Why do athletes and movie stars get paid so much money?"
A. Even if it's true that celebrities are greedy, that doesn't do much to advance your child's knowledge of labor economics. It may be hard to accept the fact that sports stars earn more than teachers, but it isn't hard to explain.

It's just a simple matter of supply and demand for workers. There's a big demand on the part of team owners and fans for top players, but there's a very limited supply. So their salaries are bid up. There's also a demand for teachers, of course, but many more people are available to fill those positions, so school districts aren't forced to bid up their salaries as high (nor could they afford to).

Don't forget, though, that despite the glamour and the money, sports and movies are high-risk businesses. Team owners and movie producers expect superstars to more than pay for themselves through ticket sales. If a movie bombs, a star becomes a has-been. If a player is injured, his value plummets. Even if he stays healthy, he can be washed up by age 35.

In economic terms, players try to "maximize their income" before they're fully depreciated (used up) as an asset to their team. In other words, they try to make hay while the sun shines.

Why Is Money Green?

Chapter Seven

Kids think in concrete terms, so it's little wonder that many of the questions they ask about money involve hard currency and coins. "Why does all our money have to be green?" they want to know, or "Why is a nickel bigger than a dime?"

Grown-ups, of course, take money for granted and are generally clueless about its origins. "Because that's the way it's always been" is your natural response to your kids' questions.

And you're not far off the mark. In addition to being a medium of exchange (meaning that you can buy things with it), money is also a store of value (meaning that people are willing to hold on to it because they think it's worth something). To keep the public's confidence over the years, money has to be stable and reliable. That's why greenbacks continue to be predominantly green even after the government has added background tints of blue, red, and even peach to redesigned bills. But 'fess up. Even grown-ups wonder from time to time why we call a dollar a "buck," or for that matter, who decided that the dollar would be the official currency of the United States. In this chapter, which is made up of children's questions, you'll get a glimpse into the colorful past of U.S. coins and currency and the fascinating history of the language of money.

KIDS' QUESTIONS

Q. "Do we have to use coins as money, or could we use something else?"
A. People can use—and historically have used—almost anything as money, so long as it's recognized as valuable. Yap Islanders in the South Pacific used huge wheels carved of a special stone that was brought hundreds of miles over the open ocean. Native Americans used necklaces made of shells, which were called wampum; the darker the shell, the more valuable the necklace. Coins were finally settled on because the metal was valuable (many early U.S. coins were made of gold and silver), malleable (meaning it could be worked into different shapes and designs), and portable (it was easy to carry in your pocket).

Q. "Why is a nickel bigger than a dime if a dime is worth more?"
A. It goes back to when "major" U.S. coins—the dollar, half-dollar, quarter, and dime—were made of silver. The half-dollar, quarter, and dime were made in proportion to the dollar in size and weight. So the half-dollar was half the size of the dollar, the quarter was one-fourth as large as the dollar, and so on.

The nickel and the penny weren't made out of silver so their size didn't matter. They were considered minor coins—small change, you might say—and at one time could legally be used to pay only very small debts.

> **A nickel is only 25 percent nickel;** the other 75 percent is copper. In fact, a nickel has far more copper than a copper penny, which is only 2.5 percent copper. **There's no such coin as a penny;** its official title is the cent. Penny is a colloquialism that goes back to the English word pence. And there's no such coin as a nickel either. Officially, it's a five-cent piece, or a half dime.

Q. "Why is a penny made of copper?"
A. Actually, it isn't—or not much anyway. A penny is only 2.5 percent copper; the other 97.5 percent is zinc. It used to be the other way around (95 percent copper and 5 percent zinc), but in the early 1980s the value of the copper in the coin was beginning to approach the penny's face value. So the U.S. Mint, the U.S. Treasury agency that makes coins, changed the composition of the cent.

Why wasn't the penny made of silver like other coins were? We don't know for sure, although probably because it wasn't considered a major coin. The first cents were minted in 1792, and they've been made of copper in some form ever since, except for the year 1943 during World War II, when copper was needed for the war effort. That year, pennies were made out of zinc-coated steel.

But pennies haven't always looked the same. They used to be bigger than today's version. The first "small cent," which is the size of the current coin, was minted in 1856. And today's Lincoln penny first appeared in 1909, when it was issued to commemorate the 100th year of the president's birth.

Q. "On the penny, why is Lincoln facing toward the right and presidents on other coins are facing left?"
A. It's not a political statement; it's just the way the artist happened to design the coin.

Q. "Why do some coins have ridges around the outside?"
A. In the old days, when coins were literally "worth their weight" in silver or gold, people sometimes cheated by filing the edges of the coins and saving the precious metal. The ridges—called reeds—were adopted to discourage filing and to foil counterfeiting. Nowadays reeded edges help sight-impaired people tell one coin from another. The penny and the dime are similar in size, for example, so the reeded edges on a dime make it easier to identify.

Q. "Is my silver dollar really made out of silver?"
A. Not unless your coin dates back to the 1930s. That's the last time a 90 percent silver dollar was minted. No silver dollars were issued between 1936 and 1970. The last two silver dollars—the Eisenhower dollar, minted from 1971 to 1978, and the Susan B. Anthony dollar (1979 to 1981)—are "sandwich coins" like the dime, quarter, and half-dollar, made with a pure copper center and coated with a mixture of copper and nickel. Even the Sacagawea golden dollar coin, introduced in 2000, is mostly copper.

Q. "Can I use one of my silver dollars to pay for an ice cream bar?"
A. You can—but the Good Humor vendor doesn't have to take it. All coins are legal tender, meaning they can be used to buy things or pay debts. But the law doesn't require anyone to accept coins as payment. Every once in a while, for instance, you may hear about someone who thinks he or she has been unfairly ticketed for a traffic violation and pays the fine with a carload of pennies. But the joke's on the driver; the traffic court doesn't have to accept the coins.

Q. "How long do coins last?"
A. A coin in normal use can last 30 years. Coins are classified in three categories: "current," which are regular circulating coins; "uncurrent," which are worn but still recognizable and machine countable; and "mutilated," which are unrecognizable, corroded, broken, bent, fused together, or otherwise not machine countable. If you have coins in that last category, you can send them to the U.S. Mint in Philadelphia, which will redeem them by the pound at close to face value (write to the U.S. Mint, Coin Redemption Branch, 101 Fifth and Arch Streets, Philadelphia, PA 19106). But you have to send no less than one pound of coins, separated by denomination. The mint won't redeem individual coins.

Q. "Who needs pennies anyway? Why don't we just get rid of them?"
A. Congress has considered such a proposal, but it has never gone anywhere, mostly

- The word **money** comes from the Latin moneta, meaning coin or mint. The Romans themselves "coined" that word from the temple of Juno Moneta, where Roman money was made.
- **Moneta** literally comes from the Latin word for warning; among other things, Juno, the queen of the gods, was also the goddess of warnings.
- The word **bank** comes from the Italian word banca, meaning bench. Hundreds of years ago, businessmen met outside on benches to borrow money or to entrust their savings to someone to invest on their behalf.

because of opposition from the states. For state revenue collectors, pennies are crucial when setting sales-tax rates; it's much easier to raise the sales tax by a penny than by a nickel. And if the rate is, say 4 percent or 7 percent, pennies are critical to collecting the right amount of tax.

Sometimes the mint has to produce more coins even though there seem to be plenty outstanding, because a certain number of coins are lost or taken out of circulation—like that jar of pennies sitting on your closet floor. At the end of 1990, the government conducted a coin census and figured there were 132 billion cents in circulation. Since then the mint has produced billions more of the coins. Yet a number of years ago, there was actually a shortage of pennies, and the government had to appeal to Americans to get those cents out of their jars and back into circulation. (With coin-counting machines available at banks, supermarkets, and other locations, that's easier and more rewarding than ever. Put your kids in charge of gathering up loose change from around the house, and let them keep the value of the coins they turn in.)

In the old days, coins were valued for their precious metals—either gold or silver. Today they're valued for their electromagnetic properties so they can be used in vending machines. That's why they're made of a copper–nickel alloy.

Q. "Who decides which person should appear on each coin?"
A. All those decisions are made by act of Congress and the Treasury Department. The secretary of the Treasury has some discretionary power to change the design of coins but has always left that up to Congress. If Congress isn't specific about how it wants a coin to look, the U.S. Mint can decide or, if there's time, even sponsor a contest. The traditional portrait of Thomas Jefferson on the nickel was chosen after a design competition among 390 artists in 1938.

Among current coins, the design of the Lincoln penny has been in circulation the longest, dating back to 1909, when it was introduced on the 100th anniversary of Lincoln's birth. Washington began appearing on the quarter in 1932, the 200th anniversary of his birth. In the case of Franklin D. Roosevelt (the dime) and John F. Kennedy (the half-dollar), it was each man's untimely death in office that prompted his almost immediate commemoration on U.S. coins.

Q. "If I find a really dirty old coin, is it worth a lot of money?"
A. Probably not. Remember, the average coin is in circulation for 30 years, so even if you find a penny that was issued 30 years ago (which sounds like ancient times to most kids), it isn't old by coin standards. On the other hand, you aren't likely to find a coin minted prior to 30 years ago, because most of those have been taken out of circulation by collectors. What you've probably found is a dirty coin made relatively recently that is worth its face value and nothing more.

But just in case: Don't clean the coin, especially if you can't read the date. If it really is old, you'll decrease its value substantially if you polish it up. If you can't make out the date, have it examined by at least two different coin dealers. You can also get an opinion from the American Numismatic Association, 818 N. Cascade Ave., Colorado Springs, CO 80903-3279 (http://www.money.org).

If the date is readable and the coin is older than 30 years, look it up in the Guidebook of United States Coins, the so-called Red Book that is published every year and is the bible of coin collectors. Remember, though, that just because a coin is old doesn't necessarily mean it's worth a lot. Age isn't the only thing that determines a coin's value; rarity, condition, and demand are important too. A worn Indian-head penny from the early 1900s might be worth $1. But a "proof" coin from the same era, distinguishable by its brilliant mirrorlike surface and sharpness of detail, might fetch closer to $200.

Q. "If I start collecting coins, will I be able to sell my collection for a lot of money some day?"

A. Don't count on it. When it comes to collecting, you should do it for love, not money—and that advice applies to coins, comic books, sports cards, dolls, and all other collectibles. Even though it's possible to make money, the market for any collectible can be complex and fickle. In 1995 kids were searching their pockets for the so-called doubled-die cent, a coin with an imperfection that made certain features appear to have been struck twice. The first few coins discovered sold for more than $1,000, but as more turned up the price quickly dropped to less than $100.

On the other hand, collecting coins can be fun for youngsters because it doesn't take a lot of money to start buying coins that interest you—U.S. Civil War coins, worldwide coins with pictures of animals, or coins from a particular country, for example. You can even buy 2,000-year-old silver and copper coins for as little as $5 or $10 (for more information on coin collecting, contact the American Numismatic Association).

Just don't expect to be able to sell your collection for enough money to send yourself to Harvard when you're 18. You might make the car fare—but not the tuition.

Q. "What do people mean when they say, 'Do you think we're as rich as Fort Knox?'"

A. Fort Knox is a former army base near Louisville, Kentucky. Back in the 1930s, the U.S. government built a gold depository there to hold most of the gold that was owned by the government and which, at the time, backed up the value of the U.S. dollar. The outer wall of the depository was made of granite and lined with concrete as a symbol of national security and the soundness of the dollar, which was "as good as gold."

The 1913 Liberty head nickel is worth about a half-million dollars. But don't bother rummaging around in your pockets or piggy bank. Only five of the coins were struck.

The government's stock of gold is still stored at Fort Knox and has been stable for quite a few years at about 150 million troy ounces (a troy ounce is slightly heavier than a regular ounce). The price of an ounce of gold has been around several hundred dollars for years, but the U.S. gold reserves are carried on the books at $42.22 per ounce.

Q. "Does the U.S. government ever spend its gold?"

A. Nope. The government does issue a gold coin. It's called the American Eagle, and it's intended for collectors and sold as an investment, not as legal tender. But, by law, the gold that goes into those coins must be newly mined in the United States.

Q. "Do people still mine for gold?"
A. Sure. The United States produces about 9.5 million ounces a year, more than half of which comes from Nevada and California. Despite the legendary forty-niners and the gold rush of 1849, the biggest growth in the U.S. gold industry has occurred since 1980. Miners no longer use pans and picks. Chemical processes extract minute gold particles from the ore.

Even with the new gold supplies that are mined each year, all the gold in the world would fill only half the Washington Monument.

Q. "Who thought of using a dollar as the main unit of U.S. money?"
A. It was adopted by the Continental Congress in 1785, although the first dollar wasn't actually issued until a few years later (it was a coin, not a bill).

Q. "How did they decide on the name 'dollar'?"
A. The word *dollar* actually dates back to 1518, when a large silver coin was minted in Bohemia in the valley (or *thal*) of Joachim. Called the *Joachimsthaler,* the coin spread across Europe, and its name was adapted to each country's language. In Dutch, for example, it was the *daalder,* in Scandinavian the *daler,* and in English the dollar.

The Spanish peso, also called the Spanish milled dollar, was one of the principal coins in the early American colonies, along with traditional English money such as pounds and shillings. But once the United States declared its independence, the country gravitated toward the dollar, partly as a show of patriotism. The Mint Act of 1792 established the dollar as the official monetary unit of the United States, and the first dollar coin was struck in 1794 (the federal government didn't print a paper dollar until 1862).

Q. "What are dollar bills made of?"
A. A secret formula that isn't really paper at all but a combination of cotton (75 percent) and linen (25 percent). That explains why the bills can survive even when kids forget that their allowance is in the pocket of their jeans and throw them into the washer. In fact, the Bureau of Engraving and Printing—the U.S. Treasury agency that prints money—washes bills over and over to test their durability.

Q. "Why is money green?"
A. To be honest, the Treasury Department doesn't really know for sure but can make a good guess.

Back in 1861, the federal government authorized the issuance of its own paper money. But it immediately faced a threat from counterfeiters. What was needed was an ink with a colored tint that would make the bills difficult to duplicate by the black-and-white photography of the time. Such an ink was developed and patented by a man named Tracy R. Edson. The ink had a green tint, which came to be called patent green.

When U.S. currency was redesigned and made smaller in 1929, the green tint was con-

> **The "heads" side** of a coin is called the obverse; the "tails" side is called the reverse. The Lincoln Memorial is pictured on the reverse of a penny; on a nickel it's Monticello, Thomas Jefferson's home in Virginia; on the dime, it's the torch (liberty), olive branch (peace), and oak branch (strength); on the quarter, an eagle or a state symbol; and on the half-dollar, the presidential coat of arms.

tinued because ink of that color was available in large quantities, and the color was highly resistant to chemical and physical changes. Besides, by that time Americans had come to trust their money as a strong, stable currency.

Q. "Why are dollar bills called 'greenbacks'?"

A. That nickname comes from the color of the ink and the fact that it's used only on the back of paper money. Look closely and you'll see that the front of each bill is printed in black ink. The Treasury seal and serial numbers are green, but that's a different ink that's added later.

Q. "Who decided which portraits would be on each bill?"

A. The current portraits, along with the design on the back of each bill, were chosen by a committee appointed by the secretary of the Treasury in 1929.

Here's the lineup: George Washington on the 1-dollar bill, with the Great Seal of the United States on the back; Thomas Jefferson on the 2-dollar bill, with a picture of the signing of the Declaration of Independence on the back; Abraham Lincoln on the 5, with the Lincoln Memorial on the back; Alexander Hamilton (the first secretary of the Treasury) on the 10, with the U.S. Treasury building on the back; Andrew Jackson on the 20, with the White House on the back; Ulysses S. Grant on the 50, with the U.S. Capitol on the back; and Benjamin Franklin on the 100, with Independence Hall on the back.

Until the most recent currency redesign, the last significant change in the nation's paper money came in 1957, when the phrase "In God We Trust" was added.

> **Gold is stored** in the form of bars that are a little smaller than building bricks but much heavier. Each gold bar weighs 400 troy ounces, or about 27.4 regular pounds.

Q. "Can the government change the color of paper money or put a different picture on it?"

A. It could, but don't hold your breath waiting for a blue suede bill with Elvis on the front and Graceland on the back!

By law, the design features on U.S. currency must have historical and idealistic significance, may not include the likeness of a living person, and may not have sectarian significance (favoring one religion over another). The government could theoretically replace the current portraits of deceased American statesmen. But tradition and psychology would probably outweigh any popular trend. Part of the reason the dollar has endured in value, both here and around the world, is that its design hasn't changed much over the years. The government would be reluctant to shake that confidence.

The same is true of the color of money. In recent years, subtle background colors of blue, red, and peach have been added to some bills, but that was intended as an anticounterfeiting measure rather than as a fashion statement. It's true that other countries print their currencies in different colors, but Americans tend to regard those as "funny money."

The U.S. government prints more currency than do other countries, and U.S. dollars are more often the target of counterfeiters. The Treasury wants U.S. notes to be uniform in appearance so that people feel compelled to look at the bills when they're paying for something or getting change, instead of just reaching for a bill of a different color or size. By paying closer attention, you'll be more likely to spot something fishy.

Q. "Why is the government redesigning our paper currency?"

A. The intent is more to foil counterfeiters than to make it look different. In addition to the $50, $20, and $10 bills, the $100 bill is also scheduled for a facelift. Right now the government has no plans to redesign the $5, $2, or $1 bills.

Q. "How many women have been pictured on American money?"

A. In addition to Susan B. Anthony, who appears on the dollar coins issued from 1979 to 1981, and Sacagawea, the native American who served as a guide for the Lewis and Clark expedition and whose image is on the golden dollar coin, one other woman has appeared on U.S. currency—but not since 1896. Can you guess who that woman was?
a. Dolley Madison, President James Madison's wife, who saved valuable treasures when the British burned the White House during the War of 1812;
b. Martha Washington, George's wife; or
c. Clara Barton, who gained fame as a nurse during the Civil War and eventually founded the American Red Cross.
And the answer is . . . Martha Washington!

Q. "Who draws the pictures on U.S. money?"

A. U.S. currency is printed on presses using plates that are painstakingly engraved by hand by master engravers. There are fewer than 20 engravers in the country, and even in this age of computers they still work with hand tools similar to those used by Paul Revere. They're called letter engravers and picture engravers, and for each bill, one person does the signatures and all other letters while another works on the pictures and decorative scrollwork.

We've learned about the origin of the word dollar (see page 94), but the currencies of other nations often have interesting backgrounds as well. Franc comes from the Latin term Francorum Rex, or "King of the Franks," an inscription that appeared on medieval French coins. Italy's lira comes from libra, the Latin word for "pound." The mark, used in Germany, means "to mark," or "keep a tally." Yen, the main unit of Japanese currency, is also the Japanese word for "circle." The theory is that money should "circulate."

Q. "How much money does the government print every day?"

A. The Bureau of Engraving and Printing prints more than 37 million notes a day, with a face value of nearly $700 million, on its presses in Washington, D.C., and Fort Worth, Texas. Of the notes printed each year, 95 percent are used to replace bills already in circulation, and 45 percent are $1 bills.

Q. "What's the biggest bill?"

A. The $100 bill is the largest in circulation right now. The government used to issue notes in denominations of $500, $1,000, $5,000, and $10,000, but they were discontinued after 1969 because there was little demand for them. The largest bill ever printed had a face value of $100,000, but it was exchanged among banks and was never circulated to the public.

Q. "How long does paper money last?"

A. That depends on the bill's denomination and how often it changes hands. A $1 bill has an average life of 22 months. The average life span of other currency: $5 bill, 16 months; $10 bill, 18 months; $20 bill, 2 years; $50 bill, 5 years; $100 bill, 8½ years.

Q. "What does the government do with worn out money?"

A. It shreds the bills and then recycles or buries them. A stack of one year's worth of destroyed $1 bills alone would be 200 miles high.

Q. "What's that funny picture of a pyramid with an eye on top that's on the $1 bill?"

A. That's the reverse side of the Great Seal of the United States, which was adopted in 1782. At the base of the pyramid is the year 1776 in Roman numerals. The pyramid itself stands for permanence and strength, but it's unfinished, which signifies the future growth of the United States and the goal of perfection. The sunburst and the eye above the pyramid represent the overseeing eye of God.

The 13-letter motto "Annuit Coeptis" means "He has favored our undertakings." Below the pyramid is the motto "Novus Ordo Seclorum," which means "A new order of the ages" and stands for the new American era.

Parents can impress kids by telling them that the front of the Great Seal of the United States also appears on the back of the $1 bill. That's the picture of the American bald eagle behind the shield. The eagle holds in its right talon an olive branch that has 13 berries and 13 leaves. The olive branch stands for peace, and the number 13 always symbolizes the 13 original colonies. In its left talon, the eagle holds 13 arrows representing war. The eagle's head is turned toward the olive branch, showing a desire for peace.

The top of the seal represents Congress, the head of the eagle the executive branch, and the nine tail feathers the judiciary branch of our government. The 13-letter motto E Pluribus Unum on the ribbon held in the eagle's beak means "Out of Many, One."

In 1775, the Continental Congress authorized the issuance of currency to help pay for the Revolutionary War. Paul Revere, a silversmith by trade, actually made some of the first plates for this so-called continental currency. But the bills quickly lost their value, giving rise to the expression "not worth a continental."

Q. "What does the treasurer of the United States do?"

A. The treasurer of the United States, whose signature sharp-eyed kids will spot on the front of U.S. currency, is the Treasury Department official in charge of the U.S. Mint and the Bureau of Engraving and Printing. The treasurer is not to be confused with his or her boss, the secretary of the Treasury, whose signature also appears on U.S. currency.

Q. "If I accidentally tear a dollar bill and tape it back together, can I use it?"

A. Yes. You can use the bill even if you don't tape it back together as long as you clearly have more than half of the note. You can also take it to your local bank and exchange it for a new bill. That's also true for bills that are dirty, defaced, limp, or just plain worn out.

It's illegal, however, to intentionally deface a bill by doodling on it, for example. But you're unlikely to be prosecuted unless you make a habit of drawing mustaches on George Washington. In that case, your artistry may come to the attention of the Secret Service, the agency charged with tracking down counterfeiters and protecting the nation's currency.

Q. "If I only have a piece of a $1 bill, can I still use it?"

A. Not if it's less than half of the original note. In that case, your remnant is considered mutilated currency and isn't legal tender. If you want to exchange it for a new bill, you'll have to tell the Treasury Department how the money was damaged and provide evidence that the missing portion has been totally destroyed.

But if all you have is a small portion of a single bill, your chances of getting a replacement are slim. Each year the Treasury handles about 30,000 claims and redeems mutilated currency valued at about $90 million. Much of that is in the form of batches of bills that have been visibly damaged by fire, water, dirt, chemicals, explosives, rodents, or insects. Nowadays, one of the biggest causes of mutilated money is microwave damage. When their money accidentally gets wet, people try to dry it in a microwave oven and end up turning their cash into ash!

All claims regarding mutilated currency are handled by the Department of the Treasury, Bureau of Engraving and Printing, OCS/BEPA, P.O. Box 37048, Washington, DC 20013.

Like the word dollar, lots of our words for money and other financial terms have their roots in other languages.

A **doubloon,** the English word for a Spanish gold coin, comes from the Spanish word for double, because a doubloon was worth twice as much as a smaller coin called a pistole.

Picayune, a word we use to mean trifling, or of little value, comes from the French word for a small copper coin.

The word **dime** comes from the Latin word decimus, meaning "tenth." When Thomas Jefferson proposed this unit of currency, he called it the disme, a French term, because the coin would be one-tenth the value and size of the dollar.

Q. "How can I tell if a bill is counterfeit?"

A. Don't bother testing the ink to see if it smears. According to one bit of folk wisdom, a bill must be counterfeit if the ink rubs off. The truth is that genuine currency, when rubbed on paper, can leave ink smears too. So the Secret Service doesn't recommend using the ink blot test to check out a suspect bill.

Instead, you should compare the suspect note with a genuine one of the same denomination and look for any differences in the characteristics of the paper or the quality of the printing. Genuine paper, for example, has tiny red and blue fibers embedded throughout. Counterfeiters often try to simulate those fibers by printing red and blue lines on their paper, but the lines are printed on the surface of the paper rather than embedded in it.

On a genuine bill, the overall printing is sharper and more distinct. Compare especially such features as the portraits, which should appear lifelike; the clarity of the sawtooth points of the Treasury seal; the serial numbers, which should be evenly spaced and printed in the same ink color as the Treasury seal; and the border, on which the fine lines should be clear and unbroken.

If you really believe you might have a counterfeit bill, the best thing to do is to put it in an envelope and take it to a bank or your local police department.

Q. "Can I see money actually being made?"
A. If you visit Washington, D.C., you can take a tour of the Bureau of Engraving and Printing. There's no charge for the tour, but in peak tourist seasons—spring vacation and during the summer—you need to pick up tour tickets in advance on the day of your visit (call 202-874-2330 or 866-874-2330 for more information).

Two of the five U.S. Mints—in Denver and Philadelphia—are open for self-guided public tours. Contact the U.S. Mint Exhibits Office, 151 N. Independence Mall East, Philadelphia, PA 19106; 215-408-0110 for more information.

Q. "Grandma told me I could use my birthday money for 'mad money.' Does that mean I have to get mad before I spend it?"
A. Most parents probably know that "mad money" is slang for money you can blow on anything you want. But don't presume that your kids know what the phrase means—or, for that matter, that they understand any of the other colorful money idioms and adages that litter our language.

We pay cash on the barrelhead, save for a rainy day, and put in our two cents. Some expressions are intuitive, some have historical roots in everyday experience, and some we owe to Benjamin Franklin, whose *Poor Richard's Almanac* was rich in financial wisdom—"A penny saved is a penny earned," "Penny-wise and pound-foolish."

Before the federal government established an official U.S. currency, colonies, banks, and even individuals issued their own money, which often wasn't worth the paper it was printed on. Even Benjamin Franklin got into the act, printing dollars on his own press for the colony of New Jersey. With typical Franklin bluntness, the motto on the bill read "Mind Your Business."

But your children won't necessarily understand any of these expressions unless you explain them. Then if you come up totally blank and can't think of any other response to their questions, at least they'll know what you're talking about if you use one of these expressions.

By the way, the expression "mad money" came into common use in the 1920s. It referred to money a young woman carried with her on a date so that she could pay for bus fare home if she got "mad" at her escort for inappropriate behavior!

Q. "How do people decide how many French francs or English pounds a dollar is worth?"
A. The value of a dollar can change every day, and it's decided in an open market by people who actually buy and sell money. In this way, the currency market is much like the stock market or even a flea market.

To understand how this works, it helps to think of money itself as the product that's being bought and sold. Suppose you're planning a trip to Paris. You'll have to pay for your hotel, your fancy French pastries, and your tickets on the Metro (the Paris subway), but in France they don't take dollars; they take francs. So before you leave home you'll have to buy francs for the trip from a bank or a money exchange. The bank gets its francs from traders all over the world who are linked by computer.

How many francs will a dollar buy? It all depends on how many francs the traders are willing to sell. If they are eager to get dollars—

maybe because they want to buy American products or because they just like the idea of owning dollars—they may be willing to make you an attractive offer of, say, six francs for a dollar. In that case, we say that the dollar is "strong."

But if they aren't very much interested in buying dollars—maybe because they already have enough and don't want any more—they may offer you only four francs for your dollar. In that case, we say that the dollar is "weak"—and your trip just got more expensive, because you have to spend more dollars to get the francs you need.

> **You can fold a paper bill** forward and backward about 4,000 times before it will tear.

Allowances: A Hands-on Experience

When it comes to money, topic A for discussion between parents and children is allowances. First, the kids want to know if they can have one. No sooner do they get one, or so it seems, than they want an advance. And before you know it they're lobbying for a raise.

It isn't only parents and children who lock horns on this issue. Parents often disagree with each other about such things as how much to give and whether kids who get an allowance should be required to do chores in return. In fact, parents can't always agree on just what an allowance is or how it should work.

To make sure we're all on the same page, here's my definition: An allowance is a fixed amount of money children receive on a regular schedule, with the understanding that they will pay for certain agreed-upon expenses. Now that I've standardized the language, let me add that no single allowance system will work for every family. But any system will work if you follow two basic rules for success. One: Don't start giving an allowance until your children are old enough to manage it. Two: Keep the system simple so that *you* can manage it.

If you think that by denying your kids an allowance you'll be able to limit the amount of money they get their hands on, forget it. Studies show that kids who don't get allowances have access to about as much money as kids who do. In fact, I've known children to actively resist an allowance precisely because they figure they'll come out ahead by hitting up Mom and Dad for cash whenever they head out to the mall with their friends.

Because kids are apparently going to get the money anyway, it's better to have them learn to manage it themselves than nickel-and-dime (-and-dollar) you to death. With an allowance, both you and your children will actually have more control over your kids' finances—especially if you make it clear to them that the allowance isn't bonus cash but will take the place of money you normally would have spent on such things as trading cards and other collectibles, snack foods, movie tickets, mall excursions, and other kid-related expenses.

You don't need to give an allowance until your children are at least 6 years old. You don't want to rush things, and preschoolers generally don't understand the abstract idea of money anyway. Whether you give them 50¢, $1, or $2, for example, they're not quite sure how much they have or how far it will go.

Once children start first grade they begin learning about money in school, so they'll know that if they get a $1 bill, that's equivalent in value to ten dimes or four quarters. They'll also have some idea of how much their dollar will buy. If your child is 9, 10, or even older and you don't already give an allowance, it's not too late. Some parents have even started their kids on an allowance when they became teenagers as a rite of passage to becoming more grown-up.

How Much Is Enough?

When setting an allowance, you should give enough so that your children can squander it but not so much that you'll be upset when they do. Sit down with your children and decide what expenses their allowance will have to cover. Depending on their interests, 6-year-olds, for example, might start with small items such as stickers or other collectibles, art supplies, hair bows, or mini racing cars. You might expect an 11-year-old to pay for his or her own movie admissions and refreshments.

Don't underestimate a child's cost of living. When my children were younger, we all got a humorous lesson in kiddie inflation from Lamb Chop, the puppet on the TV show starring the late Shari Lewis and her animal friends. In one episode, the lovable lamb was negotiating for a raise in her penny-a-week allowance. "Do you buy anything?" asked Shari. Retorted Lamb Chop, "If I save it for 12 weeks, I can blow it on a pack of gum." Shari and Lamb Chop eventually settled on 7¢ a week. But if you're going to leave room for a pack of gum, your children will need a little more than that.

When you and your children settle on an allowance, be open and realistic about what you expect the money to cover. You might want your 11-year-old to pick up the cost of after-school snacks with his friends and games at the video arcade, but figure that basic expenses for clothing and school supplies are your responsibility. By the time your child is 15, however, it's reasonable to expect him or her to be kicking in for clothes and the cost of the French Club ski trip. It's a help to ask other parents how much they're giving. Ultimately, though, you can't let an "expert" or your neighbor down the street make your decision for you; you will have to go with your own instincts and values.

It's tough to get hard numbers on how much allowance youngsters actually receive. According to the results of a recent survey by Yankelovich Youth Monitor, 6- to 8-year-olds get $6 a week; 9- to 11-year-olds, $8; 12- to 14-year-olds, $11.30; and 15- to 17-year-olds, $19.30.

But those are just guidelines, and I'm happy to offer a few of my own. I think first-graders need at least $1 a week to do any serious spending or saving; even $2 (or more) wouldn't be out of line. As children get older you can adjust that amount upward depending on how much of their own expenses you expect them to cover.

Giving kids a weekly allowance that's equal to their age is another option, but many parents feel that's too much for younger children. My own recommendation is to start with a weekly base allowance equal to half a child's age, so that a 6-year-old would get $3 a week and a 10-year-old, $5. Most parents I talk to feel comfortable with the half-age figure. And, again, you can adjust it up or down based on the cost of living in your area and what you expect your children to pay for.

Interestingly, the vast majority of kids surveyed by Yankelovich Youth Monitor said that in addition to allowance, they get extra money for things like trips to the mall and the movies. But that defeats the purpose. Certainly for older children, those expenses should be built into the financial responsibilities that come with the allowance, so kids can make decisions about how to parcel out their money (and aren't bumming 20 bucks from you every time they leave the house).

Negotiating a Raise

Now it's time to take a break in your reading and hand this book over to your kids. I'm about to tell them how to pry more money out of Mom and Dad (take a sneak peek if you wish, so you'll be prepared).

Kids, if you want a surefire strategy for convincing your parents you need a raise in your allowance, here's my advice: Don't whine. No, your parents don't live in the dark ages. And, yes, they know how much things cost. They're the ones paying the household bills, remember? In fact, maybe they're reluctant to give you a raise because they feel they can't afford to.

Instead of complaining, take the initiative to make a list of your income and expenses (use the Money Record worksheet on pages 122 and 123). If you find you're saving zilch and squandering all your money on snacks and entertainment, you're not going to win sympathy—or extra cash—from your folks. Instead, try the needs-versus-wants exercise beginning on page 118; it may help you cut back on the unimportant stuff and save for the big things you really want. Your parents may be so impressed by your initiative that they'll give you a raise even if you don't actually need one.

If you have bigger expenses—lunches, transportation, clothes—and are having trouble making ends meet, talk with your parents, or maybe take them on a shopping excursion to scope out the situation. Don't expect them to spring for the latest—and most expensive—wardrobe, but you may be able to squeeze out a few more bucks if you're willing to compromise on less expensive shoes in order to buy the most fashionable jeans. Maybe your parents will increase your clothing allowance if you're willing to accept more responsibility for buying your clothes.

One 11-year-old told me that when she wants a raise in her allowance, her parents make her come up with three good reasons why. So start thinking. Hint: "Because I need the money" doesn't count. (Now you can hand this book back to Mom and Dad—or read on if you're curious.)

No Bailouts

Don't be surprised if at first your children blow their whole allowance on candy, trading cards, and arcade games. Just bite your tongue and keep a firm grip on your wallet. You, of course, have the right to veto any purchase that's unhealthy, unsafe, or in violation of your family's principles. Outside of that, though, you have to expect your kids to go a little wild, at least at first. But they should calm down once they realize that no more money is forthcoming to bail them out.

In my experience, kids will spend unlimited amounts of money so long as it's yours. When their cash is on the line, you may be surprised at just how tightfisted they can be. Here's a real-life exchange between a father and his 8-year-old son, who were observed at a toy store. As they were leaving, the boy picked up a plastic toy and tossed it on the checkout counter. If he wanted it, his father told him, he'd

DEAR JANET

Q. I have two children, ages 7 and 10, and would like to start giving them allowances. Is it okay for parents to keep track of how they spend it?

Q. Should I start my kids' allowance with deductions for taxes, savings, medical insurance, and the like to teach them about finances? Of course, the take-home pay would be close to what the actual allowance would have been without the deductions.

A. Each of you has an interesting twist on the subject of allowance, which just goes to show that there's no one-size-fits-all system for every family.

But successful systems do have several things in common: They're simple enough for both parents and children to manage; they're age appropriate; and they give kids the opportunity to make their own decisions. Based on those criteria, each of you will have to address potential pitfalls to make your ideas workable.

In the first case, keeping track of the kids' expenses would mean work for you—and violate the "keep it simple" principle. If cash seems to slip through their fingers, you could help the children monitor their own spending. But resist the temptation to tell them what to do with the money.

In the second case, if your youngsters are still in elementary school, hitting them with taxes and medical insurance may be a bit overwhelming. Still, your idea is intriguing. To make it work, I'd keep it as streamlined as possible by limiting the deductions. Come up with a gross number that, when reduced by, say, 20 percent for taxes and 5 percent for health insurance, equals the actual allowance, out of which kids could save 10 percent.

have to pay for it himself. Replied the boy: "You don't think I'd spend my money on that junk, do you?"

Linda Jessup is the founder of the Parent Encouragement Program, a parent support group in suburban Washington, D.C., that teaches practical approaches to child rearing. She and her husband, David, also developed a cradle-to-college system for teaching their own seven children how to manage money. A cornerstone of their plan was to stand firm and let the kids get out of their own tight corners. Imagine, for example, a situation in which a child is invited to a birthday party but has run through his allowance and doesn't have enough to buy a present (one of the expenses the allowance is supposed to cover). "We tended not to give loans," explained Linda, "so we would discuss his choices and the advantages and disadvantages of each." He could, for example, not go to the party because he didn't have a gift. Or he could give something of his own that his friend liked. Or he could make a card and enclose a promise to buy a gift in the future. He could give a gift of service and offer to help his friend clean his room or let him ride his bike. "We also allowed kids to go without a gift and suffer any social consequences," said Linda. "Not surprisingly, that problem tended to correct itself."

Doing Good

Parents often ask me if they should force their children to save part of their allowance or give a portion to charity. It would be ideal if youngsters were to show both forethought and thoughtfulness on their own with a little encouragement from you. But if saving and giving are important values you want to teach your kids, by all means, have them set aside a portion of their allowance for those purposes (and any others on which you put a premium). In the Jessup household, each child was expected to tithe 10 percent and put at least twice that amount into savings, just as their parents strove to do (see Chapter 9 for more tips on getting your kids to save money).

match savings

Work for Pay NO

One of the most controversial issues regarding allowances is whether you should expect kids to do chores in return. Pose this question to a roomful of parents and you'll find they split into two camps. On the "yes" side are parents who don't want to hand money over to their children without getting some elbow grease in return. For these parents, pay without work sounds too much like a free lunch. And, besides, they can't figure out any other way to get little Billy to make his bed.

In the "no" camp are parents who feel that kids should do chores for free because they're part of the family; if they make the mess, they should clean it up.

Q. Here's the situation: My daughter was teasing her older brother while he was doing his homework. He picked up the TV remote control and threw it at her. She heaved it back. But her aim was off and she broke our kitchen window to the tune of an $80 repair job. My son says it's not his fault that his sister has rotten aim and that she should have to pay for the damage. What do you say?

A. Your daughter may have started the skirmish, but your son escalated hostilities when he threw the remote control. Once a projectile was involved, the conflict was out of control and there was no predicting the outcome. Both of them should share in paying reparations.

Paying for chores also risks creating a gang of little mercenaries, who respond, "How much will you pay me?" every time you ask them to help unload the groceries or set the table. And some children simply aren't motivated by money, so cash won't coax them into taking out the trash. After years of speaking with parents about this issue, I have concluded that there's an even more fundamental flaw in a system that's linked to chores: It can be an administrative nightmare for Mom and Dad. If Little Billy's income is dependent on work completed, you'll have to go to the trouble of coming up with a pay scale per chore and monitor which ones actually get done. If Little Billy makes his bed on only four days out of seven, do you give him his weekly dole? And what if one week he decides that he doesn't need any money, so he doesn't do any work? In my experience, many parents end up handing over the money even if their children don't do the work, so the system fails.

Consider Your Goals

To help you find a workable solution to the allowance-for-chores quandary, I offer a couple of alternatives.

1. IF YOUR MAIN GOAL IS TO TEACH YOUR KIDS TO MANAGE MONEY (AND I CONFESS THIS IS MY PREFERENCE), give them a basic allowance that isn't linked to chores but is tied instead to certain spending responsibilities. As I've mentioned earlier in this chapter, you might require them to pay for their own video games, movie tickets, trading cards, or other collectibles. It's the easiest system to manage, yet the allowance isn't just a handout; it's directly tied to financial "jobs" your kids are taking over from you. If you still want to teach them the value of working for pay, you can always let them earn extra cash for extra jobs such as raking leaves, washing the car, or cleaning the garage. That also gives youngsters a way to supplement their basic allowance.

How do you decide what expenses your kids should cover? It doesn't matter how much or how little they have to pay for so long as they have to pay for something. Their responsibilities should depend on their age and your expectations. Some parents give their children a relatively small allowance and consider it mad money. Others hand out a bigger amount, out of which older kids are expected to pay for such basics as school lunches or clothing. Either system can work if you follow a few general rules:

- **Start small,** especially with younger children. Put them in charge of the single thing they most like to spend your money on, whether it's comic books, video arcade games, or popcorn at the movies.

  One mother, who is an artist, often took her 7-year-old daughter, Roxanne, to museums, where the child loved to buy trinkets from the gift shops—with her mother's money. Mom finally told Roxanne that she would have to use her own allowance to buy souvenirs. As if by magic, Roxanne became more conscientious about bringing money with her—and the price of the souvenirs she purchased dropped drastically.

- **Anticipate conflicts.** Suppose you expect your children to pay for their own tickets when they go to the movies with friends. Then suppose your whole family goes to see a movie as a holiday treat. Who pays? One mom and dad decreed that on family outings parents would pay for the tickets—but the kids would have to buy their own refreshments.

  In another case, a mother wanted to encourage her 9-year-old to read without going broke buying books for him. She agreed to pay for up to $5 worth of books when Sam brought home the monthly order form from his school book club. Above that, he was on his own.

2. IF YOU'RE SET ON MAKING CHORES THE QUID PRO QUO FOR GETTING AN ALLOWANCE, go ahead and do it. But to make the bookkeeping easier—and to make the connection between work and pay more direct—consider paying your kids as soon as a job is done to your satisfaction instead of waiting for a designated payday. Or consider putting your children in charge of keeping track of chores completed. If they fall down on that job, their pocketbook takes a direct hit.

To avoid turning your children into little money-grubbers who refuse to do anything without being paid, expect them to do a couple of basic chores—making their beds, cleaning their rooms—for free. If they ask how much you'll give them in return for making their

OK to pay extra for reasonable extra effort jobs.

DEAR JANET

Q. I don't like the idea of just handing over an allowance to my kids, and I'd like to link the money with chores. Any suggestions on how to do this successfully?

A. Keep it simple. Try one of these strategies:

■ **Choose a chore.** Attach a value to household jobs and let your kids select the ones they want to do. This plan works best with children who need or want money. If they don't, the work may not get done.

■ **Point system.** Invest in a big calendar or bulletin board and have your kids tally a point each time they do something helpful around the house. At the end of the week you can award, say, 10¢ a point. This plan works best for younger children who do

fairly simple tasks that are roughly equal in value, such as making beds or setting the table.

■ **Negative option.** Put your kids' allowance—say, $5 a week—in quarters in a glass jar (or use dimes for a smaller amount). Each time your children don't respond to your request for help, take out a quarter. At the end of the week, they get to keep what's left.

■ **On the spot.** Here's a tip from a mom who required her children to keep their rooms neat in exchange for their allowance: She paid the money every Saturday in each child's room. If the rooms were spic and span at that time, the kids got the money; if not, they didn't.

bed every day, tell them what I tell my children—they'll earn your undying love and affection. You will ease the tension with a little humor and put a more positive spin on household tasks—which, you can remind your kids, everyone in the family (including you) pitches in to do without pay.

Two Families' Systems

The Norton family has always used a strict fee-for-service system with their two children. The Nortons don't pay for certain "family" chores, such as doing the dishes or keeping one's room clean, but they put a price tag on jobs that a cleaning service or a neighborhood teenager might be hired to do: emptying the wastebaskets, cleaning the bathroom, raking the leaves, washing the car. It's the children's responsibility to keep a record of everything they have done and to present their parents with an itemized bill by 9:30 each Sunday morning. Then they immediately deduct 10 percent for their weekly tithe. Both of the Norton children were adopted, at the ages of 8 and 6, from difficult family backgrounds, and the chore idea started out as a way to give them a sense of family structure, said Dad. But it has had unexpected benefits. When little brother was old enough to take over the job of emptying wastebaskets, "he felt great," recalled Dad. "He was getting to do something his big sister had done."

Carol McCarter adopted a different system when her son, Matt, was in seventh grade. Carol's story started out as a classic case of an allowance "system" that was too open-ended. Matt got $5 a week, but had no fixed instructions about what the money was supposed to cover. He regarded it as extra cash that his mother gave him on top of everything else, so he would fritter it away and then come back and ask for more. "We were always arguing about money," said Carol.

Tired of bickering, she finally gave in to his requests by increasing his allowance to $50 every two weeks. That may sound like a lot, but $20 of the total

DEAR JANET

Q. My husband is always slipping our kids a couple of dollars to get them to practice their music lessons or sports. I don't like the idea, but he says it's not a lot of money and it will give them an incentive to work harder.

A. Your husband is probably wasting his money. If your children like what they're doing, they don't need any other reward. If they don't like what they're doing, maybe they should be playing a different musical instrument or sport.

If you can't get your husband to change his tune, try getting him to change his system. Instead of simply paying off the kids

in cash, suggest that he reward them with "music money": For every 15 minutes spent practicing, they earn, say, $1 in music money. When they've accumulated 20 music dollars, they're entitled to a new CD or a trip to the movies.

Young sports enthusiasts often have their eye on a new tennis racket, soccer bag, or baseball glove. In this case try "sports cents": For every 15 minutes of practice, you credit your athletes with 100 sports cents. Once they've accumulated enough cents to pay for the coveted piece of equipment, you agree to spring for it.

was earmarked for school lunches. And the rest was specifically designated to pay for most of Matt's expenses, aside from clothing: movies, other entertainment, snack food, fishing equipment ("an endless need," said his mother).

With the allowance tied to financial responsibilities, Matt learned quickly that he had to manage it carefully to make it last. (He tried cutting back on lunch, but his appetite for food turned out to be greater than his appetite for other stuff.) When he discovered that he actually spent more during the summer, he began setting aside a portion each month toward a "summer fund." He used to have a bank savings account with nothing in it; suddenly he began saving for a fishing trip to Montana, starting with money he earned over the summer by watering plants.

"I had said all this to him many times before, but it was my money instead of his that was paying for things, so it just never worked," said his mom. "Now his savings have a purpose, and the best part is he came up with it; I didn't."

Which just goes to prove what I always say: Kids will spend unlimited amounts of money as long as it's yours. When it is suddenly their own cash that's on the line, it becomes a whole new ball game, and everybody wins.

Getting the Jobs Done

If you don't pay your kids, how do you get them to do chores? You could simply try asking, especially if your children are still young. Many parents anticipate doing battle on the chore front, but unless you and your kids are barely on speaking terms, they should respond to your request. A friend of mine told me that when he was a boy, his mother had a surefire way of getting chores done. "She would ask me, 'Will you please do me a favor?'" said my friend. "How could I say no? I'm 40 years old and it still works."

Also remember that you're the one in charge. "If you project self-confidence in your relationship with your children, you won't have to rely that often on gimmicks to get them to do what you want," said John Rosemond, family psychologist and author. "Put your cards on the table, then walk away and let your child come to grips with the hand." Rosemond recalls an incident that occurred when his own daughter was a teenager and he asked her to wash the dinner dishes. She protested that she had too much homework; he replied that she had time for both. Again she refused. "I got up, looked at her and said, 'You know and I know that you're going to do the dishes, so there's no point in wasting any more time.' I walked out and she did the dishes."

Even if you're not a trained professional, this is worth trying at home. If it doesn't work, try another tactic. You might, for example, let your children have a say in choosing the jobs they have to do. That will probably cut down on the complaining and give them a vested interest in doing the job correctly. After all, your purpose in requiring your children to do house-

DEAR JANET

Q. My son is 4. I know that's a little young to start an allowance, but I got tired of having him ask me to buy chewing gum. So I started giving him five quarters a week, one of which goes into his savings jar. The rest is his to spend. He has his eye on a pair of kids' rollerblades, and he already had $17 in spare change in his bank, so I told him if he saved his four quarters for four Mondays, he'd have enough to buy the skates. (I'm willing to kick in the difference).

So far it's been working. He's chosen to save his money instead of spending it, and when we went to an amusement park, he didn't ask for any souvenirs once he realized he'd have to pay for them. But I'm wondering if this will continue once he has the skates and has less incentive to save.

A. Your son is a little young to be getting an allowance, but you're doing a number of things right: giving him quarters instead of dollar bills, which makes money more concrete and easier to understand, and setting a realistic savings goal—four weeks is about as long as a 4-year-old can wait.

It will be an eye-opener for him when he has to surrender all his money for the skates, but that's a lesson too. If he doesn't start saving again right away, don't worry. Just make sure he continues to use his own quarters to buy what he wants. Not having him bug you for gum any more will be an accomplishment in itself.

hold jobs is to teach them responsibility and to get help with some of the things you just don't have time to do. So why settle for mundane tasks that don't take much time anyway? Give them bigger jobs that are potentially more interesting—and more likely to get done:

SANTA'S HELPERS. Children as young as, say, 7 or 8 can wrap a stack of gifts or help trim a tree. What does it really matter if the paper is torn and the ribbon is askew? Grandparents, aunts, and uncles will love their gifts all the more. So what if one branch is sagging under the weight of 20 ornaments? You can always move them after the kids are in bed.

KITCHEN AIDES. Put your kids in charge of planning and preparing dinner once a week or breakfast on Sundays. The next time you have to come up with four dozen chocolate chip cookies for the class Halloween party, let your children do the baking.

WATER BABIES. Put them in charge of watering the garden, washing the car or the (low) windows, hosing the deck—any outside job that requires water (preferably from a hose or sprinkler), especially when the weather is hot.

WARDROBE MASTERS. Make your kids responsible for at least sorting and putting away (and possibly even washing) their own clothes. Trust them to pack their own suitcases for family trips. (Just check to make sure they've remembered underwear.)

PARTY PLANNERS. Anticipation is half the fun, so let them write the invitations, plan the games, put the treats in the goodie bags, make the poster for pin-the-nose-on-the-witch, and help serve the food.

The point is to raise your parental expectations. Author and family counselor Eda LeShan once told of a friend who had to be out of town for a few days and put her 10-year-old in charge of taking telephone messages. "That's pretty sophisticated for a 10-year-old, but the child was very proud of being trusted to do it." One mother agreed to let her 11-year-old son take money from her purse for a comic book, only to find it was a special issue that cost $40. She kept the book until he worked off the debt—by helping her install drywall in his bedroom.

Routine Tasks

Children also feel more comfortable with what's expected of them when it's part of a daily routine. Chances are you already have a schedule for getting your kids to do their homework or getting ready for bed, so you just have to make chores part of the drill. Making the bed goes with brushing teeth in the morning, and clearing the table or taking out trash goes with doing homework at night.

When the older of his two sons turned 5, one dad I know gave the boy (along with his birthday gifts) one chore to do. Another job was added each birthday. By age 7, young Jason was responsible for making his bed, setting the dinner table, and doing his homework. "It was a mark of maturity," said Dad, "and we made it a matter-of-fact expectation that he did the job." My friend figures it's just like the real world: "Some managers think you can't get workers to do anything unless you pay them," he said, but setting high standards and expecting them to be met works too.

"I Won't Do It"

If your children flatly refuse, much as they might refuse to eat their peas at dinner, their behavior could be a symptom of a power struggle that you may be able to defuse by talking things out. (For example, you might say: "Just as everyone in the family is expected to sample at least three bites of all the food that's on the table, everyone is expected to pitch in and do his or her share of work.") If not, you may have to fall back on those few time-tested and well-chosen words: "Because I said so and I'm the Mom/Dad." That strategy might be more successful with younger children than with adolescents, to whom you could propose a deal: Tell them that until they make the beds/vacuum the floor/give the dog a bath or whatever, you will not take them to the soccer game/movies/shopping mall or wherever. It shouldn't take more than one or two missed matinees for them to get the message.

Or, like the Jessups, you may be able to think of a more creative solution. By age 11, all of the Jessup children were expected to be jacks of all trades, able to do the laundry for the family, prepare a simple, well-

---

DEAR JANET

Q. I never liked the feeling of giving an allowance (it seems like welfare) and have found a much more interesting way to teach my 7-year-old about money. Instead of doling out a couple of bucks a week, I pay her a percentage of whatever money she can muster from gifts or handouts. That is, each week the Bank of Daddy pays her 5 percent on what she has accumulated, and she records the earnings in a pretty notebook that she picked out. She suggested that she open a bank account when she gets to $60.

A. You have developed a great system for encouraging your daughter to save, but you could use a bit more discipline on the earnings side. Letting her depend solely on gifts and handouts is too haphazard.

She sounds mature enough to handle an allowance, and it doesn't have to seem like welfare if you hand over responsibilities with the cash (as outlined in this chapter). You could also pay her for extra jobs she does around the house. Having a steady source of income could also stimulate her inclination to save. The Bank of Daddy may have to rethink that 5 percent interest rate.

balanced meal, and do the marketing. Starting at age 5, each child was given a weekly job, which the child had a hand in choosing. For example, a child might go "into training" to learn how to vacuum, cook, or make lunches. If the child chose vacuuming, "I'd ask what days I could count on having it taken care of, and I'd expect it to be done at that time," said Linda. If it wasn't, "I'd point out to the child that he or she chose the job and ask what the problem was." Sometimes the solution was as simple as a gentle reminder—one child hung a sign from his own bedroom doorway to jog his memory—or trading jobs with someone else.

But sometimes Mom had to take matters into her own hands. Once, when Linda was dissatisfied with the performance of her kitchen and trash crew, she prepared a sign, complete with vicious-looking flies, announcing that the kitchen was closed by order of the Jessup Health Department. When the kids arrived home after school ravenous for snacks, Linda told them the kitchen was unsanitary and she wasn't willing to cook there. It proved to be a smart strategy: four of the kids put together a team-cleaning effort and the kitchen was reopened.

One final piece of advice about chores: Things should get better. When your children are 6, they'll leave their wet towels crumpled on the bathroom floor. When they're 13, they'll leave them crumpled in the closet. But by the time they're in college, they should have the presence of mind to hang them neatly— even if it is over the doorknob.

Needs and Wants

As children approach their teenage years, it's not unreasonable to expect them to manage their allowance on a monthly schedule—and not unusual for them to run out of money before payday. Even though they seem like irresponsible spendthrifts, your kids may simply be having trouble budgeting. It's often tough for kids (and grown-ups) to tell the difference between things they need and things they want, and to set priorities. Here's an exercise that will help:

- **On a sheet of paper, have your kids write down** their total monthly (or weekly) income from all sources—allowance, jobs, gifts. Then have them write down everything they are expected to buy with their money and what they would *like* to buy. Give them free rein to include everything from pencils to a Porsche.
- **A week or so later, pull out their papers again.** Have the kids break the big list into two smaller ones: the boring stuff they have to buy (such as school supplies and lunches, toiletries, and whatever else you've agreed on) and all the fun stuff they want. Tot up expenses in the have-to-buy column, compare it with total monthly income, and see how much is left.
- **In another week or so, go back to the lists.** Now that your kids know they have, say, $10 a week to spend on the fun stuff, they can see that if they use the money to buy a CD every couple of weeks, they won't be able to afford the new jeans. If they must have the jeans, CDs will have to wait.

Seeing all this in writing and over the course of a few weeks somehow makes it easier to categorize the items on a wish list as "must have," "can wait," or "in your dreams." It may suggest other possibilities as well—a part-time job for your kids or even a bigger allowance. If none of this works, maybe your children really are irresponsible spendthrifts. Cut them back to a weekly allowance until they're more mature.

A Clothing Allowance That Works

By the time children reach their early teens, they ought to be on their own to buy birthday gifts or an occasional article of clothing for themselves. As noted in the preceding section, it may be time to see whether they can handle an allowance monthly rather than weekly. And by the time they're high school juniors or seniors, they could be managing a seasonal clothing budget—say, twice a year, in the spring and fall, or quarterly.

Does that mean you can trust them not to buy a black leather jacket with lug nuts hanging from the collar? Not necessarily. But if you've done your job, you should be able to trust them to buy that jacket on sale. When your kids begin begging for a clothing allowance, tell them you will consider it if they earn the privilege by passing a shoppers ed course of your own creation.

Lesson one is taking inventory of every article of clothing they own, including underwear, socks, and pajamas.

Lesson two is having them make a list of all the things they need (because the clothes are falling apart or no longer fit) as well as things they want (because they're trendy and cool). Then tell them what you think is a reasonable allowance—the amount you'd typically spend on their clothes each season, for example.

With the help of catalogs, lesson three is letting them practice matching a new wardrobe with the available funds. With luck, they'll learn that (1) they can't possibly afford five silk shirts or (2) they'll have to shop in cheaper catalogs. Both are valuable lessons.

Now your kids are ready for a dress rehearsal by going with you on a shopping trip. To make the task less overwhelming, limit your itinerary to, say, three stores. Add your own commentary along the way: How to spot a bargain at sales or off-price stores; how to select clothes that won't fall apart in the wash; how to choose items that are stylish but not faddish, so they'll last more than one season. Tell them what, if anything, you won't finance.

DEAR JANET

Q. We believe that giving our children an allowance is welfare. So we have helped them become "self-employed" by printing business cards for them and finding appropriate jobs for them to do. They help me file in my home office, sweep out my business storage, mow lawns for neighbors, and babysit. We "let" them work only after the family chores are done.

A. Your work-for-pay system is noteworthy because the work can be paid for on a job-by-job basis, which is convenient to keep track of.

The final exam is an excursion on their own. Don't grade them on their choice of styles and colors—you'll have to live with those within the limits you've set—but on how well they manage their money. It's okay to splurge on a silk shirt as long as they find a great deal on jeans or buy their quota of socks. If they shop smart, reward them with a seasonal allowance.

I gave my son, John, his first clothing allowance when he was 16. We agreed on $200 for summer clothes, and he set off on his own. He bought shorts and several T-shirts from Old Navy and a collared dress shirt at Abercrombie & Fitch. Total cost: $140, and John carefully counted into my hand the $60 he hadn't spent. (Daughter Claire, who was 14 at the time, went along on that shopping expedition and was proud to have used her own money to buy a pair of warm-up pants on sale from Abercrombie.)

You can always tailor a clothing allowance to your own situation. Lest kids skimp on undies or go overboard on a leather jacket, some parents continue to buy the basics, such as underwear and coats, or dispense money in more manageable monthly chunks.

DEAR JANET

Q. I recently read an article written by a mother who had put her teenagers on a strict allowance of $5 a week. She admitted that the amount was artificially low, but she bragged about what a great exercise it was in self-discipline. What do you think of this as a treatment of children suffering from overconsumption?

A. It might work as shock therapy, but it's not a long-term cure.

Putting kids on a starvation budget is as bad as overindulging them. An allowance is supposed to teach them how to make re-sponsible decisions about controlling their appetites for CDs and pizza. Rationing their income limits their ability to make decisions—and encourages them to pig out later.

Unless those kids are wearing rags or holding down jobs of their own, it's likely that Mom and Dad are still paying a big chunk of their expenses. Strict allowance aside, the kids might agree with Bart Simpson's rejoinder to Homer and Marge's typically lame attempt to persuade him to earn some money of his own: "Room and board are free, and Santa brings the rest."

The idea is to teach your kids how to function in the marketplace so that when they're legally able to shop with their own credit cards, they'll show both good sense and good taste.

Good Grades, Good Pay

When it comes to rewarding kids for good behavior or good grades, let them know you're proud of them by giving them a hug, a word of encouragement, or a special treat such as stickers or a later bedtime—anything but money. That way, the virtue of doing their homework or getting good grades becomes its own reward, and they learn the personal satisfaction that comes with a job well done.

Sometimes money can be too powerful a motivator for parents to resist. Frustrated by the lack of response when she asked her two new stepsons what was going on in school, one woman offered to pay the boys 25¢, up to 50¢ a day, every time they reported something new they had learned. "That encouraged them to think back over their day; it got them using their minds," she said. When the boys kept forgetting to put on their seatbelts, she started a game: first one buckled up gets a quarter. "Boy, what a turnaround," she laughs.

Using money as an incentive can be appropriate if you give small amounts under the right circumstances. For example, reward your kids after the fact for behaving well at the supermarket instead of promising them money ahead of time if they don't throw a tantrum. It may seem like splitting hairs, but the former is more of a reward, the latter an out-and-out bribe.

Payment for grades is a particularly touchy issue. In their heart of hearts, parents suspect that they shouldn't be rewarding their kids' academic efforts with money. But they want their children to do well in school, and if coming across with some cash will do the trick, they figure it's a small price.

Again, pay the kids a compliment, pay the tuition at the college their good grades will get them into, but don't pay them money. Buying grades, or any other good behavior, distracts kids from the sense of accomplishment that should be their real reward. Besides, it can get expensive. And if you're trying to control your children's behavior with money, you're

---

A MONEY RECORD FOR KIDS

Use this worksheet to keep track of your money. At the beginning of the month, start writing down the money you receive and the money you spend. At the end of the month, you'll see whether you came out even (you spent as much as you received), ahead (you spent less than you received and have money left over to add to your savings), or behind (you spent more than you received and might have had to borrow money from Mom and Dad to pay for something). You can do this for a whole year by making 12 copies of the worksheet (record any cost of using the copier at the library under Odds and Ends, below).

The worksheet may help you decide that you want to spend your money differently next month. Maybe you want to increase your income by asking for more odd jobs around the house. Perhaps you will spend less on snacks so you can save up for a new pair of skates.

But remember, just because something is listed on this worksheet doesn't mean you have to buy it—or that your parents will let you. Besides, they may expect you to use part of your allowance to buy school lunches. They may expect you to save some of your money and give some of it to help other people or your place of worship. It's a good idea to write down those amounts first thing each month so you'll set them aside and not spend them on something else.

Month   _____

WHERE MY MONEY COMES FROM

My allowance $ _____

Odd jobs   _____

Babysitting, paper route, and so on   _____

Gifts   _____

Money borrowed from my parent(s) (or someone else)   _____

My Total Income $ _____

WHAT I SPEND MY MONEY ON

Money I owe my parent(s) (or someone else)   _____

My savings (savings account or piggy bank)   _____

doomed to failure because eventually they'll earn their own.

I do know of cases in which parents have successfully used money as compensation for grades. One dad worked out a complex set of financial incentives that rewarded his 11-year-old son for improved grades, even if the grades weren't As. A mom set aside time

My church or other charity (like UNICEF)	_____
Gifts for my family and friends	_____
Lunch money	_____
Clothing I help pay for	_____
School supplies and fees (class parties, science projects, and so on)	_____
Snacks (sodas, chips, candy, gum)	_____
Fun stuff I pay for	
Books, magazines, and comics	_____
Toys	_____
Things I collect	_____
Special stuff for my room (posters and so on)	_____
Entrance fees (for the skating rink, rec center, and so on)	_____
Club dues and uniforms (Girls Scouts, 4-H)	_____
Art and craft supplies (including taking pictures)	_____
Holiday costumes (Halloween)	_____
CDs and DVDs	_____
Video and computer games	_____
Movies	_____
Other outings (amusement parks, museums, zoos, and so on)	_____
Souvenirs and postcards	_____
Odds and ends	_____
My Total Expenses	$ _____
My Total Income	$ _____
Minus My Total Expenses	− _____
Money Left Over	$ _____

every week to go over schoolwork with her first-grader and paid him $1 for every perfect paper. But money seems to work best as a motivator when it's used in small amounts over limited periods of time; the longer you do it, the less effective it is. Your goal should be to wean kids from cash just as you eventually weaned them from treats when they learned to go to the potty.

Even in the situations noted above, factors other than money were at work. In the first case, the 11-year-old admitted that he was also influenced by a conscientious teacher who prodded him to do better. In the second case, Mom's interest and approval probably had as much of an effect on her son's performance as the money. Paying a compliment will buy better results than paying cash.

Although promising a reward ahead of time is risky, a spontaneous blowout after the fact to celebrate a good report card is always a morale booster. Go ahead, treat your scholar to a banana split or even dinner at the restaurant of his or her choice.

The Parent Giveth, the Parent Taketh Away

When your kids misbehave, it's better to make the discipline fit the deed than it is to dock their allowance. If they fight about the TV, it gets turned off. If they dawdle in doing homework or getting ready for bed, they don't play video games.

Still, monetary disincentives have been known to do the trick if you use them strategically. (Translation: Hit 'em where it hurts but not too often.) When the Dalton family moved to a new house with a laundry chute, the children got it into their heads that cleaning up their rooms meant tossing all items of clothing into the chute. Tired of fishing her kids' clean clothes out of the laundry bin, Peggy Dalton told them each item of clean clothing would cost them 10¢. That did the trick. Another mom fined her kids 25¢ for every wet towel or article of clothing found lying on the floor.

It would also be appropriate to make your children pay if their carelessness causes damage that money can fix. When Sam and Sophie Dalton got into a friendly tussle while they were wearing their church clothes, Sophie's tights were ruined—and Sam was responsible for replacing them. If the damage is more extensive—for example, your kids break a neighbor's window after being warned repeatedly not to play ball so close to the house—it's their responsibility to apologize and offer to pay for at least part of the repair costs.

To discipline your children, try using some of the same strategies you'd use to get them to do chores, chief of which is the force of your own authority. If your kids pay attention to you in general and want your approval, just telling them what you expect of them—and indicating that you'll be disappointed in them if they don't deliver—can get them to do what you want.

That doesn't mean you should wield dictatorial power. Kids are more inclined to cooperate with you if you're open to them when they have a problem or complaint. But deep down parents know that their children are only as disciplined as they themselves are and that kids will push as far as they can. When parents draw the line, kids are stopped; when parents slide, so do kids. It's too exhausting to draw the line all the time, so you have to pick and choose your confrontations. To gain leverage, you may have to resort once in a while to tech-

---

ALLOWANCE BOOKS AND SOFTWARE

- *The Kids' Allowance Book,* by Amy Nathan (Walker Publishing). Cartoon illustrations and quotes from other children help to entice young readers.
- *Kids' Allowances: How Much, How Often, and How Come,* by David McCurrach (http://www.kidsmoney.org). Geared toward parents, with an allowance workbook for kids.
- *Kidsca$h* (http://www.kidscashmanagement .com). A basic spiral-bound ledger in which kids can keep daily and monthly records of how much cash they get (from allowance, found money, gifts, earnings) and what they spend it on.
- *Family Bank* (http://www.parentware.org). A software program that's a kind of Quicken for kids. You open an account into which you can credit a child's allowance and pay interest on the balance. When kids want real money out of the account, they print out a check that you cash.

niques like time-out or grounding or the "if . . . then" gambit: "If you do 'X', then I'll be forced to respond by doing 'Y'."

Whatever you do, do it sparingly. Even good, effective tactics can lose their impact if they're overused. If you're basically insecure, your kids will sense that. Like the boy who cried wolf, you'll find that your attempts at taking charge will eventually lose their effect. You don't want to be forced into buying your kids' cooperation only to find yourself in the position of the parent who lamented of her teenage son, "The only way I can control him is with money."

And Now, for Your Regularly Scheduled Allowance

If you lose track of when you've given your children their allowance (and you suspect they're always trying to squeeze an extra week's worth out of you), get into the habit of paying them on a regular schedule, preferably a quiet weekday—maybe even your own payday—instead of the hectic weekend. You might also consider Sunday night, so the kids don't blow the money over the weekend. Same goes for giving kids a raise in their allowance. Agreeing in advance on an annual allowance review to take place on the child's birthday or the first day of school will save your child the trouble of nagging you and save you the pain of having to listen.

In my own case (as described in Chapter 1) I decided to use a checkbook system in which I credit my kids' accounts with a monthly allowance. They write me checks as they need money and earn interest on any balance they carry over to the next month. Some families have come up with other creative and inexpensive solutions. One mom simply took scrap paper and made her two sons "coupon books," each with 52 dated coupons, one for every week of the year. Each coupon was good for a weekly allowance payment, and Mom agreed to pay the kids on demand for each coupon they turned in, even if they turned in more than one at a time. But each coupon could be used only once.

A Word of Encouragement

To test the financial smarts of America's youth, the Jump$tart Coalition for Personal Financial Literacy administers a periodic exam to high school seniors. In an interesting sidelight, students who reported receiving a regular allowance scored slightly lower than the group as a whole. If an allowance doesn't improve a child's financial literacy—at least as measured by this exam—should parents bother to give one?

Yes, yes, a thousand times yes. The Jump$tart study also showed that young people who are inclined to save money didn't score better on the exam, yet we consider thrift a virtue. So, too, are the day-to-day money management skills required to manage an allowance successfully.

Of course, there are limits to what an allowance can do. An allowance will not teach kids that they could lose health insurance if their parents become unemployed (a question that fewer than one-third of the students answered correctly on the test). It will not teach kids that stocks are likely to have a higher average return than savings accounts over an 18-year period (a fact that less than 20 percent of students knew). It will not teach kids that legal liability on a lost or stolen credit card is limited to $50 (just 18 percent of the seniors got that right).

But nothing beats an allowance for teaching kids how to separate wants from needs, set priorities, and make their money last from paycheck to paycheck.

If you have tried allowance systems but have never been disciplined enough to make one stick, don't be too hard on yourself. You don't have to duplicate any system down to the last wonderfully organized detail. Just pick and choose the tips that will work best in your household. Instead of starting an allowance when his children were 6 or 7, for example,

John Rosemond didn't bother with one until they were teenagers. Then, said Rosemond, "we used the allowance to represent the fact that we were going to give the kids expanded autonomy over their lives."

You wouldn't want to offer money as a reward all the time, but used judiciously it can work. One family created an inventive system to encourage their daughter to practice the piano. For every half hour of toil, she earns 1 "piano dollar," funny money with Beethoven's visage subbed for George Washington's. When she accumulates 20 piano dollars, she's treated to a meal at the fast-food restaurant of her choice.

If you don't have the time or the discipline to construct an elaborate system, concentrate on whatever is most important to you, whether it's teaching your kids to manage an allowance, do chores, or contribute to charity. If you do nothing else, at least talk to your children about money when the opportunity presents itself, such as when you're withdrawing cash from the bank machine or paying bills. One father has walked his kids through their tax returns, taken them to rental property he owns and discussed the responsibilities of landlords and tenants, shown them his credit report, and even talked about the virtues of prepaying a mortgage. Said Dad, "I can't think of anything I wouldn't share with them."

KIDS' QUESTIONS

Q. "Jessie's getting 'lowance, so why can't I?"
A. Younger siblings catch on more quickly to everything (as you're already painfully aware), so sibling rivalry is one exception to my rule about not giving preschoolers an allowance. If you're going to give your older child, say, $1 or $2 a week, go ahead and give younger brother or sister 50¢. Chances are he or she won't understand how much that really is, so you might be able to get away with a quarter. The point is, give a token amount so he or she doesn't feel left out. And don't feel obliged to give anything unless your preschooler asks.

Q. "How come my friend Christopher's allowance is bigger than mine?"
A. Resist the temptation to tell your kids that Christopher's parents must have more money than you do. Your income shouldn't be the only factor, or even the main one, that determines your children's allowance.

Tell your kids up front that their allowance will be based on three things: how much you can afford to give, what you expect them to pay for, and how much money you think they can comfortably handle. If they bring up the subject again, you have a ready-made reply to rattle off.

In asking this question, your children may be dancing around what's really on their minds. They may be fishing for a raise in their allowance. Or they may be trying to keep up with the Jones kids.

If you really can't afford to come up with more money, that can work to your advantage. What counts isn't the size of the weekly dole but the experience kids get by making it

last. If you have to limit your children's income because your own is stretched, that's a lesson in real-world economics, and your kids will be better off for learning it. With more money to spare, Christopher's parents will have a tougher time teaching him the value of a dollar.

Q. "Can I have an advance on my allowance?"
A. Most times it's best to say no. You can bet that your children hope you'll forget about any money you've advanced them, so you'll need to keep meticulous records or have a steel-trap memory.

Besides, an allowance is supposed to help kids learn about deferred gratification. If you expect your children to save their own money to buy CDs, it's self-defeating to advance a couple of weeks' worth of allowance so they can buy the hottest release today.

That being said, I know there will be times when some kind of loan seems reasonable—especially if your kids don't ask too often and are generally responsible money managers. Rather than giving them an advance, however, simplify your bookkeeping by lending them the money for a specific purpose and a specific payback period. When one young man asked to borrow $250 from his parents to buy a bicycle, he also presented them with a list of extra chores and special jobs he could do to earn money to pay off the loan and even offered to pay $50 interest. He earned $100 by painting his grandmother's porch and made all the money over the course of one summer.

What you're trying to avoid is a permanent pattern of borrowing money that keeps your children chronically in debt and leaves you confused about exactly how much they owe.

Q. "If I don't spend all my lunch money, can I keep it and use it for something else?"
A. That may sound like a reasonable deal, but think about what you're getting yourself into. If your child habitually avoids the cafeteria, she doesn't need lunch money, which becomes a de facto raise in her allowance. If you think a raise is in order, give her one. If not, stop shelling out money for phantom lunches and keep packing those bologna sandwiches.

Lunch money appears to be a hot button among many parents. Here's a sampling of the mail I received in response to a column about older children paying for their own school lunches:

I disagree that children should pay for their school lunches with their own allowance. Snacks, concert tickets, and special trendy clothing can certainly be financed through the allowance or the child's financial assets. But food, clothing, and shelter are typical categories that are the traditional responsibility of parents.

In your recent column you included lunch money in a child's allowance. This should never happen. I have too often seen middle school and high school youngsters skipping lunch or just buying a snack in order to save money for other things they wanted.

As a parent it is my duty to provide lunch. There is always lunch money in the designated drawer if my children decide

they do not wish to pack their own lunch. They are expected to return any change to the drawer if they eat light. The kids do what they wish (within reason) with their allowance, but the lunch money does not belong to them.

If you're going to make older children responsible for managing their lunch money, you'll have to provide extra money over and above their discretionary income to cover the expense. If you suspect your children aren't up to the challenge or would starve themselves to buy a new pair of jeans, rethink your strategy: Dole out lunch money one day at a time, require kids to return any unspent cash, or bag the lunch money—and bag the lunch. (Note: Many school cafeterias have solved this problem by issuing student debit cards. Parents deposit a certain dollar amount in a school account, and students draw it down for lunch. The cards don't work in vending machines.)

Q. "Will you buy me that [fill in the blank] if I pay you back when we get home?"
A. Don't fall into this trap. As with advances on allowance, your kids are counting on you to forget about the debt. If you do cave in, at least hang on to the item you bought until the kids come across with the cash.

Q. "How much will you pay me to stay out of the way during your party tonight?"
A. Don't dignify this one with any answer. Rewarding your children for doing something good is tricky enough; paying them off for not doing something bad is simply blackmail.

Penny-Wise: Kids and Saving

When Caitlin, the daughter of a friend of mine, was in first grade a number of years ago, she forgot to return a library book at school. Told that she would have to pay a ten-cent fine, Caitlin sighed, "There goes my college fund."

That about sums up most young children's view of saving: clear that something good can come of it but a little fuzzy about the details. Banks, for example, can be scary places for kids, who see their money swallowed up and are sometimes horrified to learn that if they deposit, say, a $10 bill, they won't get the same $10 bill back.

And let's face it: Saving in general can be a downer, especially for children, who crave instant gratification. If saving is spinach and spending dessert, which would your kids choose? To teach them that thrift is a virtue, you have to sugarcoat the vitamins. Let kids savor their savings. As my son observed when he peeked over my shoulder while I was writing this chapter: "Saving can be dessert, too, if you save for something you want." Whatever your children crave, let them spend the cash even if the purchase cleans them out.

Reward their efforts. Save for America (http://www.saveforamerica.org), the nationwide school-based saving campaign, rewards students with stickers. Frequent depositors qualify for bigger prizes such as cameras, books, and CDs. "Kids in grades K through 3 get really excited," said Stephan Avena, president of Save for America. "We think that if we can get them to stick with it for three years, they'll continue the habit."

At home, one of the most effective incentives you can give is to offer to match—anywhere from ten cents on the dollar to dollar-for-dollar—whatever children put aside on their own.

Look at what happened to Greg G. When he was was 7 years old, Greg signed up for a school saving program and started squirreling away $10 to $20 a week—money he got from doing jobs around the house and practicing the piano. By the time he was 10, he had more than $1,000. Not satisfied with the rate of interest he was earning in the bank, Greg withdrew most of the money and began diversifying into a mutual fund and stocks, even as he continued to replenish the money in his bank account. While some kids his age were frittering away their allowance on Big Macs and Mickey Mouse T-shirts, Greg was buying shares in McDonald's and the Walt Disney Co. While other kids were paying to see basketball games, he bought a piece of the Boston Celtics.

What turned Greg into a supersaver? "I got excited about what the money would grow into and what I'd be able to do with it when I grew up." How would he advise parents to get their kids hooked on

---

DEAR JANET

Q. To get my 8-year-old interested in saving, I offered to match anything he put in the bank. But the deal was he couldn't spend the money on toys—he had to save for a major purchase down the road. So far, he hasn't put in a penny. I can't believe he won't take the match.

A. Would you take a 100 percent match for your retirement plan if your employer told you that you could never stop working?

For an 8-year-old, a toy is a major purchase, and even a few weeks can be an eternity. Setting up unrealistic rules about what your son can buy took away his incentive to save.

Try this strategy: Tell your son that once he gets a minimum of $100 in his account, he can spend additional money on anything he wants (within reason). You can gradually raise the minimum balance, but as your son gets older, his goals will become larger and more expensive, his time frame longer, and the match more attractive.

saving? "Make them excited about it too." To raise a generation of supersavers, give them a reason to save. To keep them interested, reward them for their efforts. To guarantee their success, devise a system that makes saving easy.

Eyes on the Prize

Kids today have more reasons to save than did their predecessors a generation or two ago: such big-ticket items as designer clothing or video equipment and games that their parents are reluctant to buy. If you are feeling in a generous mood the next time your son simply must have a pair of $120 sneakers, offer to pay a portion of the price if he picks up the rest of the tab. Making this kind of a deal is a win-win situation: You save money and get the psychological satisfaction of saying no to what you probably consider a ridiculous request; he learns to save money and gets the psychological benefit of hearing you say that two-letter word. The younger the child, the smaller and more immediate the goal should be; it ought to be something—a toy car or a set of paints—that the child can reach within a few weeks. As young Caitlin showed in the example at the beginning of the chapter, college, though certainly worthy, is a fuzzy concept in the far-away future.

One Family's Savings Goal

Older children can move on to bigger, more expensive goals. You can even make saving a family project. For the Coogans of Pennsylvania, the catalyst that got them into the thrifty frame of mind was a first-ever family vacation to Florida. Ray Coogan is disabled by a chronic illness. His wife, Trudy, is a hairdresser. Of the five Coogan children still living at home, four are teenagers with part-time jobs. They all decided to pool their money for the trip south to visit another Coogan child.

DEAR JANET

Q. My 10-year-old daughter has her heart set on buying a laptop computer for kids that costs $100. I don't object to her buying it if she uses her own money, but I'm afraid it will take her too long to save that kind of cash, and she'll end up discouraged. Should I try to talk her out of this?

A. You sound more discouraged than your daughter does. If she understands the terms and is willing to give it a try, let her go for it.

It is a big goal for a young child, but you could lend her a hand (without actually lending her any money) by breaking it up into more manageable chunks. For every $10 she saves, for example, you might offer a $5 match. Give her opportunities to do extra chores so she can earn the money more quickly.

If your daughter only makes it to $50 and then loses interest, she'll still have saved $50 to spend on something else. And that's not bad for a 10-year-old.

As organizer and chief cheerleader, Ray Coogan set a relatively low initial goal of $2,500. He figured meeting it would be such a morale booster that everyone would be encouraged to aim even higher and extend their stay in Florida. All working family members were given a savings goal and offered a bonus: For meeting their goal quickly or making an extra effort (by requesting extra work hours, for example), they would be rewarded with an additional $25 in spending money for the trip.

Ray held weekly family meetings to track their progress. "It wouldn't have worked if we hadn't had him to spearhead the whole thing and light a fire under everyone," said Trudy. Within three months the Coogans had saved $4,000 and were on their way in a rented van. Next year, maybe they'll head west.

Play Numbers Games

If you really want to get older kids psyched up about saving, dazzle 'em with numbers—in particular, the magic of compound interest. (Interest, of course, is the money a bank pays you for letting it use your money; compounding means that you also earn interest on the interest paid, which gives your savings an extra boost.) Youngsters are turned on by the idea that over time their money can grow. In one money management course for high school students, the most popular chart in the workbook is the one showing that a relatively small amount of money can grow into a big pile. To wit, if you sock away $2,000 a year in a tax-favored retirement account for nine years starting at age 22 and earn 9 percent on your money, your $18,000 will grow to $579,000 by the time you're 65. (By the way, 9 percent isn't an unreasonable rate of return. The Standard & Poor's 500-stock index has returned a tad over 10 percent annually, on average, since 1926.)

For a dramatic illustration of the magic of compounding, Harold Moe, coauthor with wife Sandy Moe of *Teach Your Child the Value of Money*, performs a trick that is guaranteed to knock the socks off everyone from young kids to adults. It works like this: Raid the penny jar or go to the bank and load up on pennies—say, $10 to $20 worth. Then take out a checkerboard and place one penny on the first square in the first row. Double the number of pennies in the second

---

DEAR JANET

Q. Our very responsible and hardworking son is managing to earn and save a good deal of money for an 11-year-old. The immediate issue is a new electric scooter to replace his still-working scooter that is only a year and a half old. Should we discourage him from buying a new one, which he wants, or mind our own business?

A. Assuming you don't have any objection to the scooter itself, remind your son that his old one still works and ask him to consider whether he really wants to spend his money on a new one. If he says yes, then go ahead and let him do it. He had the discipline to make and save the money, so he should reap the rewards—and feel the pain of parting with his hard-earned cash.

square and continue doubling them until you reach the end of the first row, at which point you'll have 128 pennies. Then point to the remaining pennies and ask your audience to guess how many will be left after you've filled the checkerboard by doubling the amount of pennies on each square. After a suspenseful pause, announce triumphantly that there probably isn't enough money in the whole world to complete all 64 squares. (When my son saw this principle demonstrated on a kids' video about money, he was so bowled over that at first he refused to believe it was true.)

With older children, you can go on to more math legerdemain. The rule of 72, for example, states that dividing 72 by the interest rate you're earning tells you roughly how long it will take your money to double (and dividing 72 by the number of years in which you want to double your money will tell you how much interest you need to earn). If you're earning,

DEAR JANET

Q. When I was a teenager, my parents provided for all of our needs and most of our wants so that we would not be tempted to spend our earnings. I had saved $10,000 by the time I graduated from high school. Now I also want my kids to save lots of money. My son recently received $150 for his birthday. I took the cash and put it in his savings account, somewhat to his dismay. We give him an allowance and make him put nearly half of it in the bank. I will also encourage him to save virtually all of his high school job earnings for college. What do you think about this approach?

A. Although I strongly agree that children should help pay for college, I have a couple of reservations about your approach. By requiring your kids to save so much of their money, you're giving them fewer opportunities to make choices about how to spend it. And that's also an important financial skill.

Instead of paying for "all their needs and most of their wants," as your parents did for you, I'd make your children use their own money to cover at least some of those expenses, especially as they get older. That might mean saving a little less, but it would give them a more well-rounded experience.

And I must say that whisking all your son's birthday money off to the bank was a bummer. No wonder he was dismayed. C'mon, Mom. Next time let him blow some of it on something he wants.

DEAR JANET

Q. My 13-year-old daughter wants to buy a treadmill. She's willing to use her own money, but those things are expensive. Is there any way I can help her get the money more quickly without making the purchase myself?

A. I can think of several ways to give your daughter an incentive to save (as outlined in this chapter), but I can't help wondering why a 13-year-old girl needs a treadmill in the first place. At that age, running around the block is more fun, healthier, and a heck of a lot cheaper.

---

say, 6 percent, your money will double in about 12 years.

By the time your kids are in high school, they should be able to use the table on page 146, which shows how much a deposit of $10 a month will grow at various rates of interest over different periods of time. You can easily use the chart to calculate how quickly you can get rich with any monthly deposit (or use an online savings calculator, such as the one at http://www.kiplinger.com/tools).

A Spoonful of Sugar

No less a light than Sir John Templeton, the mutual fund pioneer and advocate of long-term saving, has observed that "learning to save is so important that parents should reward their kids for doing it." One of the most effective rewards you can offer is an incentive system in which you match all or part of your child's savings. This tactic works well with children of all ages but especially with teenagers, who might be saving for a big-ticket item such as a car or a class trip.

Rewards themselves don't have to break the bank. Sometimes a pat on the back is all it takes to push a child in the right direction. Consider the enthusiastic students who participated in the saving program at one elementary school in New York City. What made them do it?

- **Hillary:** "It's a cool thing to do," said Hillary, who also advised parents to take extreme measures if kids let their allowances burn a hole in their pocket: "Keep part of their allowance. When they ask for more money, don't give it to them."
- **Kenny:** "I never had a bank account before, and when I got the notice from school, I said to my mom, 'Please let me have one.' Parents should tell their kids, 'What happens if your father loses his job and has to borrow money?'"
- **Rachel:** "I thought I would like to save for college, so I started the banking program, and I usually put in $2 every week." But she might raid her account for something special—like one of the dolls from the American Girl Collection.

As in all other aspects of teaching kids about money, *your* attitude is critical. One of the biggest reasons students don't participate in school saving programs is lack of interest on the part of parents. First National Bank of South Miami has sponsored Twiglet,

---

DEAR JANET

Q. I'm 14, and when I picked up your book from the library, I was surprised and a little angered when you suggested that parents should be so involved in their kids' finances. I've always had my own bank account. My parents said, "Save," but we didn't discuss or enforce it. On my own, I set (and reached) a personal goal of $1,000 in my account. Kids can be just as effective savers on their own as when they are "managed" by their parents.

A. Let me assure you that 14-year-olds aren't always as effective in their saving habits as you are. Reaching a goal of $1,000 is an achievement at any age, and I salute you.

Even though it was your initiative and self-discipline that got you to your goal, you also apparently had guidance from your parents, who encouraged you to save and probably helped you open that bank account. I agree with you that parents should never try to "manage" kids. But they do need to offer advice. In any family, teaching and learning financial values is a team effort.

a school bank that's run by students, at David Fair-child Elementary in South Miami. In First National's experience, some children who are gung ho about the program lose interest when their parents don't share their enthusiasm. "Either the kids don't get an allowance or the parents don't give them money to save," said a spokesperson.

Still, school banking programs, which were ubiquitous a generation or two ago and then all but disappeared, are making a comeback (see the sidebar on page 142 for information). And there are several dozen student-run credit unions in high schools around the country. One of the most active is the Gateway Credit Union–Kent Denver Branch at Kent Denver School in Englewood, Colorado, which was started in 1984. Over 60 percent of the students have credit union savings accounts, with an average balance of about $1,500. Open daily before school and during lunch periods, the credit union is run by three dozen students and faculty adviser Donna Duvall-Serrano. "Lots of kids bring in some of their allowance and deposit it," said student president Brett Perlmutter. "Just having the credit union there teaches kids about saving."

Systems That Work

Key to the success of any saving regimen, whether for kids or adults, is getting into the habit of doing it regularly, and that means making it as painless as possible. Among younger children, banks often conjure up an image of a place that takes your money but doesn't give it back, so saving is best begun at home, where kids can keep an eye on their cash and watch it grow. For the same reason, children will be frustrated to see their money swallowed up by a piggy bank that can be opened only by a well-aimed hammer.

Better to make the money more accessible—in a jar or plastic bag, perhaps with a picture of whatever they're saving for attached as an incentive. One inven-

---

DEAR JANET

Q. I am 13 years old and am working on becoming as "money savvy" as I can be. I'm not sure I agree with all of your tips. For example, matching children's savings could instill the false idea that they only need to provide for themselves halfway and can do whatever they want with the half that you are making up for. When the child gets to high school, for instance, he may expect you to pay for half of all his purchases, from gas to clothes to dinner for his date. The lesson you have been teaching could easily end up being damaging in his later life.

A. Wow. You are already one money-savvy kid, with a unique perspective. Having considered your point, I still think parents can match a child's savings without setting up false hopes as long as they do it right.

In your letter you mix together two different things, saving and spending. The match is an incentive to put money aside and is completely optional; parents can choose to offer one or not and can select the amount. On the other hand, gas, clothes, and dates are expenses, not savings. Parents should make it clear how much they'll pay for and how much will come out of the kids' own income, from jobs or allowance. In each case, the key is to set the rules up front so everyone knows what to expect.

---

tive 11-year-old kept each bill carefully displayed in a photo album (and even folded the bills around the edge of the page so that half appeared on one page and half on the next—a convenient way to double your money).

I'm a big fan of fun savings banks for kids (and I have an extensive collection of my own). One year my sister bought my son Peter a large, round metal bank painted like a baseball on the outside; open the hollow sphere in half, and the inside is painted with a ballpark scene—grandstand, spectators, and a game in progress. The bank became one of Peter's favorites, in which he squirreled away the change from purchases he made, as well as unclaimed coins he found around the house. "You know what I like about my baseball bank?" he asked out of the blue one day. "I like it when I think that I have $10 now, but in a year I could have $100 or $200."

If your children are disciplined enough to save a portion of their allowance on their own, congratulations! Some kids are natural savers, occasionally to the point of hoarding their cash. That's just as unhealthy as not saving anything, and you may actually have to prod them to spend their money. If, on the other hand, your children are among those whose money burns an immediate hole in their pocket or pocketbook, you may have to exert some parental pressure to save. But as always, keep things simple.

For example, you might require your kids to save 10 percent of their income; deduct that amount at the time you give them their allowance, and drop it into their bank or glass jar. Some families adopt a more elaborate system, in which the kids divvy up their money into separate pots for spending, saving, investing, charitable giving, or other purposes. But this is more complicated and tougher for many families to manage.

Another alternative is the spare-change method, which lets children spend their bills but encourages them to save their coins (which eventually can be turned in to the bank). At our house, we had a system in which the kids were allowed to keep cash they received as gifts, but had to deposit checks in their savings accounts. It worked well but had one unexpected consequence: Our teenage son was shocked when he learned that you could actually deposit cash in a bank. "I thought banks only took checks," he told his flabbergasted parents.

Although they may grouse about it, your children will appreciate any discipline you impose. Here's a letter I received from 10-year-old Madeline: "Every time I get money I will spend it on every toy that I see. But then I see things for my room, and clothes that are more important than toys. I don't know what to

---

DEAR JANET

Q. My 9-year-old not only saves all his money, but he also keeps it in his room and counts it every night. He has over $200, and I want him to open a bank account, but he won't part with the cash. Am I raising a Scrooge?

A. Humbug. He's probably a typical 9-year-old who worries that if he puts his money in a bank, he'll never see it again.

Try appealing to his hoarding instincts by pointing out that a sum that large needs safe-keeping, and that banks will pay him for allowing them to take care of his money. Don't insist that he put every cent in the bank. Let him keep $50 or so to spend on things he wants. Learning to spend money wisely is just as important as learning to save.

do. I can't think of a way to save money." A fourth-grader named Jonathan actually preferred that his parents hang on to his allowance and give it to him once a month instead of every week. "When you get it in bigger amounts it seems like you get more, and you don't spend it all at once on baseball cards and other stuff like you sometimes do if you get it in small amounts," said Jonathan. "It's much easier to save that way."

When your kids want to hang out at the mall with their friends, suggest that instead of taking all their money with them, they take exactly what they need to play a couple of video games, get a snack, or buy a pair of jeans. What they don't have they won't spend.

How to Open a Bank Account

Eventually your kids will be old enough, or accumulate money enough, to be introduced to the fine points of a real bank savings account. In fact, one study shows that parents use savings accounts as their primary tool for teaching money management to children. Be aware, however, that although financial institutions pay lip service to teaching the value of thrift, some of them can be decidedly unfriendly to kids.

"For the past four years, our bank has been taking a $7-per-month service charge out of the savings accounts of our 10-year-old twins," one dismayed parent wrote to me. "The bank manager said that they add service charges if the account balance is less than $2,500. Our sons have faithfully deposited money over the years, hoping to watch their accounts grow as they earned interest. But they've been disappointed. Should we take our accounts out of this bank?"

As fast as you can, I advised. That's the best way to demonstrate

HELPING KIDS SAVE

In the school-based Save for America campaign, PTA volunteers collect children's coins at school once a week and record the deposits on the SFA Web site. SFA then sends the record of deposits electronically to a participating bank via the Federal Reserve System (the actual money is still delivered in person to the bank). Save for America, adopted in 48 states, has garnered more than $125 million in 25 years. If you'd like to get your school in on the action, visit http://www.saveforamerica.org.

A TAX TIP FOR COSIGNED ACCOUNTS

Make sure your child's Social Security number is used as the tax identification number on any account on which your name also appears as cosigner. That way, interest earned will be treated as your child's income for tax purposes.

Children can make up to $800 in investment income in 2005 without having to pay any taxes. Income between $800 and $1,600 will be taxed at the child's rate. But if your child is under 14, income above $1,600 will be taxed to him or her at your rate, even though the child is the principal owner of the account. That's the so-called kiddie tax, and it's intended to keep parents from ducking taxes by shifting income to their children. After your children reach 14, however, their income is taxable at their rate.

your unhappiness with the bank's policy, which, unfortunately, isn't uncommon. But not every financial institution is so punitive. Many community banks, credit unions, and national institutions offer special programs for kids. Don't be shy about inquiring at other financial institutions in your area, or shop at an on-line bank (such as ING Direct (http://www.ingdirect .com; 800-ING-DIRECT, which offers its Orange Savings Account with no minimum balance and no fees).

If none of your local banks rolls out a welcome mat, you can also open an account at the kids-only Young Americans Bank (303-321-2265; http://www .theyoungamericans.org). Young Americans is headquartered in Denver, but it accepts accounts by mail from all 50 states.

Bank policies covering accounts for minors vary among states, banks, and even branches, depending on state law and banks' own preferences. As long as kids can sign their name, some banks will allow them to own accounts and make both deposits and withdrawals. More commonly, however, you'll probably have to cosign or set up a custodial account. In that case, you control the account, and your child may not be able to make withdrawals without your signature.

One notable exception is Young Americans Bank in Denver, where all customers are under the age of 22. For kids under 18, Young Americans sets up joint

Check out tax requirements for kids updated info

accounts in the name of both parent and child, with two signatures required for all transactions. Parents actually need their children's authorization to make a withdrawal. The bank will also let you sign a release allowing your kids to make withdrawals on their own. Other financial institutions sometimes offer a similar option, so ask about it if you want your children to have more control over their own money.

No Withdrawals Allowed?

Once your children have put their money into the bank, should they be able to get it out—to buy those $120 sneakers, for example—or should they be required to keep it there for longer-term goals? That depends. For many children, being able to withdraw their money to pay for something they want provides most of the incentive to save in the first place. Just getting your kids to put money aside is a major victory. They should be allowed to savor their reward, even if means depleting their savings on something you personally wouldn't have bought. And they can always build their account back up again.

An exception to this rule might be the case of a teenager with a part-time job. In that situation, it would be appropriate for you to require him or her to save a portion of her income for college. Or you could compromise by requiring your children to maintain a certain minimum balance above which they can make withdrawals.

Saving for Your Kids

Aside from teaching children the value of thrift, plenty of parents, grandparents, and other generous relatives want to save on their kids' behalf. I was bowled over when I received this e-mail from a young man who dubs himself "Dr. Frugal": "I have an 8-year-old niece and two nephews, 11 and 4. My brother and I would like to open an account for them that we both could drop money in and to which other relatives could contribute as well. I am 22 and my brother is 21, so we don't have much money to spare. Would you recommend that we go with a savings account, or is there something else we should consider?"

It's a rare 22-year-old who has the foresight, discipline, and thoughtfulness to do what this young man wants to do for his niece and nephews. Some day they'll appreciate having Dr. Frugal for an uncle.

The quick answer to his question is that there's nothing wrong with starting a garden-variety savings account. It's easy, convenient, and safe. The same is true of U.S. savings bonds, Series I, on which the interest rate adjusts with inflation. You can purchase Series I bonds in small denominations at financial institutions or online at http://www.savingsbond.gov.

If you're willing to take on more risk, you always have the option of opening a mutual fund account for the kids, and investing in the stock market certainly makes sense for young children (for much more on kids and investing, see Chapter 10). If you can't come up with the minimum initial investment many mutual funds require—often several thousand dollars—you could open a bank savings account and then transfer the money when you reach the minimum. Or if you're able to invest on a regular basis, many funds will let you open an account with as little as $50 a month.

If college saving is your goal, you have even more choices that come with tax benefits to boot. With the Coverdell education savings account, for instance, you can invest as much as $2,000 a year per child in stocks, bonds, or mutual funds and use the tax-free earnings to pay for private high school expenses as well as college.

At least until 2010, you can also get tax-free earnings for college expenses by opening an account with a state-sponsored 529 college savings plan. Open an

> ## A BANK FOR YOUNG AMERICANS
>
> **Young Americans Bank** (3550 East 1st Ave., Denver, CO 80206; 303-321-2265), which offers savings accounts, checking accounts, credit cards, and loans, has mail-in customers from all 50 states and about a dozen foreign countries. The average savings customer is 9 years old and has a balance of approximately $500. Write or call for more information.

account in your home state (or anywhere else) with as little as $25 a month. Most states let you choose from a slate of investment options geared to a child's age (for more on these plans, go to http://www.savingforcollege.com/kiplinger/plan_details.php and http://www.savingforcollege.com/kiplinger/plan_comparison.php).

HOW YOUR MONEY WILL GROW

You can use this table to figure how much to save or invest to accumulate a specific amount by some future date. Say you and your daughter are planning for her to save $5,000 by the time she starts college six years from now. Assuming that she could earn 8 percent on her savings and investments, how much should she put away monthly? Find the place in the table where six years intersects with 8%. Divide that number—926—into your goal of $5,000. The result tells you that your goal is 5.4 times the total generated by a $10 deposit every month. Your daughter will have to set aside $54 each month to reach the goal on time, assuming an 8 percent return.

YEAR	2%	3%	4%	5%	6%	7%	8%	9%	10%	11%	12%
1	$121	$122	$123	$123	$124	$125	$125	$126	$127	$127	$128
2	245	248	250	253	256	258	261	264	267	270	272
3	371	377	383	389	395	402	408	415	421	428	435
4	500	511	521	532	544	555	567	580	592	605	618
5	631	648	665	683	701	720	740	760	781	802	825
6	765	790	815	841	868	897	926	957	989	1,023	1,058
7	902	936	971	1,008	1,046	1,086	1,129	1,173	1,220	1,268	1,320
8	1,042	1,086	1,133	1,182	1,234	1,289	1,348	1,409	1,474	1,543	1,615
9	1,184	1,241	1,302	1,366	1,435	1,507	1,585	1,667	1,755	1,849	1,948
10	1,329	1,401	1,477	1,559	1,647	1,741	1,842	1,950	2,066	2,190	2,323
15	2,101	2,275	2,469	2,684	2,923	3,188	3,483	3,812	4,179	4,589	5,046
20	2,953	3,291	3,680	4,128	4,644	5,240	5,929	6,729	7,657	8,736	9,991
25	3,895	4,471	5,158	5,980	6,965	8,148	9,574	11,295	13,379	15,906	18,976
30	4,935	5,842	6,964	8,357	10,095	12,271	15,003	18,445	22,793	28,302	35,299

KIDS' QUESTIONS

Q. "I have $35 in my piggy bank. Can I spend it all on a building set?"

A. Let your kids spend their money, even if you think they're blowing it all on one overpriced toy. If they have exercised the self-discipline to save in the first place, they deserve a reward.

Parents should certainly retain some veto power over how children dispose of their own money. You may not want them to have inline skates, for example, because you think they're too dangerous, or a video game system because you don't want them to be parked in front of the TV all day.

But price alone shouldn't be the deciding factor. Even if the coveted item is expensive relative to your children's allowances, let them splurge so long as the purchase is otherwise suitable. Gazing upon the vast emptiness in their piggy banks will be a lesson in itself.

Q. "Why don't you just go to the bank machine and get some money?"

A. Control your impulse to point out that money doesn't grow on trees. That old chestnut may be colorful, but it's not very useful. Your children already think cash pops out of bank machines, and now you've really confused them.

Tell them instead that bank machines don't actually print money (which is what your kids may think). Explain that the bank is like a big piggy bank: You get paid for working at your job and you deposit your paycheck into your bank account for safekeeping. When you get money from the bank machine, you're actually taking money out of your own account. When the account is empty, it's empty—just like your children's piggy banks.

Q. "How does a bank machine work?"

A. You don't have to be a technological wizard to take a stab at this one, even if it's only to assure your child there isn't a person inside the machine dealing out $20 bills. Here's all you need to know:

- An ATM is like a computerized teller.
- You talk to the computer with your bank card, which tells the machine who you are. The machine then calls your bank to find out if you have enough money in your account to cover the amount of cash you're requesting. If so, the machine gives you the cash. If not, you're out of luck.
- How does the cash actually get into the machine? It's loaded there by bank employees or outside security firms. Sometimes machines are "cashed up" several times a day, because banks don't like to load them with large amounts. But over a long holiday weekend, for example, machines will hold more cash than normal.

Your Kid, the Investment Guru

Don't make the mistake of thinking that investing in the stock market is for adults only, sort of like an R-rated movie. On the contrary, it's more like PG-13. Children that age or younger are able to understand how the market works and, with a little parental guidance, become successful investors. Nicole W. was only 9 and in the fourth grade when she noticed that she had earned a disappointing $11 on a $500 certificate of deposit (CD). When the CD matured, she was champing at the bit to invest her money in a stock—preferably one that was about to split so that she could get more shares. "Nicole is on her way; I just hope I can keep up," said her mom, Rita.

Kids who own stock are in the minority among children, but they're a vocal and savvy group. I have interviewed a 12-year-old who publishes his own investment newsletter and runs his father's individual retirement account, a teenage daytrader, and a junior high student who started to invest after playing a stock market simulation game as a class exercise.

In my experience, the children most likely to take an interest in stocks fall into three categories:

1. **Kids who already have their own savings accounts** and start to notice that when interest rates are low, their money doesn't grow very fast
2. **Kids whose grandparents, parents, or friends invest** in the stock market
3. **Entrepreneurial kids who have earned** several hundred dollars or more at a job or business and have

bigger plans for their money than keeping it in a bank account.

Although they have a nodding acquaintance with Wall Street, children don't always understand its twists and turns—nor, if truth be told, do many adults. I'm bombarded with requests from parents and grandparents for material specially written to help children get started in the stock market.

The first thing parents and kids should understand is the principle of a market: Sellers ask a high price for their wares, buyers bid lower, and they reach an agreement somewhere in the middle. And that's it. No matter how complex they sound, no matter how sophisticated their computers, all markets are fundamentally the same, whether you're buying and selling stocks, baseball cards, or foreign currency. And the goal of an investor is always the same too: buy low, sell high.

With that bit of knowledge in hand, you're ready to begin. If you have any budding investors around the house, hand them this book (after you've finished, of course). The following pages are written for all would-be Wall Street tycoons—such as a young man named Jonathan H. By the time he was 15, Jon was

DEAR JANET

Q. We bought stock in Wendy's for our 14-year-old son and 6-year-old daughter, and they contribute their own money to buy more shares. Lately, however, my son has been saving for a Boy Scout trip, so his sister's holdings are catching up with his. Should we make up the difference?
A. Keep up with your investments on your son's behalf, but don't worry about his own. Part of learning to manage money is setting priorities, and your children have made

choices that make sense for them. Your son is obviously a thrifty young man. Even if his stock account is growing more slowly right now, he'll have a great time on the Boy Scout trip. And he'll have the satisfaction of knowing that he paid for it himself.

Because your daughter is younger, she has fewer choices when it comes to parceling out her money. But when she gets older and wants to save for space camp or a ski trip, the family books will balance.

managing his own $10,000 portfolio, "more than his father and I had when we got married," his mother told me. Jon built up a core of reliable blue chip stocks, including AT&T and IBM, and he also owned some personal favorites, such as Topps and Reebok.

To support his investing habit, Jon earned $20 a week working at a health-food store and got an additional $5 to $10 in allowance and gift money. All of it went into a bank account from which he could make his own withdrawals without his parents' cosignatures. Not that he made many withdrawals for things other than investments. Jon saved most of what he got and reinvested all his stock dividends in more shares.

All this started with ten shares of AT&T purchased for him by his father when Jon was 7. "This taught him how to make money by becoming the owner of a company," his dad told me. "He used to get angry at other telephone commercials." For Jon, the real investment bug bit a little later, when he was 10 and wanted to collect Topps baseball card sets as an investment. "I told him he could invest in the cards or the company," said his dad. He chose the company. His shares split several times and turned out to be a "super investment."

Kids as Stock Pickers

Buying your children shares in a company is the best way to get them started in the market. Investing in only a few shares can be expensive as far as commissions go, although there are ways to minimize your costs (see the discussion beginning on page 159). But the lesson you're teaching is priceless and the options limitless. The beauty of it is that you don't even have to be an expert stock picker; you can let your kids do the choosing. Jonathan's strategy: "Look at which clothes kids are wearing in school, find out what recording labels they're listening to, what kind of CD players they have. When I go to the mall, I go to the toy stores and shoe stores and ask what's selling fastest."

DEAR JANET

Q. Our 10-year-old daughter will earn about $300 this year in dividends and interest. Does she have to file an income tax return? If so, can she get away with filing a 1040EZ because she's a child?

A. The answer to your first question is easy: No, your daughter doesn't have to file a return. Because all her income was "unearned"—meaning it came from dividends and interest rather than from a salary—she can make as much as $800 in 2005 without owing tax or having to file a return.

But the answer to your second question is not "EZ." Assuming your daughter's income did meet the filing threshold, the type of form has nothing to do with age. What counts, among other things, is the source and amount of income.

You can't use the 1040EZ if you have any income from dividends or capital gains, or more than $1,500 in interest income. In that case, your daughter would probably have to file Form 1040A. And if she also had income from capital gains, she'd have to file the 1040 long form and a Schedule D. You can always skip lines that don't apply.

When young people like Jonathan speak, even old pros like Peter Lynch listen. Lynch, the star money manager whose expertise at the helm of Fidelity Magellan helped make it the largest and most successful mutual fund in the country, observed in his book *One Up on Wall Street* that "the best place to look for the tenbagger (a stock that appreciates tenfold) is close to home—if not in the backyard then down at the shopping mall." When Lynch's three daughters came home from the mall raving about the Body Shop, the British company that specializes in soaps, skin-care products, and perfumes, Lynch did some checking and concluded that the company "would become a money machine." He bided his time until he could buy when he felt the price was right.

I don't recommend that youngsters invest in penny stocks, so-called because they typically sell for less than $1 a share. Their low price makes them attractive to kids, but they're issued by companies that have a short or erratic earnings history, they aren't listed on any stock exchange, and public surveillance is spotty. They're a gamble, not an investment.

How to Scout a Stock

Kids can be fickle customers, so there's no guarantee that the latest fad will be around long enough to make a success of the company that created it. If you're serious about getting your children started in solid stocks with growth potential, you, and they, will have to do some research on the companies. And that's where many parents feel they are on shaky ground. 'Fess up—you may not even feel comfortable explaining to your kids what it means to invest in the stock market or helping them follow the price of a company's shares in the newspaper stock tables.

Relax. It isn't all that difficult, and you don't have to go it alone. This book can help and so can a clever little volume called *Ump's Fwat, an Annual Report for Young People,* available online at http://www.Powellendowment .org. Ump, by the way, is a caveman and the Mickey Mantle of his day in a primitive game called fwap that bears an uncanny resemblance to baseball. Fwatters toss rocks into the air and slug them with a club, or fwat. Ump's fwat was much coveted by the other fwatters, so he had an idea: Why not start a company to make and sell fwats? Thus might the first capitalist have been born.

Cave dwellers interested in investing in Ump's Fwat Co. didn't have access to all the information that you do when it comes to researching prospective stock picks. You can get annual reports and other information for free by contacting a company directly. Then you can get independent analyses by consulting these trusted sources:

- **Value Line Investment Survey** (800-833-0046; http://www.valueline.com), a one-stop encyclopedia covering nearly 2,000 U.S. companies with an enormous database and trenchant commentaries. A subscription is expensive, but you can consult it at no charge at your public library.

- **Standard & Poor's** (800-852-1641; http://www.spoutlook.com) provides data and commentary on more than 1,000 companies in its *S&P Stock Reports,* which is also available from your public library.

- **Financial publications** such as *Kiplinger's Personal Finance, Money, Smart Money, Forbes,* and *Barron's* are invaluable and easy-to-use sources. And, of course, the Internet is a gold mine of information on investing (for just a few sources, try http://www.kiplinger.com, http://www.finance.yahoo.com, or http://www.marketwatch.com). In Ump's day, shareholders might have tracked the ups and downs of Ump's Fwat Co. by scanning the stock tables in the *Gnu Yerk Times* or the *Welp Strit Journal.* So can you. Don't be intimidated by what at first looks like endless gibberish. The tables are easy to interpret—and are much admired by math teachers for the practice they give kids in using decimals and percentages. For a detailed look at how to read and interpret the stock tables, see the illustration on page 155.

To Market, to Market

Forget price-earnings ratios and market capitalization. When I spoke with a group of eighth-grade students about the stock market, the kids cut right to the chase: "How long does it take to sell a stock, and when do you get your money?" they wanted to know.

Investing was definitely a weak link in their knowledge of personal finance. Some had a vague understanding of what it means to own stock, but that was about it. And no one could tell me what a dividend is.

HOW TO READ THE STOCK LISTINGS

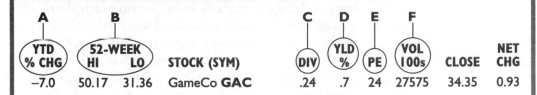

A	B			C	D	E	F		
YTD % CHG	52-WEEK HI	LO	STOCK (SYM)	DIV	YLD %	PE	VOL 100s	CLOSE	NET CHG
−7.0	50.17	31.36	GameCo **GAC**	.24	.7	24	27575	34.35	0.93

A. The YTD percentage change reflects the stock price percentage change for the calendar year to date, adjusted for stock splits and dividends over 10%.

B. The 52-week high and low columns show the stock's highest and lowest price during the preceding 52 weeks plus the current week, but not the latest trading day.

C. The dividend listed is the latest annual dividend paid by that stock.

D. The yield is the stock's latest annual dividend expressed as a percentage of that day's price.

E. The price-earnings ratio is the price of the stock divided by the earnings reported by the company for the latest four quarters.

F. The sales figures are the unofficial daily total of shares traded, quoted in hundreds (two zeros omitted).

Source: *The Wall Street Journal.*

Then, as part of their algebra class, the students began taking an hour or two a week to participate in SMG2000, the online version of the Stock Market Game. Sponsored by the Securities Industry Foundation for Economic Education (212-618-0519; http://www.smg2000.org), the school-based game gives teams ten weeks to turn a virtual $100,000 into a winning portfolio.

The game's ten-week time frame is a bit of a handicap because it encourages students to shoot for a quick profit. As an informal observer and occasional guest lecturer, my goals were to give the kids a longer-term perspective, make sure they at least learned how the market works—and teach them what a dividend is. I also wanted to see how well a school could fit the game—or any other financial curriculum—into a day that's already packed with so many demands on a teacher's time. (Hint to PTA groups or individuals who want to introduce financial education into local schools: Find an interested teacher and give him or her materials to work with. You can get a slew of curriculum references through the Jump$tart Coalition for Personal Financial Literacy, http://www.jumpstartcoalition.org.)

WHAT ARE BLUE CHIPS?

The term blue chips was introduced in 1904 to mean the stocks of the largest, most consistently profitable corporations. It comes from the blue chips used in poker—always the most valuable ones.

It took at least one class period for the students to become familiar with the software—how to find ticker symbols, enter trades, and look up company descriptions. The kids liked the *Washington Post* site (http://www.washingtonpost.com) because they were familiar with the newspaper and because the user-friendly business section gave capsule news reports on each company, plus a chart showing price trends over recent months.

Right off the bat it was clear that when it came to picking stocks, the kids had more basic concerns than technical analysis. They were surprised to find out, for example, that Old Navy, the popular clothing chain, is actually owned by Gap and that some of their favorite companies—notably Hallmark and Mars—weren't publicly traded (one team mistakenly ended up with shares in Hallmark Capital, a bank holding company). When they sell stock, they wondered, to whom do they sell? What does it mean when you hear that the market went up or down? And who is Dow Jones anyway?

Playing the game in the fall and hoping for a boost from seasonal sales, the kids bought Hershey

(Halloween candy), Sony (video games for the holidays), and even Anheuser-Busch ("Seasonal depression may make people drink more," observed one young investor). But the kids were too skittish to invest their entire $100,000. And often they didn't buy anything because team members couldn't agree on a stock (shades of adult investment clubs).

By the end of the game's third week, it was clear the seasonal strategy wouldn't pan out the way they had hoped; most of the stocks hadn't moved much one way or the other. With only seven weeks left, the kids were beginning to think they might have to try something else to get a big price bounce. "We're looking for stocks that are down," said Diane, whose group ended up buying Disney at a price way off its 52-week high.

As it turned out, the kids didn't get a big-enough bounce. During the ten-week contest, the market rose an impressive 14 percent, mostly on the strength of a run-up in technology stocks. But the kids finished what to them was a disappointing 283rd out of nearly 400 student teams in the state of Maryland, making a profit of about $1,100. Even though their instincts to go with proven consumer-products companies rather than bet on the latest highflier probably cost them the contest, over time they stand a better chance of reaping impressive returns with fewer sleepless nights.

The students' experience was instructive in other ways as well. "You can't predict the market," said Diane. "We should have used more of our money," said Allison. "Just because something new comes out doesn't mean people will buy it," said Andrea. "I learned not to let other people manage my money," said Anthony, with a sidelong glance at his teammates. (A number of kids preferred their teacher's go-it-alone alternative, in which each student chose a single stock and tracked it with paper, pencil, and the newspaper stock tables.)

As for me, I was glad they finally understood that a dividend is a stockholder's share of the profits a company earns.

A Family Investment Club

At home, some parents and grandparents have made investing a family affair. Betty Taylor of Kansas City, Kansas, started an investment club that included four generations of her family, including her father, her three children, and her grandchildren. "The youngest ones owned stock when they came into the world," said Taylor.

Each member of the club, grandkids included, could contribute. Only those 18 or older got to vote on which stocks the family would buy and sell, but the younger children had significant input, often based on their considerable intake of things like frozen yogurt. The family invested in TCBY when it was a fledgling firm, watched as the stock price rose with the popularity of frozen yogurt, and then bailed out when lots of other companies cut in on the craze and the stock price faltered. "It was a great way to teach the children that once a company has a niche, competitors come in," said Taylor.

She also taught the children to invest in a few good stocks instead of spreading their money over a lot of companies (the family's portfolio generally included eight to ten stocks) and how to handle a proxy vote: "We told them to vote for the management if they liked what the company was doing and against it if they didn't."

When the children were between 8 and 12 years old, they learned to look up a stock in *Value Line* or color a chart tracking a company's earnings for the past ten years. Taylor encouraged the teenagers to read a company's annual report, especially the report for the preceding year "so they could see what the president's goals were and whether he met them." When one of her granddaughters returned from a school trip to Russia, Taylor sat her down and debriefed her

---

START YOUR OWN CLUB

For information on starting an investment club as well as basic information on investing in general, contact the National Association of Investors Corp. (http://www.better-investing .org; P.O. Box 220, Royal Oak, MI 48068; 248-583-6242). The annual membership fee is $50, or $20 for young people 18 and under.

---

on which American companies had established a presence there.

Low-Cost Stock Investing

Once parents (or grandparents) are sold on the idea of investing for their children or grandchildren, they run smack up against a big challenge: how to buy small amounts of stock without paying big commissions. As the *Kiplinger's* expert on kids and money, I can't tell you how often I'm asked questions like this: "Each of my three lovely children has a few hundred dollars, with which I would like to buy a few shares of stock to use as an investment and a teaching tool. Where can I go to buy stocks a few shares at a time, as cash permits, with discount commissions? Stock that they can identify with would be my first choice, such as Coca-Cola, McDonald's, or Walt Disney." Then there's this related question: "How should I go about starting a dividend reinvestment plan for my 5-year-old grandson and soon-to-be-born granddaughter?" (As its name indicates, a dividend reinvestment plan, or DRP, lets you reinvest stock dividends to buy additional shares in small increments.)

One of the best ways to purchase stock in small amounts is through the online broker ShareBuilder (http://www.sharebuilder.com). Terms can change, but as of the time this book went to press, the commission was a low $4 per trade. And there's no investment or account minimum or inactivity fee.

Another nice touch is that ShareBuilder lets you buy fractional shares of stock. So if the questioner above invested, say, $200 for each of his three children in a stock trading for $16 a share, each of them would own 12¼ shares (less the $4 commission).

To keep costs low, ShareBuilder bundles its trades and makes purchases periodically, so you won't necessarily get the most current price. But as long as your children intend to hang on to their stock—and they should—the purchase price shouldn't be a big factor. ShareBuilder executes sell orders in real time and charges a higher commission—another inducement for your kids to hold on to their shares.

You also have the option of bypassing a broker altogether by investing in any of the hundreds of companies that are willing to sell you stock directly. For a listing of those companies, visit the online site NetstockDirect (http://www.netstockdirect.com).

Minimum investment requirements, fees, and other plan details vary from company to company. Of the three companies mentioned above, for example, all have direct-purchase plans. But as of press time Coca-Cola offered the best deal: a minimum initial investment of just one share with no enrollment fee. McDonald's, on the other hand, required a minimum initial investment of $500 and charged a setup fee of $5. Walt Disney was the most expensive, with a minimum initial investment of $1,000, a setup fee of $10, plus a commission of two cents per share.

No matter how you purchase your shares, once you own stock in a company, you can join its dividend reinvestment plan if one is available. Besides automatically reinvesting your dividends, a DRP lets you buy additional shares of stock.

The Temper Enrollment Service specializes in purchasing the number of shares needed to enroll in a DRP—sometimes as few as one, which lets you bypass high minimums for company-direct plans. Temper will also set up your DRP. For information on fees and terms, go to http://www.directinvesting.com.

Another direct-investing option is the Low Cost Investment Plan of the National Association of Investors Corp. (NAIC) (http://www.better-investing .org). NAIC members can purchase shares in a selected number of companies. Membership costs $50 a year

DEAR JANET

Q. My 11-year-old son has $120 saved in his bank account, but he doesn't like the low interest rate he's getting. He would like to invest his money in the stock market. Can he invest such a small amount?

A. Yes, your son can invest such a small amount (as discussed in detail in this chapter). The bigger question is, should he. If this is his entire life savings, or if he has plans to buy a new bike, a video game system, or something else that catches an 11-year-old's eye, he should keep the money in the bank, where he can get at it easily. But if he isn't going to need his money and really wants to invest in the stock market, go for it.

for adults, or $20 for young people 18 and under, and includes other NAIC publications and services.

A Web site called OneShare.com specializes in delivering a single share of stock in certificate form that's suitable for giving as a gift or hanging on a wall (the company will even frame it for you). OneShare charges $39 for an unfolded stock certificate. That may not be a bad price for a piece of art, but it's steep if what you really want to do is invest in the company; you can do that for a lot less.

Mutual Funds Made Easy

Besides shares of common stock, Jonathan H., the tycoon mentioned at the beginning of this chapter, owned shares in mutual funds. Investing in a mutual fund isn't as direct as buying shares in an individual company, so the concept isn't as easily grasped, especially by younger children. And as a hands-on learning experience, it isn't as exciting as being part-owner of a specific company. But as an investment, it has lots of advantages.

What you are doing is pooling your money with that of other investors. The fund's professional money managers take all that pooled cash and invest it in a portfolio of stocks (or bonds) that is designed to achieve a specific objective. Growth funds, for example, invest in companies that have the potential to grow (along with the price of their stock) but do not pay much in the way of dividends. Income funds concentrate more on bonds and other investments that pay interest, along with the stocks of companies that pay consistent dividends. Although growth funds are riskier than income funds, they are more appropriate for children, who have plenty of time to ride out the market's ups and downs.

Mutual funds can be ideal investments for small investors, and that includes kids, for a number of reasons:

■ **You get instant diversification** that isn't otherwise available to small investors who don't have the money or the inclination to invest in a dozen or so individual stocks.

■ **You can purchase no-load funds**—funds that charge no up-front sales fee—directly from the fund management company.

■ **You can invest with as little as $50 a month** or less if you sign up for an automatic investment plan.

Whether youngsters invest in stocks or mutual funds, they have lots of time to recover when the market hits the skids. Over time, investing in growth stocks or in a growth-stock mutual fund will give them a better return than will any other investment. Going back to 1926, large-company stocks have had an average total return (increase, or appreciation, of share price plus dividends) of around 10 percent a year; the total return on small-company stocks has averaged around 12 percent. You can't argue with those numbers, which beat all other financial assets.

SCOUTING THE WINNERS

As with stocks, you can track daily price changes for mutual fund shares in the stock tables of your newspaper. The illustration on page 164 shows you what to look for. A number of personal finance and business magazines provide regular coverage of funds and rank their performance. Among the most popular periodicals: *Kiplinger's Personal Finance, Money, SmartMoney, Business Week, Forbes,* and *Barron's.*

Other publications, available for sale or through your local library, provide comprehensive fund directories and performance data:

■ **Individual Investor's Guide to the Top Mutual Funds.** Compiled by the American Association of Individual Investors. Includes risk ratings and portfolio holdings. Updated annually (625 N. Michigan Ave., Suite 1900, Chicago, IL 60611; 800-428-2244).

■ **Morningstar Mutual Funds.** Expert analyses of individual funds, updated every other week by Morningstar Inc. (225 W. Wacker Drive, Chicago, IL 60606, 800-735-0700; http://www.morningstar.com).

■ **Value Line Mutual Fund Survey.** A biweekly publication analyzing the performance of about 1,500 mutual funds. (Value Line Publishing; 220 East 42nd St., New York, NY 10017, 800-535-8760; http://www.valueline.com).

How to Pick a Fund

Dear Janet: How can I find mutual funds that will let my kids personally invest in their own accounts?

Dear Janet: Aloha from Hawaii! My toddler daughter often receives money for her birthdays and special holidays, and it is starting to accumulate. We're new to investments for children, so we are not sure if we can open a custodial account for her. We already have a college fund set up, so this will be her money to use when she gets older. Where should we start to invest? Mahalo!

Dear Janet: I'm only 12 years old, but I'm into investing. I just wanted to know some good funds that are directed toward kids.

My e-mail box is crowded with questions from parents (and kids) about how to choose a mutual fund for children.

First off, let me make clear that kids can personally invest in *any* mutual fund. If a child is under 18, you, as a parent, would have to set up a custodial account (easily done) with you or some other adult as custodian (see the sidebar on page 166). After that, children can contribute their own money from gifts or earnings, or you and other family members can invest on their behalf.

Of the thousands of funds available, only a half dozen or so have actually marketed themselves directly to children. And that was primarily during the heyday of the 1990s bull market, when every fund was a winner and expansive management companies were willing to spend money on kids.

With a more sober stock market, fund managers are less willing to be so generous. And, frankly, after the bull market boom, the funds themselves didn't perform particularly well. The lesson: Don't pick a mutual fund because it's aimed at kids but rather because it's a good fund. For children, look for funds that invest in a broad range of growth-oriented companies and have performed well over time.

HOW TO READ THE MUTUAL FUND LISTINGS

Most daily newspapers publish mutual fund tables in the business pages. Here's a guide to interpreting them:

- **NAV** is net asset value per share, what a share of the fund is worth.
- **Net change** is the change in the fund's NAV from the preceding day.
- **YTD percentage return** is the fund's return for the year to date.
- **3-year percentage return** is the fund's return over the preceding three years, expressed on an annual basis.
- **p** next to the fund's name means that it charges a yearly 12b-1 fee to cover the mutual fund company's cost of marketing, sometimes including commissions to bro-

kers. Funds may be listed as NL, even if they charge this fee.
- **r** means that the mutual fund may charge you a redemption fee (or back-end load) when you sell. These fees may be permanent or temporary, as with a contingent deferred sales fee, which may start as high as 6 percent and decline gradually the longer you keep your shares. A fund can have a redemption fee but still be called no-load.
- **t** means that both p and r apply.
- **x** and/or **e** stand, respectively, for ex-cash dividend and ex-capital gains distribution, meaning that the fund has just distributed income to current shareholders. That day's NAV will be reduced by the amount of the distribution per share.

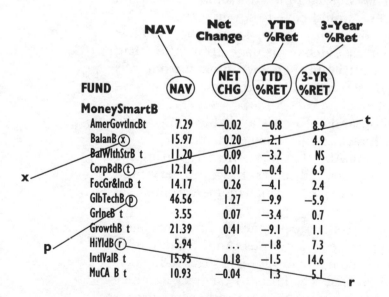

Source: *The Wall Street Journal.*

An excellent choice would be Vanguard's Total Stock Market Index fund (800-635-1511), which invests in companies representing the entire stock market. Another broad-based fund is T. Rowe Price Spectrum Growth (800-638-5660). To keep current on other mutual fund selections, go to http://www.kiplinger.com.

A Word about Risk

Jonathan H. had some words of advice for would-be Wall Street tycoons: "Leave your investments alone; if you buy and sell a lot, you'll be murdered by commissions." And steel yourself to take a loss. "I was fully aware I could lose every single penny," Jonathan told me.

Getting your kids to save at all is great; getting them to appreciate the risks and rewards of various kinds of investments is icing on the cake. Just like adults, they'll have different tolerances for risk and make different choices, depending on how much money they have and what they want to use it for. Here's a rundown on their options:

GARDEN-VARIETY BANK SAVINGS ACCOUNTS. Still the best place to stash money earned from paper routes or babysitting. Your kids won't get rich fast on the interest they earn, but bank accounts are convenient and the money is safe so long as it's insured by the Federal Deposit Insurance Corp. (FDIC) or the National Credit Union Administration.

BANK CERTIFICATES OF DEPOSIT. These pay a higher rate than a regular savings account, but in return your children will have to promise not to touch their money for a certain period—most commonly, six months, one year, two and a half years, or five years. Also, CDs can require a minimum deposit of several hundred dollars. They're insured by the FDIC up to $100,000.

MONEY MARKET MUTUAL FUNDS. Instead of investing in stocks, these mutual funds invest in the "money market," which is a collective name that describes all the different ways in which governments, banks, and corporations borrow and lend money for short periods. The interest rate changes every day, but it's generally higher than it is on regular bank accounts, especially when rates are rising. And your kids can get their money whenever they want it, although they (or you, on their behalf) will have to transact business by mail or phone. Money market funds aren't insured; how-

THE INS AND OUTS OF CUSTODIAL ACCOUNTS

Minors can't own assets in their own name, so if you want to save or invest on behalf of your children—or if the kids want to do it on their own—you'll need to set up custodial accounts. These generally come in two varieties, depending on the law in your state: the Uniform Gifts to Minors Act (UGMA) or, more commonly, the Uniform Transfers to Minors Act (UTMA). Opening one is as easy as checking a box when you open a mutual fund or brokerage account. All you need to do is name the child as beneficiary and an adult (typically you) as custodian.

Custodians have a legal right to manage and invest a child's assets and to spend them on anything they consider appropriate for the "use and benefit" of the child. That can include school tuition, summer camp, a personal computer, even clothing, so long as those expenditures don't take the place of a parent's legal support obligations. And under no circumstances may custodians spend a child's assets on themselves.

How will anyone know how you spend the money, you might ask. It may be that no one will. But it's the possibility of getting caught, along with the pricking of your conscience, that's expected to keep you in line. The larger the amount of money, the greater your incentive to stick to the letter of the law. A tax audit could trigger a review of the accounts—and the IRS would probably be inclined to look closely if a custodial account held a large balance one year and a significantly smaller one the next or showed considerable activity. Using the money for your own purposes would make you liable for taxes on the earnings. In addition to facing tax consequences, you have a fiduciary responsibility to the child as custodian of the account. If you misuse the assets, your child could sue you to recover the funds.

Giving money or other assets to children results in a couple of tax breaks for you. You can give as many people as you wish annual gifts of $11,000 each without having

ever, they're regarded as one of the safest uninsured investments around. Minimum balance requirements can be steep, but there are always exceptions that allow investors in for less money or waive minimums altogether. For older kids with money and savvy, money market funds can be an alternative to a bank savings account.

STOCKS AND STOCK MUTUAL FUNDS. Over time, these offer the greatest rewards and carry the greatest risks.

to pay gift tax. If both you and your spouse join in the gift, you can give away $22,000 a year. That can be an attractive estate-planning tool for parents and grandparents who would like to distribute assets from their estate before they die. Note, however, that even though donations to charities can be deducted on your tax return, gifts to individuals cannot.

Nevertheless, you do gain certain income tax advantages. In 2005, the first $800 of earnings from assets held in a child's name is tax free (that figure will rise in the future with inflation). The second $800 is taxed at the child's rate, which for dividends and capital gains is currently as low as 5 percent for those in the lowest tax bracket. For children under age 14, investment income above $1,600 is taxed at the parent's rate. Older kids always use their own tax rate.

Custodial accounts have a couple of drawbacks. Assets given to a child belong to the child irrevocably. That means you can't get them back, but the child can get them as soon as he or she reaches the legal age in your state. Fortunately, most states have raised that age to 21 or even older, making it less likely that kids will squander the money on a sports car instead of paying their college tuition.

Assets held in your child's name can also affect your eligibility for college financial aid, because schools usually expect a bigger contribution from a student's assets than from a parent's. But don't let financial aid eligibility alone determine whether you save in a child's name. Some parents prefer to set up an account in a child's name as a convenience. That way, they can keep college funds separate and make it easy for other family members to contribute to a college account. Parents going through a divorce may prefer that assets be held in a child's name (with a neutral third party as custodian) so they don't become a bone of contention. And grandparents sometimes prefer to give assets to their grandchildren rather than to their grown children.

When chosen well, they can be the best alternative for kids who are saving for a long-term goal.

The PG Factor

Back during the peak of the 1990s bull market, a number of teenage investors made headlines by running afoul of the Securities and Exchange Commission (SEC). In one case, a 15-year-old from New Jersey was nailed for stock fraud on the Internet after he bought cheap shares in small companies, hyped the stock in misleading e-mails, and then sold at a profit. When I was interviewed about this case by a concerned TV news reporter, I was asked how we could possibly keep other kids from pulling the same stunt. After all, the object of the stock market is to make money, so why not do it any way you can?

I told the reporter that a full-blown bear market would put a damper on incipient day traders—and eventually that's exactly what happened. In fact, during the depths of the bear market at the beginning of

---

DEAR JANET

Q. Do you really think it wise or even necessary for 12-year-olds to be fiddling with stocks and investing? I question whether at that age they fully grasp such concepts as price-earnings ratio or market share. I sometimes read about kid investors and wonder whether it's really something they'd do if given a choice between sitting down with a spreadsheet versus video games or Barbies or even a book.

A. I fully expect (and fervently hope) that any typical 12-year-old would rather sit down with a video game or a book than a spreadsheet (Barbies would probably be passé by that age). That being said, however, investing is a natural extension of saving. It's important to teach kids about both, and it can be done in age-appropriate ways. When my son, Peter, played a stock market game in school, the most complicated thing he did was look at charts showing company performance—and throw a sharpened pencil at the financial pages. But Peter ended up building his $100,000 portfolio into $116,000 in two months. What he learned, he said, was that "good things come to those who wait. I held the same stocks, except for one, for the whole game." Not a bad lesson.

the 2000s, reporters did an about-face: How could we convince young people to invest at all, I was asked, when the market is so lousy?

What's needed in each of these situations is the "PG" factor. The New Jersey teenager reportedly was hailed as a folk hero by friends and family members, including his parents, who looked the other way as he raked in his ill-gotten gains. But touting stocks is just as wrong as cheating on your taxes or hiring someone to take your SAT exam, and kids need to hear you say that (for a longer discussion of financial ethics in the wake of Enron and other corporate scandals, see Chapter 16).

At the other extreme when the market skids, it's important that kids (and adults) not lose heart. Call it the "$" strategy of investing: $tarting young to $teadily invest $mall amounts of money in $olid companies is the $urest way to make a million bucks. Think children are too young to appreciate that lesson? Think again. I was once asked to judge an essay contest in which high school students wrote about someone they considered to be a successful investor. I was blown away by how many of the teens cited family members:

- **Ben O.:** "My aunt first introduced me to investing when she opened a mutual fund account for me. I was somewhat intimidated by the idea of investing what I had worked hard to earn. However, I was glad to be introduced gradually to the whole process of the stock market by someone I knew."
- **Annie D.:** "When I was 11, my family had a competition to research and pick ten stocks and record the progress of each over a two-month period. My dad and I ended up winning, but that was beside the point. The competition taught me to look for certain things in a stock, like growth and earnings. Invest only what you can afford to lose."
- **Morgan K.:** "One lesson I learned from my father is never to panic. With investing, you must remember that you are in it for the long run."

DEAR JANET

Q. I'm a volunteer with the Big Brothers Big Sisters organization. My "little brother," who's 12, is bright, curious, and a pleasure to be around.

Recently, I introduced him to basic concepts of investing and encouraged him to create a list of companies in which he would like to own shares. That eager beaver listed about 25 solid companies or industries. If that wasn't enough, he took the time to summarize the minilecture I had given him about how to read the financial pages. I was amazed that he had nailed it after just one discussion.

Can you recommend a few investment resources for youngsters to nurture this budding CEO?

A. Be happy to. I get similar requests frequently but not always with such an uplifting story attached.

Publications for Teenagers
- *Stock Market Knowledge for All Ages,* by Susie Vaccaro Hardeman (Ten Speed Press).
- *Street Wise: A Guide for Teen Investors,* by Janet Bamford (Bloomberg Press).
- *TeenVestor: The Practical Investment Guide for Teens and Their Parents,* by Emmanuel Modu and Andrea Walker (Perigee).
- *The Motley Fool Investment Guide for Teens,* by David and Tom Gardner, with Selena Maranjian (Fireside).
- *Wow the Dow!* by Pat Smith and Lynn Roney (Fireside).
- *Young Money magazine* (http://www.youngmoney.com).

Web Sites
- *http://www.fool.com/teens.* Teen site from the Motley Fool.
- *http://www.better-investing.org/subjects/youth.* Youth site from the National Association of Investors Corp.
- *http://www.smg2000.org.* School-based investing game with virtual portfolios.

Games for Teenagers
- *Mr. Bigshot* (board game or CD-ROM; http://www.mrbigshot.com). The computer version of this stock-picking game features snappy graphics and music and a wisecracking announcer. Players can choose between two real companies—disguised here as "Big" and "Shot"—and follow their fortunes, deciding whether to hold or sell.
- *Mutual Mania* (http://www.mutualmania.com). Starting with $25,000, players circle the board assembling portfolios and landing on spaces that require them to respond to market-shaking events.

Books for Middle School Kids
- *Growing Money: A Complete Investing Guide for Kids,* by Gail Karlitz and Debbie Honig (Price Stern Sloan).
- *Stock Market Pie,* by J.M. Seymour (DynaMinds Publishing).
- *The Young Investor: Projects and Activities for Making Your Money Grow,* by Katherine R. Bateman (Chicago Review Press).

- **Isaac S.:** "My grandmother was a second-grade teacher, but she lives as comfortably now as any retired oil tycoon, with most of her income coming from money she invested. Her greatest feat, however, was helping one teenager (me) realize the value of investing."

- **Michael O.:** "My mom's primary rule of investing is to pay yourself first, even if it is only a few dollars a week. Mom followed this rule over the last 29 years, and today my parents are well on the road to a secure retirement. This has made Mom my financial guru."

Way to go, Mom.

Turn page for Kids' Questions→

KIDS' QUESTIONS

Q. "If I have a share of stock, does that mean I have to share it with someone?"
A. Not exactly. Owning a share of stock in a company means that you own a part of that company—a piece of the action, so to speak. As one of the owners, you're entitled to a share of the money your company makes after all its expenses are paid—its profits. If you're a shareholder in Nike, for example, you stand to profit each time someone buys a pair of Nike sneakers.

Profits are paid out in the form of a dividend, which is like the interest you earn on a bank account. Banks promise to pay you a certain rate of interest. Dividends, on the other hand, aren't guaranteed. The size of a dividend all depends on how much money the company makes. Sometimes even a profitable company doesn't pay dividends. Instead, it puts all its profits back into the company so that it can grow even bigger.

When you're a stockholder, you can make money in another way, too. If your company does well and its stock becomes more valuable, the price of your shares will go up. If you paid $15 for a share of stock, for example, it might go up to $20 or even higher. On the other hand, your company may not make much money or could even lose money. If that's the case, it may not pay a dividend, and the price of a share of stock could fall from, say, $15 to $10 or less. That's the risk of investing in the stock market.

Q. "Can kids buy stocks?"
A. Yes, they can. Minor children (usually children under the age of 18) can't own stock directly. But all you have to do is ask your parents to fill out a simple form to open a custodial account—which means their name appears on the account along with yours.

With their parents' help, children can buy shares in any of the thousands of companies whose stock is bought and sold on stock exchanges, such as the New York Stock Exchange (NYSE), the Nasdaq market, or the American Stock Exchange (AMEX). Once you have opened an account with a stockbroker (a person who buys and sells stocks for customers), all you have to do is call your broker and tell him or her how many shares of which company you'd like to buy (or go online to do the same thing).

Q. "How much does stock cost?"
A. The price is set by the market, and it all depends on how much buyers and sellers think the stock is worth that day. Some stocks sell for less than $10 a share, others for more than $100 a share. If you're interested in buying stock in a particular company, you can check to see how much its stock has been selling for by looking up the company alphabetically in the stock tables section of any newspaper or online. Stock tables have lots of small type and look long and boring, but they're really pretty easy to use once you know what you're looking for. (For some instructions on reading the stock tables, see page 155.)

Q. "How do I sell a stock?"
A. The same way you buy one, only backwards. You call your broker and tell him or her to sell your shares (or you enter your sale with an online broker). You'll get the market price of the stock that day.

But you shouldn't get into the habit of selling stocks frequently. You'll have to pay a commission on each sale, just as you do when you buy a stock. And that could eat up any profits you might have made if the stock has gone up in price.

Q. "But what if the price of my stock goes down?"

A. That can be an even better reason not to sell. The price of your stock is almost guaranteed to fall at some time. Maybe your company will go through a period when business isn't so great. Sometimes the whole stock market goes down because people are less enthusiastic about holding stocks.

But the best way to make money in the stock market is to buy shares in good companies that have the potential to grow and hold on to them. Over time the stock market tends to rise, with downward blips along the way. When a stock price drops, young investors should follow the same strategy as adults: Ask yourself if you still like the company and think its future looks good. If the answer is no, go ahead and sell your shares. If the answer is yes, hold on—and maybe even buy some more. Remember the secret to making money in the stock market: buy low, sell high. It may take a while for prices to rise again. But if anyone qualifies as a long-term investor who can ride out ups and downs in the market, it's a 12-year-old.

Q. "Who is Dow Jones? They talk about him on TV a lot."

A. Actually, your question should be "Who *are* Dow Jones?" "Dow" is Charles H. Dow and "Jones" is Edward D. Jones. In the 1880s, they founded the newspaper that later became the *Wall Street Journal*. In 1896, Mr. Dow began

calculating the average daily price of 12 stocks. By the 1920s, the editors of the *Wall Street Journal* were tracking the stock prices of 30 big industrial companies every day. The 30 stocks chosen are representative of the broad market and of American industry.

What the editors did was add up the 30 stock prices and divide by a number to get an average price (it gets complicated here because they didn't divide by 30, but you don't have to worry about that). The average price they came up with was called the Dow Jones industrial average (or Dow, for short). Looking at movements in the average was a way of measuring whether the stock market as a whole went up or down. A rising Dow means stock prices went up; a falling Dow means they went down.

The Dow Jones industrial average became so popular that even after all these years, it's reported every day in the news. It's done by computer now, but the procedures are the same as those Charles Dow developed over a century ago. New companies are added to the average, and old ones removed, when it seems appropriate. General Motors is one firm that has been included since the 1920s; other companies among the elite 30 are Johnson & Johnson, Procter & Gamble, General Electric, ExxonMobil, Home Depot, and Microsoft.

Q. "Wow! I just got a 3-D Derek Jeter baseball card! Is it going to be worth a lot of money someday?"

A. Don't get your hopes up too high when it comes to making money by investing in the collectibles market. Old baseball cards are valuable if there's interest in the players and if the cards are relatively rare and in mint condition. (That probably lets out most of your parents' cards if they flipped them, stuffed them in their pockets, or wrapped rubber bands around them. So don't let your parents blame Grandma for tossing them out.) Nowadays, with millions of cards being produced (and carefully preserved by kids with an eye to making a killing in the market), it's less likely that prices will shoot up in the future. Even if some do, it's tough to predict which players will generate the most interest a generation from now.

Collect for love, not money. There's a market for just about anything you can collect—Beanie Babies, Hot Wheels cars, McDonald's Happy Meal toys—but markets are fickle. There's no guarantee you'll be able to sell your treasures at the time you want the money and for the price you think they're worth. Kids, especially, can be taken advantage of. There are success stories, of course—like the young man who got hooked on collecting comic books when he was 4 and at 18 sold his collection of 10,000 books for $6,000, enough to pay for his first three semesters of college.

But any money you eventually make should be an unexpected bonus; the real pleasure should come from the thrill of the chase that is part of building and enjoying a collection.

If you still harbor the hope that some day all that work will pay off, the best you can do is:

■ Focus on items popular with kids between the ages of 10 and 17. That's the time in their life that people like you will try to recapture when they're 30; they won't remember much before the age of 8.

■ Treat collections gently. Better still, if you have the space and the cash, buy duplicates of some items—one to play with and one to keep in its box. The container can easily double an item's value.

■ Look for collectibles with tie-ins to movie or television characters or well-known personalities, whether it's Ronald McDonald or G.I. Joe. That's what makes an item memorable.

Of Lawn Mowing and Milkshake Stands

When my son Peter was 10 years old, he had an idea for a summer business that would, as he put it, "make some major cash." Along with his friends, Mickey and T.J., he would set up a stand at the corner and sell milkshakes. I didn't want to burst his bubbling enthusiasm, but I wasn't quite sure how this scheme would shake out. Would there be enough traffic at the end of our cul-de-sac to generate any business? Just how did they plan to get the electric milkshake maker down to the curb? And how would they keep the milk cold and the ice cream frozen?

Not to worry, Mom, Peter patiently assured me. Since this would be a three-man operation, he would stay in the house making the shakes, Mickey would man the stand to make sure nobody took anything, and T.J. would shuttle back and forth delivering the drinks. And, of course, they'd do it on a Thursday afternoon, the busiest day of the week for the piano teacher up the street.

My initial misgivings were perhaps typical of many parents with entrepreneurial kids. You'd think we'd be happy to nurture our children's interest in the free enterprise system. After all, the extra cash would help free us from the enterprise of keeping the kids in clothes, cosmetics, and video games. And the kids might even lay the foundation for their life's work. Business tycoon Warren Buffett bought stock at age 12, made enough money to pay taxes at 13, and bought a farm in Nebraska before finishing high school in Washington, D.C. Computer king Michael Dell started his empire in his college dorm. Nowadays especially, when jobs are constantly in flux and every member of the workforce has to be a little entreprenurial just to keep pace, it's important for kids to know that working for yourself is an alternative to working for a company or joining a profession.

But instead of encouraging our children's grand schemes, we're often tempted to find the flaws in them—perhaps because we're afraid that we'll end up spending lots of our time minding the kids' business. But as Peter reminded me, children can be satisfied with small successes that don't necessarily require much in the way of parental input.

Several days after our conversation, I got an excited phone call from my son while I was at work. On the spur of the moment, he and his buddies had set up their stand at T.J.'s house (on a busy corner) and cleared $21—not bad for a few hours work, even after they had paid me back for the milk and ice cream they used. T.J.'s mom contributed a long extension cord so they could make the shakes outside, and they kept the milk and ice cream in a cooler. They charged $1 per drink (the $1.25 banana special wasn't a big seller) and netted a few extra dollars from customers who tipped them for their good service.

If they did it again, Peter decided, he would plow some of the money back into the business in the form of a bigger sign. I figure that as long as I don't rein him in, he could be well on the way to achieving his goal of being the second-richest man in the world behind Bill Gates—but only by a penny. "Bill Gates made Microsoft," Peter once told me. "You can't dump a legend."

The ABCs of Capitalism

Why are we parents sometimes reluctant to teach our kids entrepreneurial skills? Often because, unless we're in business ourselves, we don't feel comfortable in the role. If truth be told, many Americans would probably be hard-pressed to explain the economic system that makes their country tick (and some might even feel vaguely guilty about it).

But peel away the layers of econospeak and the system really is quite simple. In fact, scratch the surface of the average American and you'll find an itchy capitalist. With the possible exceptions of eating and breathing, nothing is more instinctual than making money. Consider, for example, that American institution, the fundraiser—specifically, a fundraiser undertaken a number of years ago by my children's nursery school. The school was a nonprofit cooperative run by the 30 families whose children attended. For several years demand for nursery school slots exceeded supply, so the school enjoyed a long waiting list and a modest budget surplus. One year, however, a new day care center down the road siphoned off customers; as a result of the lower than expected revenue from tuition, the school faced a deficit of about $300.

How to close the budget gap? We couldn't cut expenses because most of our costs were fixed. Besides, our problem wasn't a bloated budget but a revenue shortfall. The quick and dirty expedient of a special midyear assessment was dismissed; consumer resistance would be too great, and it would breach the informal contract agreed to in the fall when tuition rates were set. The idea of raising money through an auction or a book sale was more appealing but was rejected as not feasible. Our potential market—the 30 co-op families and members of the church at which the school was located—was too small. What we had to do, everyone agreed, was tap a larger market at the lowest possible cost.

Someone proposed a bake sale at a local shopping center, and that drew a flurry of interest. It had a number of advantages: a commodity product that everyone was familiar with and that wouldn't suffer for not having a brand name; ease of entry into the market (we could set up shop in front of Sears); no need for outside financing because parents would be investing the cost of materials (we'd bake the cookies).

A MODEST PROPOSAL

To lend a hand to all those tweens who'd like to work but don't necessarily want to start a business of their own, I'd like to make a modest proposal that middle school and junior high guidance offices act as a link between parents and other adults who are looking for help and kids who are looking for a job.

I know counselors have a lot on their plates, so I'm not suggesting anything too elaborate or time consuming. But I think schools are a natural place for adults in the community in need of assistance to post their job descriptions.

In order to get access to this list, students would have to fill out for the school a sort of preliminary résumé. Besides giving pertinent information about themselves, they'd also have to give some thought to what kind of work they'd like to do, where and when they'd be available, and what skills and qualifications they have to offer—everything from making good grades to participating in extracurricular activities or sports to volunteering.

That would help youngsters focus their search. In return, they could get job leads from the guidance office, along with tips on how to polish their résumé and impress prospective employers—valuable job-hunting skills that will give them a leg up when they get a little older and head out into the workplace for real.

Another parent suggested a 50-50 raffle. Once the idea was explained—the winner gets 50 percent of the take—we were quick to see the potential. A ticket allotment of, say, $20 per family would go over better than an assessment because people would have a chance to make a return on their investment. Besides, we could sell tickets at the bake sale.

Eventually, the raffle idea had to be scrapped because of regulatory difficulties: the church whose name the nursery school bears frowned on gambling. But the bake sale was a go. The goal, of course, was to maximize profits—or, as our bake sale organizer put it, "The more we bake, the more we make." But we also had to determine the market-clearing price of homemade brownies and pineapple upside-down cake. In pricing my own nut roll pastries, I rejected a cost-plus approach; how could I put a price on my grandmother's research and development? Instead, I opted for market-based pricing: I called my mother in Pennsylvania and asked how much nut rolls fetch in bake sales there. Sell them for $5.50 each, she told me, and not a penny less than $5. Allowing for the higher cost of living in Washington, I figured we could get $6 easily.

We did. We also got $4-plus for cakes and did a brisk business in a scrumptious chocolate and cream cheese concoction called black-bottom cupcakes (25¢ each, five for $1). We rotated our stock from the back of the table to the front, ran specials on slow-moving items, and after four hours liquidated what little remained of our inventory with a special closeout sale. ("You couldn't even buy a mix at these prices.") The black-bottom line: a profit of $263.50.

And that's the economy in a nut roll.

Are Entrepreneurs Born or Made?

Everyone seems to agree that there's an entrepreneurial "type"—glad-handing extroverts who are convinced they've built a better mousetrap and have no qualms about ringing doorbells and telling total strangers all about it at great length. No room here for shy, quiet kids who'd rather fiddle with computers or doodle in a sketchbook.

It's true that some personality traits can increase your chances for success as an entrepreneur. It helps to be well organized and dependable, and to enjoy your work, for example. But building high-tech mousetraps and talking a blue streak aren't necessarily on the list. While Linda Menzies was researching her book *A Teen's Guide to Business,* which she coauthored with Oren Jenkins and Rickell Fisher (Master Media), she talked to 13- and 14-year-old teens "who had done so much that they made me feel old at 21," said Menzies. "I thought they'd be geniuses who had invented something, but they were just teens who had a good idea."

I've had much the same experience in my encounters with young entrepreneurs. Carrie H. used $80 from her savings to set up shop making hand-painted aprons and personalized ornaments during the holiday season. Melissa A. sold jams and jellies made with grapes from her aunt and uncle's

DEAR JANET

Q. My 7-year-old son has been very envious of his older sister's bigger allowance and cat-sitting money, so he took the initiative to make some money of his own. I thought you'd enjoy seeing his marketing pitch:

"I am selling paper fish. Buy one for 25 cents. On Friday, buy one, get one free for 50 cents. You could get three for 75 cents, because you get one, and then you buy one and get one free. Ordering is free, too! Your fish stuff all comes with instructions about how to make a clam! Sadtisfaction garinteed. [sic]"

I figure he'll grow up to be either a brilliant entrepreneur à la Bill Gates or a deft inside trader!

A. Either way, he'll make lots of clams!

California vineyard. Molly E. founded the Reflect-O-Light Co. to paint reflective house numbers on curbs—the very same thing her grandfather did to earn money back in 1947.

Walk into an average classroom of 13-year-olds and ask them for ideas on how to earn money, and it's likely that half will say babysitting and the other half lawn mowing. Bonnie Drew, author with her husband, Noel, of *Fast Cash for Kids* (Career Press), breaks it down even further. "I go to a school to speak to the students, and maybe 2 of 30 kids in a class are real entrepreneurs, by which I mean interested since the age of 4 or 5. Five aren't motivated by money at all. But the others might be motivated to become entrepreneurs if they had a specific goal and you got them at the right time." The catalyst could be a long summer vacation when they're looking for something to fill the time, a burning desire for a video game system that you're not willing to buy—or just a good idea about how to earn some extra money.

Peter's milkshake stand wasn't his only entrepreneurial venture. At one point he was heavily into collecting Pokemon cards, when that was a red-hot fad among kids his age. Then he had the inspiration to sell his collection and make a profit. I never understood the rules or the rationale of Pokemon, but I quickly found out that it was a great tool for learning about business.

Peter assured me he could sell his cards at school as long as he limited his business hours to recess. I gave him permission with one restriction: To avoid being accused of taking advantage of younger children, he should limit his sales to less valuable cards that were only worth a dollar or two.

That was Peter's first brush with market regulation. When I picked him up from school the next day, he couldn't stop chattering about the other capitalist principles he had picked up:

■ **Market-clearing price.** "I told them it was first come, first served, and I wouldn't play favorites," said

Peter. "If two people wanted a card, whoever brought more money would get it."

■ **Ease of entry.** Peter might have been able to make more money if I had taken him to a local mall or flea market to set up a table, but "it was easier just to sit on the curb and open my card book."

■ **Profit margin.** As he watched his sales boom, Peter calculated that he could buy 11-card packs at the 7-Eleven for around $3 each, then resell them at school for $4 and pocket the difference.

■ **Cost of doing business.** Peter carefully counted out four quarters to repay me for taking him to the store to buy his cards in the first place.

■ **Money-back guarantee.** Peter offered one to protect himself from teary-eyed children with buyer's remorse, but no one went back on a deal (and no irate parents called us).

All told, Peter was satisfied with the $55 he made. He retained most of his earnings in his savings account and reinvested some of his profits in new packs of cards, which he decided to hang on to. They're still in his closet—perhaps appreciating in value?

Super Ideas at School

Sometimes it's a school assignment that plants the seed of capitalism—like the one that inspired Ronni Cohen's fourth-graders at Burnett Elementary School in Wilmington, Delaware. Cohen instructed her class of entrepreneurs (defined by the students as "people who take risks and make choices so their company can make a profit") to invent devices that make it easier to eat pasta. The kids also had to come up with a marketing plan to sell them. On the day I visited, Ian was showing off his Super Duper Spaghetti Scooper, a gizmo made of a tea strainer with a spoon attached at the other end (for eating spaghetti without losing the sauce). Using a hardhat, a clothespin, and Legos, Courtney had created an elaborate pulley to hoist the spaghetti off her

DEAR JANET

Q. Last summer my daughter, Diana, who is 14 years old, wanted to go on a trip to Washington, D.C., with a church youth group. Both her mother and I gave our consent, but we felt it was important for her to earn part of the needed $650.

Diana had in the past done babysitting and occasional lawn mowing. However, these jobs weren't going to provide her with the needed money in the short amount of time she had before leaving. We encouraged her to be creative and think of ways she might earn the necessary money quickly.

After much thought, she hit upon the idea of selling baked goods. She enjoyed cooking and felt this would be something she could do. We encouraged her to scale down this idea to something more manageable, such as cooking only certain items. She decided on cookies.

Diana negotiated with us to contribute the ingredients as our contribution to her trip. She then went to her computer (another hobby of hers) and developed an order and price list, which she distributed at church, among family and neighbors, and at her mother's and my workplaces.

The orders started flowing in. The cost of the cookies was $3 to $5 per dozen, and she was able to earn over $900 in under four weeks. The business would have continued had she not gone on her trip and then started summer school.

She kept an account of what she spent on ingredients and her net profit would still have exceeded $700 had we not contributed the ingredients.

A. Diana deserves a pat on the back—and so do you for helping to channel your daughter's energy into a project that she could manage and then taking a businesslike approach to your own contribution. You provided support without doing the actual work.

plate. All of the children could rattle off the "factors of production" that they had used in building their inventions: "materials," such as tape, glue, rubber bands, string, and empty soft drink bottles; "capital," or equipment that could be used again on other jobs, such as screwdrivers, scissors, and staple guns; and, of course, "labor"—their own and that of various family members.

Each child had also done a marketing survey for his or her invention, measuring supply and demand at various prices and graphing the results to come up with a market-clearing price, the point at which supply meets demand. Eventually the kids voted Josh's creation—a fork attached to an electric screwdriver—

as most marketable and launched into a discussion of how to drum up demand for it: "Have a catchy ad." "Decorate it." "Make a small one for little kids." "Think of other things it can do, like whip potatoes, roast marshmallows, and dig holes to plant seeds."

Closer to Home

School programs can provide the spark, but it's up to parents and other adults to fan the flames. Parents, family members, and other entrepreneurs have the most influence on a child's decision to start a business, according to a survey of high school students attending a conference for teen entrepreneurs at the University of Pennsylvania's Wharton School. You don't need to be in business yourself; giving your child an opportunity to earn money around the house may be encouragement enough.

After all, kids get their first taste of the world of work by making their beds and picking up their toys. As they get a little older, they learn that their parents are willing to pay them to do more grown-up jobs, such as raking leaves or shoveling snow. One day it dawns on children that *other* people will pay them to rake *their* leaves and shovel *their* snow, and suddenly Mom and Dad have a fledgling entrepreneur on their hands.

Something as straightforward as a family yard sale presents all sorts of entrepreneurial possibilities. One family gave its teenage son the food concession at its regular yard sales. He sold coffee, soft drinks, and popcorn and made $25 or $30 in a couple of hours.

When Bonnie Drew's two sons were young, they helped organize family garage sales. On trash pickup days, older son Jon would get up early and scavenge neighborhood castoffs for old bikes and bike parts. Then he'd rebuild the bikes and sell them at garage sales of his own. Kids began bringing their bikes to him for spare parts and repairs, and by the time he was 14, he was running a business fixing small engines. Younger son Robby, a "totally different personality," would buy boxes of candy at a warehouse store and then resell it to neighborhood youngsters. A musician, he eventually organized his own band. Whatever children end up doing, the impetus comes from home. "That's where they get the confidence," said Drew.

When I have interviewed successful young entrepreneurs, the first thing to impress me has been their enthusiasm and enterprise. They all capitalized on simple ideas that took advantage of their talents and interests. When you talk to these kids, you want to smack yourself in the forehead and say, "Why didn't I think of that?"

The second thing to impress me has been their close family bonds. "You can't be laid back with a child like this," said Mary Gluck of her daughter, Erica.

When Erica was 7 years old, she wanted to earn money so badly that she threatened to sell her teddy bears on the sidewalk. Then she had a better idea. She went to the two brothers who ran the pasta shop her family patronized and got the okay to sell their pasta at weekend farmers markets near her home.

The entire Gluck family joined in the enterprise. The first week they bought 120 packages of pasta at $1.25 each and sold them for twice that. Erica's pasta sold out, and Erica's Pasta, her business, was born.

Erica had a flair for aesthetics, setting up food demonstrations and getting customers to try new

ENCOURAGING YOUNG ENTREPRENUERS

Lots of programs are available at all grade levels for teachers who want to introduce kids to entrepreneurship. Ronni Cohen's project, described on pages 181–183, was part of "Choices and Changes," sponsored by the Delaware Center for Economic Education. Every state has its own such agency; to locate yours, contact the National Council on Economic Education (1140 Avenue of the Americas, New York, NY 10036; 212-730-7007).

things. The business became so successful that it eventually expanded into a full-time family enterprise run by her parents. In addition to pasta, the company sells other food products and cookbooks with recipes Erica helped her dad whip up (http://www.pastapress.com).

"What Can I Do to Earn Money This Summer?"

- *Dear Janet: I'm 11 and I want a job. People say I'm too skinny to walk dogs. Can you help me?*
- *I want a job over the summer to get my dad off my back. I'm sure that I can do a lot of stuff, but I don't think people will give me a chance.*
- *I am 13 and want to get a summer job to earn some cash. I've thought about it, but I can't really come up with any good ideas. Can you help me?*
- *If you have any suggestions for a job in Baltimore, please help me out.*
- *I need money and I want a job so I don't sit around and get fat.*
- *I am 13 and I want a job. I know I'm young, but I think I can take it.*
- *I need money for a paintball gun. Do u [sic] have any suggestions?*

Judging by the deluge of e-mails I receive from kids like the ones above, lots of 11- to 13-year-olds are admirably eager to become productive members of society—and astonishingly clueless about how to do it. Some seem to think there's a magic formula for making a quick buck. Well, there is a formula, but it isn't magic: A little imagination to find a need, plus lots of elbow grease to fill it, equals less time on your hands and more money in your pocket.

Children under 14, who can't yet legally work at traditional summer jobs in stores and restaurants, are perfect for the service economy. If they're having trouble coming up with a need to fill, that's where parents come in: give them some idea of the services adults would be willing to pay for.

For example, kids who are "too skinny to walk dogs" could feed pets and take in mail when their neighbors are on vacation, wash cars, or carry trash cans and recycling bins to and from the curb each week. Enterprising youngsters can give a new spin to old standards such as mowing lawns or babysitting. Instead of just cutting the grass, they could sign up clients for full-service yard work, such as watering plants or hosing decks (anything that can be done outside with water is a hit with children). Add leaf raking and snow blowing, and a summer lawn service becomes a year-round venture.

Instead of waiting around for babysitting jobs on Saturday night, kids could organize a daily dinner-time play group that gives harried parents an hour or two of free time. Or sign up all their friends who babysit and match them with people in need of sitters, so parents only have to make one phone call.

One enterprising 12-year-old offered his services as waiter, busboy, and gofer to an aunt who was giving a dinner party. Seven hours later he went home

DEAR JANET

Q. We live in a tourist community, and last summer my children made a lot of money selling Kool-Aid and angle worms (great combination, huh?). They each had over $150 before the Fourth of July. The idea is they learn to earn. I love giving my kids things, but we can't really afford a lot with a big family, and I know the kids are more careful with spending money when they earn it.

But friends of mine think I'm denying my kids the fun of being given gifts for no reason. My contention is that you don't have to buy your kids' love by getting them stuff they only play with for a minute and then throw aside, but I still feel like a prude.

A. Kool-Aid and angle worms—I can't think of a better summertime treat. Your kids are ingenious, not to mention rolling in dough.

Refusing to buy your kids toys and expensive clothes every time they walk into a store does not make you a prude. It makes you a good parent (and you can tell your friends I said so). Of course, it's always fun to surprise your kids with treats for no reason. But who says they have to be expensive? In my experience, all it takes is a Slurpee from 7-Eleven.

with a pocketful of cash. Two 11-year-olds hired themselves out as parents' assistants at birthday parties, helping to take pictures and entertain the young guests.

Your children will be happiest and most productive if they do something that taps their special talents or interests. If they're good at computers, they could tutor other kids or adults who need help. One brother-sister team shared a job reading aloud to a handicapped child in the neighborhood. If they're artistically inclined, they could make and sell jewelry or refrigerator magnets. One young lady made more than $100 during her summer at the beach by selling necklaces she made out of colorful fishing lures.

Young children don't have wheels, but they don't need to go too far afield. They can make funky fliers and target likely customers in the neighborhood— families with young children or older people who'd appreciate having someone else haul those trash cans.

To keep up the kids' enthusiasm, keep their jobs manageable and fun. Primary school children still think in concrete terms—money can be exchanged for things. So they get a kick out of selling stuff, any stuff—old toys, pictures they draw, cookies they bake, and, yes, even lemonade.

You may have to put in a little time helping them bake the cookies or choose sale items that they won't want back the next day. But you don't have to spend days constructing an elaborate stand or hours minding the store. The kids will be happy to sit by themselves at a card table in your front yard for an hour or two and make $5.

Getting Started

Lots of kids who babysit or mow lawns are already in business for themselves; they just don't realize it. Officially, their work becomes a business when they earn at least $400 a year, because that's when the self-employment tax kicks in. Unofficially, it becomes a business when they begin to take it seriously by giving it a name, making fliers, handing out business cards, or generally being more professional and more formal about the way they run it.

PUTTING IT ON PAPER. In adult businesses, the first crucial step is to draw up a business plan, a blueprint of the business that describes in detail the product or service you're going to offer, your target market, advertising strategy, potential competitors, and financial projections. For kids, of course, that has to be scaled down, and lots of youngsters may be turned off by the task.

But they'll stand a better chance of success if they at least ask themselves some basic questions, such as what their business will do, who it will serve, how much they'll charge, how much they'll have to pay in expenses, and how they'll promote it. Their "business plan" can be as simple as a one-page worksheet with those headings (see the list of questions on page 194).

Older teens can be more detailed and more ambitious. Author Sarah Riehm (*The Teenage Entrepreneur's Guide,* Arco; out of print) recommends that they decide on a period (will it be a summer or year-round job?), set up a work schedule, separate their costs into those that are fixed and those that are variable, establish prices, and estimate how much business is expected each month.

Kids should think about who their competitors might be and set goals for the business that are specific, reasonable, and measurable. For example, "I want to be the best lawn service in Center City" is good, but "I want to achieve 100 percent customer satisfaction with no refunds" is even better.

RAISING CASH. A service business won't require much in the way of start-up capital, which kids will probably be short on. If they do need to raise cash, encourage them to rustle it up themselves by doing extra jobs around the house or holding their own yard sale. You can help finance the venture, but it's more important for you to provide moral rather than financial support. Kids shouldn't expect their parents to be their main customers, provide unlimited free phone time, or furnish raw materials at no charge. If you're going to set up the table and provide the pitcher, the lemons, the sugar, the water, and the cups, you're entitled to more than a free glass of lemonade.

SELLING THEMSELVES. One of the toughest steps for kids to take is the one that leads to that first door. Carrie H. "felt uncomfortable going door-to-door . . . so I marketed my crafts by setting up a booth at my local grocery store and at my softball games."

Kids who offer a service should be prepared to encounter skeptical adults who don't believe that young people are disciplined or dedicated enough to follow

---

BUSINESS IDEAS FOR KIDS

I've culled this list from the books recommended in the box on page 197. Once your children have identified ideas of interest, they can use the questions on page 194 to choose endeavors that are appropriate for their age, ability, and resources—including how involved you want to be. The lesson here is to match your children's skills, hobbies, or talents with money-making opportunities.

- ❑ Window washing
- ❑ Curb address painting
- ❑ Outdoor painting (outdoor furniture, fences, doghouses, porches, decks, or storage sheds)
- ❑ Garage cleaning
- ❑ Lawn mowing
- ❑ Pool/driveway cleaning
- ❑ Housecleaning
- ❑ Carpet cleaning
- ❑ Plant watering
- ❑ Pet grooming
- ❑ House-sitting
- ❑ Picking up papers and mail for vacationing neighbors
- ❑ Pet- and plant-sitting

- ❑ Helping people move (packing, cleaning up)
- ❑ Golf caddying
- ❑ Bike repair
- ❑ Birthday clown/entertainer
- ❑ Birthday party planning
- ❑ Tutoring
- ❑ Typing/word processing
- ❑ Buying and selling used books
- ❑ Sign making and painting
- ❑ Gift wrapping
- ❑ Errand service, including grocery and dry-cleaning delivery
- ❑ Messenger service
- ❑ Flier distributor
- ❑ Odd-jobs agency set up with other neighborhood kids

through on their promises. It wouldn't hurt if young entrepreneurs were to prepare a written résumé with details about their school or work experience and references customers could contact. Being polite will win adults over and so will dressing neatly. Even if you're selling a lawn service, don't show up in an old T-shirt and cutoffs. Instead, wear a neat polo shirt or, better yet, a T-shirt imprinted with the name and logo of your business.

That kind of sight advertising also helps kids who would rather die than ring a doorbell. So does a not-so-silent partner in helping spread the word. As noted earlier, shyness needn't keep kids from starting a business. At some point, however, they'll probably have to make direct contact with prospective customers. And when they do, Bonnie Drew has some advice on how to be a super salesperson: Use the same powers of persuasion you use on Mom and Dad when you're trying to get them to take you to the ice cream store or buy a new bike:

- **Tell customers all the reasons they should buy** your product or service and how it will help them.
- **Tell them why they need your service right away.** Instead of asking them if they want you to carry their trash cans to the curb, tell them when you can start.
- **Don't give up if they say no.** If they say they don't have time right now, ask if you can come back. If they say they don't need the service, ask if they know someone who does.
- **If they say yes, do the job promptly,** courteously, and thoroughly. And always say thank you.

Mistakes Kids Make

Kids will be kids, even if they're entrepreneurs. At a time in their life when they're particularly self-absorbed, it's often tough for them to live by the principle that the customer is always right.

Not being professional enough in their attitude—by showing up late, acting rudely, or speaking crudely—

is perhaps the biggest mistake children make, and it's the surest way of alienating skeptical adults. Following are some of youngsters' other foibles, with advice on how to correct them.

BECOMING BORED. It's typical of kids to get excited about something, jump in with gusto, and quickly burn out. If you recognize your children in this picture, encourage them to start their business as a short-term venture during summer vacation or over a holiday. With the end in sight, they can get out gracefully if they lose interest.

GETTING IN OVER THEIR HEADS. Here are the three biggies:

1. **Underestimating the cost.** A big problem even for adult entrepreneurs, being short of cash is best avoided by choosing a business in which your kids' biggest investment is their own effort. If they do need equipment—say, a computer to print fliers or a lawn mower—they should use what they have or borrow what they can instead of buying something new, shiny, and expensive.

2. **Underestimating time.** For young children just starting out, ten hours a week is enough to devote to a business. Before they start, they should draw up a schedule to see when they can best fit in the time; working weekends and once or twice on weeknights is plenty. After all, they're still kids, and they need time just to have fun.

3. **Overestimating their strength.** Children can be tempted to take on a job that's too physical—moving furniture, for example—or just plain unrealistic—mowing ten lawns in two days. Making the effort to think through a business plan, even a rudimentary one, can help here. So can the timely intervention of Mom and Dad.

MILKING THE BUSINESS. Many kids, after all, start working to make money, and they're tempted to spend everything when it may be prudent to plow

DEAR JANET

Q. I thought it was enterprising and educational when my son and his friend, both in second grade, decided to have a yard sale of old toys and split the proceeds. As it turned out, my son contributed all the toys, and his friend ended up buying them. That would have been okay—but then the friend showed up and asked for his share of the proceeds! I felt that wasn't fair to my son, but I didn't want to interfere because a deal is a deal.
A. It's a raw deal if the parties involved are confused about the terms. Don't be afraid to help straighten things out.

You could have volunteered to go over all the transactions and count out the money. If your son's friend was unhappy about being long on toys and short on cash, you could have asked your son if it would be all right for his friend to return some of his purchases. Or you might even have paid him a small "salary" for helping out at the sale. If kids are going to learn a lesson about money, it might as well be how not to cheat—or be cheated.

some money back into the business. Starting a lawn service by borrowing Mom and Dad's mower is fine, but if the business takes off, it's time for kids to consider investing in a machine of their own.

OVER- OR UNDERPRICING THEIR PRODUCTS OR SERVICES. Kids often don't have a good sense of what their costs will be or what their services are worth.

As in the bake sale example that introduced this chapter, young entrepreneurs have a couple of options in setting prices. In the so-called cost-plus approach, they tot up the cost of any raw materials they might need (such as cleaning supplies for washing cars), add in how much they want to make, and come up with a figure. In the market approach, they find out what competing businesses are charging and set their prices accordingly. Their competitors can be anyone from the kid down the street who's also mowing lawns to a professional lawn care service. Sarah Riehm recommends that a kid-run business should charge 25 percent to 30 percent less than its professional competition. One rule of thumb for youngsters who make products is to charge twice the cost of their materials.

Zillions, the consumer magazine for kids mentioned earlier but no longer published, once asked hundreds of children what they had earned on summer jobs. The survey turned up a two-tier pricing system: one (lower) price for parents and another price for everyone else. To set their prices, kids asked other kids what they were charging or sought advice from their parents. Some enterprising youngsters visited customers in advance and set their prices based on the difficulty of the job. One babysitter upped her fee if the kids seemed unruly—and if they looked "really bad," she didn't take the job.

Children can also ask potential customers how much they're willing to pay, or they can do some informal market research by surveying their parents and other adults. That can work to a child's advantage because adults often put a higher value on the service than the child does (see the question on page 194). If the price is too low, the kids can bargain or turn down the job. (For a fun lesson in how *not* to set prices, look for the video "The Gravelberry Pie King," in which Fred Flintstone becomes a pie tycoon by selling Wilma's famous gravelberry pies for a price that doesn't cover the cost of the ingredients.)

Should you pay your own kids for doing some of these jobs? It depends. You shouldn't pay your 13-year-old to stay with younger siblings for an hour or so after school while you run errands. But you should expect to pay for a Saturday night job, as he or she could easily land a paying gig. You could, of course, negotiate for a family discount.

DEAR JANET

Q. When, if ever, is it appropriate for kids to take money for helping neighbors with chores (babysitting, taking in mail while they're away, shoveling snow)? We have a neighbor who sometimes offers my daughter money when she gives him a hand. I don't want her to expect to be paid for being nice.

A. It might be more charitable for your daughter to help out for free, but don't let her give away her services too cheaply.

A lot depends on the circumstances. Suppose your daughter is visiting a neighbor with younger children when the neighbor has to make a quick trip to the supermarket and asks your daughter to stay with the kids. In that kind of spur-of-the-moment situation, it should be understood that your daughter is pitching in to be neighborly. No compensation is necessary.

If, on the other hand, your neighbor calls a week ahead of time to ask if your daughter can babysit on a Saturday night, that would be considered a formal job for which pay is appropriate.

If kids pitch in spontaneously, they could be rewarded spontaneously with a slice of chocolate cake or a glass of lemonade but not necessarily with money. Kids need to learn there's a distinction between volunteering their services and working for pay, and each has its time and place.

QUESTIONS KIDS SHOULD ASK THEMSELVES

What will I do?

When will I conduct my business? _____

Summers only? Year-round? _____

What will the name of my business be? _____

Is there a need for my product or service? _____

Who will my customers be? _____

How far from home can I conduct my business? _____

Who else is doing the same business in my
neighborhood? _____

How much are they charging? _____

Can I do the job better than the other guys? _____

How much will I charge? _____

How much time will each job take? _____

How much money do I want to make? _____

What's my goal for my business? _____

What do I need to know to do the job? _____

What kind of equipment do I need to do the job
and where can I get it? _____

How much money do I need to start my business? _____

What kind of help will I need from my parents? _____

How much of their time will I need each week? _____

Do I need to hire other people to help me? _____

How will I let my customers know that I'm available? _____

LACKING CONFIDENCE. Some kids are doomed to failure because they don't really believe they can succeed. Encourage them to set their sights high while
engaging in some down-to-earth planning, and they
stand a good chance of pulling it off.

Nuts, Bolts, and Red Tape

Starting a business is, after all, an introduction to
the real world, so it shouldn't be surprising that
as entrepreneurs your kids will be introduced to
regulation, taxes, and the fine points of the law.

Red Tape

Kids will probably set up shop as a sole proprietor,
which is the easiest way to start a business: You just do
it. Federal and state child labor laws restrict the age at
which kids can get a job, the kinds of work they can
do, and the hours they can work. Under federal law,
for example, 14 is the minimum age for most nonfarm work. But the federal law applies to employer-
employee relationships. So if the kids run their own
business or are independent contractors who babysit
or mow lawns on a part-time, irregular basis for lots
of different customers, they're not covered by the law.
There are specific legal exemptions for kids who deliver newspapers, perform in show business, or work
for parents in their solely-owned nonfarm business.
For more information, visit the Department of Labor's
Web site, http://www.dol.gov.

Once youngsters have decided on a name for
their business, they should register it with the county
government through the county clerk's office. Registra-
tion is required if they're going to be doing business
under a name other than their own; it's also recommended if they'll be using their own name. In some
cities, kids may also need to get a license to operate
certain businesses; check with your local authorities.

It's possible that your kids will have to contend
with homeowners associations and local zoning ordi-
nances, which may not allow them to run a business

in a residential neighborhood, post signs on their lawn, or store equipment in the yard. In reality, however, neighbors, who tend to be the most vigilant enforcers of zoning laws, aren't likely to object to the kinds of service-oriented businesses kids are likely to start.

If your children will be selling directly to the public goods or services that are subject to state or local sales tax, they'll be expected to collect the tax. That means applying for a sales tax permit. If they'll be selling to a store for resale to the public, they probably won't have to collect the tax but may have to apply for a wholesale exemption certificate.

Taxes

If your child has net business earnings from self-employment of at least $400 a year, the federal tax law kicks into gear. Technically, your son or daughter is expected to file three tax forms:

1. **Form 1040,** the basic two-page tax return
2. **Schedule C,** to report the business income and any expenses
3. **Schedule SE,** to figure the Social Security tax on self-employment income. (Teenage babysitters are normally considered employees and are exempt from paying the self-employment tax. Newspaper carriers under age 18 are also exempt.)

Although a child claimed as a dependent on the parents' tax return can't claim a personal exemption, he or she does get a standard deduction. That deduction is either $800 or, if greater, equal to the child's earned income up to $5,000. (Those are the 2005 figures; they will rise in the future with inflation.) That means there may be no income tax due on up to $5,000 of earnings from the business. But there's no standard deduction to offset the self-employment tax. That 15.3 percent levy starts with the first dollar of net self-employment earnings. On $500 of income, this tax would cost $76.50. Check with your local Small

---

BOOKS FOR BIZ KIDS

- Daryl Bernstein's *Better Than a Lemonade Stand* (Beyond Words Publishing) describes 51 businesses, with hints on which supplies and how much time you'll need, what to charge, how to advertise.
- Bonnie and Noel Drew's *Fast Cash for Kids* (Career Press) lists 101 money-making projects for children under 16, arranged by season of the year. Also includes age-appropriate tips on how to handle the financial end of the business.
- *A Teen's Guide to Business*, by Linda Menzies, Oren S. Jenkins, and Rickell R. Fisher (Master Media Ltd.), offers anecdotes from successful teen entrepreneurs and

includes a section on how to land a job working for someone else
- *The Lemonade Stand: A Guide to Encouraging the Entrepreneur in Your Child,* by Emmanuel Modu and James B. Hayes (Diane Publishing Co.). A comprehensive guide for parents that includes chapters on legal and tax issues, business ethics, and business concepts your kids should know.
- *The Biz Kids' Guide to Success: Money-Making Ideas for Young Entrepreneurs*, by Terri Thompson and Shannon Keegan (Barron's), is aimed at teens in grades 9 through 12.

Business Administration office or chamber of commerce to see if any state or local taxes are due.

Note: If you have a sneaking suspicion that few children with such low incomes go through the hassle of registering a business, collecting sales tax, or filing an income tax form, you have a lot of company.

Points of Law

If your children's business employs other children, their working hours will have to be limited as required by child labor laws. Under federal law, for example, children who are 14 and 15 can't work more than 3 hours on a school day or more than 18 hours during a school week. Kids under 14 can't be employed at all, unless it's in an occupation that the law specifically exempts: acting or performing, delivering newspapers, or making wreaths at home (the state of Maine requested that exemption back in the 1930s, when making pine wreaths was a major state industry).

Minors can enter into contracts, but they're not legally bound to fulfill them. This may put off some

ORGANIZATIONS THAT HELP

- **YoungBiz** publishes Y&E, a magazine for teen entrepreneurs. At its Web site, http://www.youngbiz.com, you'll also find a wealth of information on workshops, camps, curricula, and educational resources.
- **The Center for Entrepreneurship** offers a variety of resources and educational opportunities for prospective entrepreneurs, including students. (Wichita State University, 1845 N. Fairmount, Wichita, KS 67260-0147; 316-978-3000).
- **Junior Achievement** works with schools and businesses to introduce students to practical economic concepts, business organization, management, production, and marketing (http://www.ja.org; One Education Way, Colorado Springs, CO 80906; 719-540-8000).

adults, who may be reluctant to do business with a minor. To reassure skeptical adults, parents could become a party to the contract (although this would also make you liable if the customer was dissatisfied with your child's product or service). The best solution is for your children not to back out of a contract.

Check to see whether your homeowners policy covers any business-related injuries, say, to customers or employees. Some policies have so-called business pursuits clauses that specifically exclude such injuries. Even if yours doesn't, make sure you're covered.

All in all, the red tape shouldn't be sticky enough to discourage kids from starting a business. Most children don't make big bucks, so the procedure is fairly simple and straightforward. "I did a little of my tax return and my mom did the rest," one young entrepreneur told me. "I didn't look forward to it, but it wasn't horrible."

Why You Should Care

The whole issue of how much, or even whether, young people should work is a hot potato (for more on that debate, see Chapter 13). But if your kids are inclined in that direction, there's a lot to be said for having them be their own boss and set their own hours in a job they enjoy doing. And it will yield dividends to you. Kids may not pay attention when you talk about being dependable, but if they lose a customer because they show up late to do the lawn, they learn a lesson parents can't teach. In addition, they learn to converse with grown-ups, use the telephone, and budget both their time and (you hope) their money.

Entrepreneurship has also proven to be an avenue for channeling the creativity and hustle of inner-city kids into productive ends. A number of organizations—including the National Foundation for Teaching Entrepreneurship in New York City and the LEAD Program at the University of Pennsylvania's Wharton School—teach business skills to at-risk youth to build their self-esteem. "A lot of these kids don't even believe they can start a business. But once they see it's a way of making money and getting praise from family and friends, they become excited and involved," said one Wharton administrator.

Zakia A., an alumna of the LEAD Program, started her own business selling lingerie at house parties and took it with her when she went to college. When Michael F. started the program at the National Foundation for Teaching Entrepreneurship, he didn't even know what the word *entrepreneur* meant. With a $25 stake from the course, he went to New York's wholesale district and bought novelty items like nail clippers and pens, which he resold to people in his neighborhood. Later he graduated to selling calculators and, finally, to teaching future entrepreneurs.

For kids (and adults) of any age, running a business provides a glimpse of the real world and a look at a career option they might not otherwise have thought of—and one that will look increasingly attractive. As traditional employers attempt to stay lean and mean, jobs have become more competitive and more vulnerable. Young people should be aware that they have the opportunity to make their own living and don't have to rely on someone else for a job. For three years in a row, teens participating in a poll on kids and careers conducted by Junior Achievement have selected a career in business as their ideal job, followed by doctor and teacher. And owning their own business appealed to more than two-thirds of the students interviewed.

Last, but not least, dreaming up a business of your own can be just plain fun. When a group of middle school students were asked what kind of company they'd like to own, Thomas O. replied that because he enjoys sports and music, he'd like to open a store called Rock 'n Jock, which would sell sports equipment and CDs. Jeremy M. would some day like to open an agency for outer-space travel. Gillian S. wants to start Woof Away, a dog spa that would "offer a day or two of fun, exercise, and relaxation for your pooch."

And Jay L. had perhaps the most fanciful idea: starting a company to make Christmas lights "that would not break or burn out so quickly."

DEAR JANET

Q. My husband and I are fortunate to live in a neighborhood where young people come to our door asking if they can mow our lawn or shovel our walks when it snows. But I'm never sure exactly how much to pay them. What's the etiquette in a situation like this?

A. Often it's my children who are the inspiration for answers in my column, but this time that honor goes to my mom.

After a big snowstorm, a neighborhood boy showed up at Mom's door asking if he could shovel her driveway. They never discussed how much he would charge, but she intended to pay him $10. When she couldn't find anything less than a $20 bill around the house, she figured his efforts were worth the price and offered him the $20.

When she did, he hid his hand behind his back. "It's too much," he mumbled. Mom pressed him to take the money, telling him he had done a good job and she wanted him to have it. He eventually accepted the cash, and both of them were happy about the outcome.

But the episode points out a valuable lesson for kids who do odd jobs and the adults who hire them: Although children should set a price for their work, they often don't, depending instead on the judgment of their employers. If you have a figure in mind, tell the kids ahead of time so you both know what to expect and can iron out any differences up front.

Don't take advantage of child labor, but don't lavishly overcompensate kids for the work they do, giving them an inflated idea of their value in the labor force. Quote a figure that you think is fair and see if that's acceptable. If not, there's nothing wrong with dickering a bit or hiring someone else.

Teens: The Early Years

When my oldest child was a freshman in high school, I figured I was still a couple of years away from the expense of prom season. Then I received a letter from the parents association at my son's high school asking me to contribute $25 (or whatever my budget would allow) to help pay for the school-sponsored postprom party. I was also told it's customary for freshman families to pony up for one of the party's grand prizes—that year a mountain bike.

The truth is, I really didn't mind ponying up. After all, it was for a good cause—keeping the kids entertained, and contained, at an alcohol-free party where they could have fun without losing control.

Unfortunately, parents don't always have such a positive influence at prom time. Even as I read the parents association appeal, out of my other eye I was scanning a story titled "Prom Night Means Teen Independence, Buying Spree for Parents and Kids" in a marketing trade publication. The prom, it seems, is the "quintessential teen event," for which teens are ready to "break away and buy, buy, buy." They shell out anywhere from $175 to $600 or more, including the dress or tux, tickets, and other extras such as corsages, hairdos, and limo rentals.

Far from balking at the expense, parents apparently encourage it. "When it comes to 'dress-up,'" marketers were advised, "parents are a key target because they share in the fantasy and are willing to pay for it."

In fact, when the Geppetto Group, a New York market research firm, interviewed teens across the country, the kids said they sometimes feel parental pressure in reverse: "My mom's been talking to me about my prom since I've been in the eighth grade. If I don't go, it will be such a disappointment to her," said one teenager in Michigan.

As children enter their teen years, their expenditures escalate and the stakes get higher—in just a few years they'll be on their own, in one way or another. But what the prom article brought home to me was that even on this ultimate night of teen fantasy and freedom, parents still are a force in their children's life and have the power to influence kids for good or ill.

What Teens Know . . . and Don't Know

By the time children become teenagers, they're hemorrhaging cash; kids between the ages of 12 and 19 are spending more than $170 billion per year of their own and their parents' money. And today's teens aren't exactly babes in the woods when it comes to things financial. They are, after all, children of the revolution that has popularized personal finance in recent years. Trouble is, what they know is often just enough to make them dangerous.

Checking Accounts

Teens know, for example, that checking accounts exist, but they don't always know how to balance one. That old joke about not being overdrawn if you still have checks is sometimes painfully on the mark. One college faculty member who has counseled students on financial matters recalls a student who came to her in tears while clutching a sheaf of checks. The student feared that the checks had bounced, but they were actually canceled checks that had been returned to her routinely by the bank.

Credit Cards

Teens know how to use a credit card to buy things, but they're not always clear on how they're supposed

---

DEAR JANET

Q. We just found out that our 13-year-old son has signed up with a mail-order music club to get eight compact discs for one cent. Now he's obligated to buy six more at a potential cost of more than $100. He doesn't have that kind of money. If he doesn't pay up, will we have to?

A. Neither you nor your son should have to pay. If you don't, however, I presume you'll return the "free" CDs. In general, minors (usually those under the age of 18) can disavow contracts like these, and their parents (or other legal guardians) can't be held responsible. Write to the music club and explain the situation. An official of one big club told me that in the circumstances you describe you'd be let off the hook: "If the parent comes and says, 'My son is a minor, and he joined without my being aware of it,' we will cancel the membership and the obligation." Sometimes parents aren't aware that their kids are piling up debts until the dunning letters start arriving. Don't be intimidated by fancy legal stationery. Write back and explain that your child is a minor, and the letters should stop. Lest kids learn the wrong lesson—that they can renege on a deal with impunity—consider imposing your own penalty, such as confiscating the CD player or charging a cancellation fee.

---

to pay the bill. They think plastic is just another form of currency and don't understand that using a card is like taking out a loan. So they're vulnerable to the experience of one of my neighbors, who went off to college, ran up $600 in credit card debt, faithfully made the minimum monthly payment, then suddenly realized she wasn't making a dent in paying off the bill. Her parents eventually bailed her out.

Saving

Teens know that saving money is a worthwhile goal—especially to pay for the expensive college education their parents have been fretting about for years—but for many of them CD means compact disc instead of certificate of deposit.

Planning for college actually provides a convenient opening for parents to introduce their kids to the fine points of budgeting, saving, and even investing. Yet when parents seek advice on how to pay for college, "very few of them bring their kids when they come to see me," one financial planner told me.

That's partly because they're naturally reluctant to discuss the family's financial situation with their children—and partly because they often share their children's casual attitudes toward budgeting, credit, and saving. But now may be the last chance for the whole family to shape up before the kids graduate and go off on their own, either to manage a household and pay bills they didn't even know existed or to attend college, where credit cards are as easy to get as pizzas at midnight—and just as habit forming.

On-the-Job Training

You don't want to disclose the details of your family's financial affairs to younger children, but teens are old enough to learn the nitty-gritty of household finances. Now might be a good time for you to adopt the strategy of one mother, who let her teenage daughter write the checks to pay the monthly bills (Mom still signed them). Even more dramatically, one father brought home his pay in cash, sat his family down with the stack of money and a pile of household bills, and asked his teenagers to parcel out the money to pay them. By the time his kids saw how little was left, they were talking about getting part-time jobs. (Note: I used this exercise myself with a family I was counseling on the *Oprah Winfrey Show*. Read about the results starting on page 228.)

Holding down a job is one way for teens to get an introduction to Life 101. Your kids will find it easier to appreciate the cost of adding them to your auto insurance policy if you can put it in terms of how many hamburgers they'd have to flip to pay the premium themselves.

Whether you want your child to work and for how many hours merits separate consideration (see Chapter 13). If you prefer that your kids concentrate on schoolwork and extracurricular activities rather than on a job, that doesn't mean they have to miss out on real-world experience. Simply holding family discussions about such financial matters as which car to buy and how to pay for it, how to cope with an impending layoff, or how much to spend on holiday gifts can give your kids an invaluable insight into the kinds of decisions they will have to make someday. And there is an immediate payoff for you. By seeking their input, you short-circuit any grousing later on if you wind up with a minivan instead of a sports car, or if the customary holiday pile is smaller than usual.

By the time your children graduate from high school, it's certainly reasonable to expect them to be able to manage their own checking account (although you will probably have to cosign for them to open one if they're under 18). At Young Americans Bank in Denver, the average checking account holder is 16, has a balance of nearly $700, and is "very responsible" about managing his or her account, said bank president Linda Childears.

Even before kids are old enough to have a checking account of their own, you can give them a simple explanation of how the process works. I once witnessed an exchange between a mother and her 8-year-

---

DEAR JANET

Q. Every year I spend hundreds of dollars to outfit my preteens and teens with clothes and other back-to-school paraphernalia. This time of year is getting to be as big a financial strain as the holidays.

A. My personal preference is that kids wear uniforms to school, which cuts down on both money spent on clothes and time spent bickering about styles. If that's not an option, try these suggestions on for size:

- **Set a budget.** The easiest way not to overspend is to establish limits in advance and give your kids a say in parceling out the money.
- **Spread out your spending.** If your kids see a nice item that doesn't fit into the budget, file it away as a possible holiday present and kill two birds with one credit card charge.
- **Don't sweat the little things.** If your child needs a lunch box and wants one with a picture of the latest TV hero, go ahead and buy the box of choice—it's a cheap thrill. So are new notebooks and pencils. Kids get a psychological lift out of starting the year with pristine notebooks and crayons that have points.
- **Recycle the old stuff.** Use old notebooks for art projects and grocery lists, and store puzzle pieces in last year's lunch box.

old, who was begging her mom to register her for a gymnastics class. Mom explained that she wouldn't have enough money until Friday. "You can write a check," said the child. "It wouldn't matter," Mom replied. "There won't be any money in the account until your dad and I get paid on Friday." The child accepted this explanation without a fuss.

Lesson one for kids, which they often pick up on their own, is that a check is a substitute for cash. Lesson two, which doesn't always occur to them, is where the money ultimately comes from to make good on the check. Lesson three is watching you write checks and subtract their value from your bank account. If they've absorbed that by the time they leave home at 18, they may run out of checks, but they're less likely to run out of cash.

The Budget Bugaboo

Like adults, teenagers need to know where their money is going. But, not surprisingly, they have even less confidence than do adults in their ability to manage their finances. A study of high school students by the National Endowment for Financial Education (NEFE) turned up some interesting findings. Only 19 percent of students said they "almost always" felt confident about making financial decisions. Only 18.5 percent said they almost always set aside money for future needs and wants. Just 42 percent strongly agreed that they even knew the difference between needs and wants. And an anemic 9 percent said they almost always set financial goals.

The study went on to show significant improvement in each category after the students had spent ten hours studying NEFE's High School Financial Planning Program. A little experience with budgeting could also go a long way here. But kids, like adults, are put off by the "B" word. In fact, people have such a distaste for its eat-your-spinach overtones that the word *budget* has all but disappeared from the lexicon of financial counselors. Instead, the focus is on dessert, in the form of a "spending plan" that's more freewheeling and less constraining than a budget. Here's how to help your teens come up with such a plan:

RECORD EXPENSES. Encourage your teens to write down everything they spend for a month, not necessarily to cut back on their spending but just to see where the money goes (they can use the recordkeeping worksheet on pages 212 and 213). They may not change their behavior, but the next time they buy fries and a Coke they'll remember that 60 percent of their money is going toward junk food.

SET GOALS. You stand a better chance of getting your teens to change their behavior if you encourage them to set goals. Saving money because it's the right thing to do is too abstract, even for teenagers. They need something to work toward, whether it's a DVD player, a college education, or a school ski trip. That gives them an incentive to cut back on the fries.

> ## DEAR JANET
>
> **Q.** Our teenager recently got a part-time job, but he expects us to continue paying his regular allowance. Should we?
>
> **A.** Not if his job is paying him what you consider to be a sufficient amount to cover his expenses. The main purpose of an allowance is to provide kids with a regular income when they don't have earnings from a job. Once they're employed, you can cut back the allowance, either all at once or gradually. Studies show that once children reach age 13, they get more of their money from jobs than from allowances, and the gap continues to widen as they get older.

MAKE GOALS TANGIBLE. Whatever goal your kids settle on, have them write it down. There's something psychologically satisfying about committing a goal to paper or discussing it with a friend; the goal becomes more real—and more likely to be accomplished.

MAKE GOALS STRAIGHTFORWARD. Sometimes it helps to have your kids divvy up their cash into different pots. The amount that goes into each pot can shift to suit your purposes. For example, there's the 70-20-10 rule—70 percent to spend, 20 percent to save for future big-ticket purchases, and 10 percent for long-term investing. Or you might choose a 33-33-33 plan for spending, short-term saving, and long-term saving, or a simple 50-50 division—or even 90-10—for spending and saving. The point is that when a spending plan is that cut and dried, it becomes more manageable and less off putting.

DECIDE WHAT'S IMPORTANT. Teens also need help with setting priorities—deciding which things they really need and which they merely want. Maybe this sounds obvious to you, but with teens you can't belabor a point. (I often think that kids define a "want" as anything *you're* willing to spend money on; a "need" is anything they have to buy themselves.)

HAVE THEM DRAW UP A LIST OF NEEDS AND CORRESPONDING WANTS. For example, they *need* school clothes but they *want* a fringed leather jacket that will exhaust their entire clothing budget. They *need* shoes; they *want* a pair to match every outfit, plus a few extras. They *need* transportation to school; they *want* a new car—and they want *you* to buy it for them.

RUN DOWN THE LIST WITH THEM AND ATTACH A REALISTIC PRICE TAG TO EACH ITEM. Writing down the numbers will make them seem more real to your kids and will give you room to maneuver. If there's $300 in your clothing budget and the kids insist on new jeans, they'll have to forgo the leather jacket (or pay for it themselves). If you're willing to spend $100 on shoes, they'll have to decide on four pairs at $25 each or two pairs for $50.

One mom who lives in Beverly Hills once told me that when her oldest son approached driving age, he assumed that being a child in residence at 90210 automatically entitled him to a car. "I'm from Cleveland," said his mother. "I told him he needed transportation, but whether he got a new car, a used car, or a skateboard depended on how much he saved, which his father and I would match." Her son saved $5,000 on his own and bought a brand-new Ford Escort.

Expanding the Allowance

As I explained in Chapter 8, the teenage years are a good time to give your kids more financial responsibility by expanding their allowance to include such big-ticket expenses as clothing and entertainment. Not only does it help them become better money managers (and distinguish between wants and needs), it can also snuff out many a potentially explosive parent-teen confrontation. Mom and Dad can't be expected to pay for rock concert tickets if money for that kind of entertainment is already built into the allowance.

"Children know the rules because they've been discussed ahead of time, so it eases parent-child tensions," explained Joan B., a mom who knows what she's talking about. When Joan's daughter turned 13, she was offered the opportunity to manage a sum large enough to cover all her expenses, including lunches, clothes, gifts, and dancing lessons (with the exception of medical care and any parties she might have, which Mom wanted to keep under her control). Her daughter was "dazed and delighted," Joan said. With her parents' help, she spent an entire summer monitoring her expenses. "It gave us something genuine and valid to talk about, instead of 'why aren't you combing your hair differently,'" said Joan.

The plan "took off and flew," and "we had zero problems with the rest of the teenage years." The arrangement stayed in effect till Joan's daughter reached 18 and left for college. It was the object of much envy on the part of her little brother, who couldn't wait till he was 13 and got the same privilege.

Of course, you can't just hand over the money and say, "See ya." When my daughter Claire was 15, I wanted to start her on a seasonal clothing allowance. Before giving her the cash, we went on a test shopping trip to see how she'd handle the $200 I had in mind for a summer wardrobe. We started at Abercrombie & Fitch, where Claire had a $50 gift certificate from her grandparents. She bought two tops, on sale for $19.90 each. She balked at paying $30 for shorts, even on sale, especially when I told her she'd have to pay the extra $20 out of her own money. She took the $10 remaining on her gift certificate in cash.

Then we headed to Gap. Claire, bless her heart, made straight for the sale rack, where she picked up a twin set: tank top for $17, cardigan for $25.

Next stop Old Navy, where Claire chose a pair of shorts for $14.50 (less than half the price of the pair at Abercrombie), a couple of matching tank tops (on special for $5 each), and a sundress on sale for $19.99.

We ended up at Sears, where Claire found two T-shirts on sale for $8.40 each and a floral print skirt for $18.

Claire's purchases came to just about $200 on the nose. She liked her name brand Abercrombie tops, but she was even more pleased that she had been able to get so many additional items by shopping at other, less expensive, stores. "This should last me for two summers," she said.

When I wrote about Claire's experience in my column, one reader took me to task for setting such a low budget. Said the reader, "$200 per season for clothes is really, really unbelievable." It's true there's no magic number that's right for every family. I'm not a diehard bargain hunter, but I do like to pay reasonable prices. And as our shopping expedition showed, that figure worked for us.

Let me also add that an allowance doesn't have to cover every item of clothing. If parents wanted to get out of the kids' apparel business altogether, they would certainly have to increase the size of the allowance. But in my experience, most parents don't turn all clothes buying over to the kids.

DEAR JANET

Q. We like our teenagers to have cell phones as a safety precaution, but their bills are atrocious. How should we handle this?

A. Pay only for basic service and have your kids cover any additional minutes they spend on the phone (including text messaging). They will quickly schedule their conversations when talk is cheapest. To hold down cell phone costs for kids, consider signing up for a prepaid service. Two plans worth looking at are Virgin Mobile (http://www.virginmobileusa.com) and TracFone (http://www.tracfone.com). For a comparison of prepaid plans, visit Myrateplan.com.

In our family, for instance, I took care of coats, shoes (up to $50 per pair), prom gowns, and special-event dresses (within reason), plus an occasional surprise. The kids budgeted for shirts, shorts, jeans, skirts, sweaters, and accessories—the things they typically bought on trips to the mall with their friends.

And don't forget the gift factor. In addition to the spring/summer and fall/winter shopping seasons, there are the holidays, when most kids get an infusion of new clothes as gifts, plus birthdays and visits from grandparents and generous aunts.

Finally, teenagers can, and should, supplement a clothing allowance with their own earnings. At Christmas, for example, I always buy bathing suits for my daughter, who is a year-round swimmer. But in the summer, when she's flush with cash from her summer job, she buys her own suits.

Again, the point is not necessarily to account for every last penny in the "parent" or "child" column but simply to give kids a stake in their wardrobe so they can learn how to make smart buying decisions. When Claire and I went shopping for a dress for the homecoming dance, I told her I would spend up to $100; anything above that she'd have to pay for. As we shopped in Lord & Taylor, she checked out the price of each dress. I was truly shocked when the salesclerk confided to me, "I have been selling homecoming dresses all afternoon, and your daughter is the first one who even looked at the price tags." Claire eventually chose a dress that was marked down below $100, so she was home free.

Kids and Cars

When your children become teenagers, one expense you probably won't be able to avoid in some form is the cost of driving. That's not to say you should buy your kids a car. On the contrary, I'm convinced that families would be better off, financially and otherwise, if teens didn't own a car of their own—even if they paid for it them-

WHERE YOUR MONEY'S COMING FROM, WHERE IT'S GOING

As a teen, you probably have a steadier stream of income—and more of it—than you did when you were a kid. Your regular expenses have probably expanded, too. So it's never too soon to start tracking where your money comes from and where it goes.

This worksheet will help you achieve your goals. Make one copy of it for each month of the year. By recording your income and expenses this month, you can identify where you'd like to make changes next month. Maybe you want to increase your income by asking for more odd jobs at home or by taking a part-time job. You could stop buying clothes or snack food for a while to save money for your class ring or prom. Maybe you want to save more for college or give more to charity.

Remember, your parents will still expect to have some say about your choices. They may limit the hours you can work each week or not allow you to buy a car. They may expect you to save a percentage of your income for college or to pay for your share of the family's car insurance bill. Fill in those regular "fixed expenses" first thing each month and set aside the necessary money.

Month _____

INCOME

Allowance $ _____

Odd jobs _____

My job or business _____

Gifts _____

Money I borrowed _____

Total Income $ _____

EXPENSES

Money I owe $ _____

Savings _____

College savings _____

Church or other charity _____

Gifts for family and friends _____

Car payments and/or insurance _____

Gas, oil, repairs, fees, and taxes _____

Public transportation (bus, subway) ———————————————

Lunch money ———————————————

Eating out and snacks ———————————————

Clothing and accessories ———————————————

Personal care ———————————————

School supplies and fees ———————————————

Telephone bills that I pay for ———————————————

Recreation and hobbies ———————————————

Sporting equipment and fees ———————————————

Entrance fees for the skating rink,

    rec center, and so on ———————————————

Club dues, uniforms, and other expenses ———————————————

Art and craft supplies ———————————————

Things I collect ———————————————

Stuff for my room (posters and such) ———————————————

Books, magazines, and library fines ———————————————

Software ———————————————

Electronic equipment ———————————————

CDs and DVDs ———————————————

Video and computer games ———————————————

Movies ———————————————

Concerts ———————————————

Other outings ———————————————

Prom (or other party expenses) ———————————————

Vacations, other special trips ———————————————

Odds and ends ———————————————

Total Expenses $ ———————————————

Total Income $ ———————————————

Minus Total Expenses − ———————————————

Money Left Over $ ———————————————

selves. Just putting your teens on the family auto insurance policy can easily double the premium. If your child owns a car of his or her own, the premium could triple. Besides, owning a car is a long-term financial commitment; your child would probably have to get a part-time job just to support it. One thirty-something man recalls that when he owned a car as a teenager, the first thing he learned to do was change the oil by himself. If he needed or wanted parts that were beyond his budget, he'd ask for them as gifts—sort of like "All I want for Christmas is two new front tires."

Money isn't the only issue here; maturity is important too. One family counselor has concluded that in his experience it's better for adolescents to have use of an extra family car than to have one of their own. "I have found that the nicest of adolescents become rigid, selfish, demanding, and difficult when they discuss 'their' car versus the 'family' car," the counselor told me. Also, it's less awkward for kids to explain to their friends that they've been grounded or can't get use of the car if it's a case of family ownership.

When John, my oldest child, got his license, he drove the family's 1994 Ford Taurus station wagon, which was so uncool it didn't even have a built-in CD player. John didn't have a year-round job, so we didn't require him to pay his share of the insurance (over $1,000 a year). And we took care of the car's upkeep.

But John had to pay for his own gas, parking, and other costs associated with his use of the car (including parking and speeding tickets). He cleaned it out and washed it (occasionally), replaced the turn signal bulbs that burned out regularly, and took it in for oil changes. When he had his first fender bender, it was his responsibility to notify the insurance company and get damage estimates.

Other parents have told me they make their teen drivers pay a portion of their insurance, or they require them to learn how to change the oil and do other routine maintenance. One dad even charged his daughter a "mileage fee" that included upkeep and depreciation.

In my opinion, any of those approaches is preferable to having a high school student get a job solely to support a car—a time-consuming and costly commitment. Worst of all is giving kids a car with no strings attached. I've heard of parents handing over title to an SUV even before their teens have a driver's license. What kids are really getting is a sense of entitlement.

Every time I write about cars in my column, I get delightful letters from readers reminiscing about their own experiences. This one is typical: "We are among those families who have not bought our kids a new car when they turned 16. However, we did hold on to a 1986 Honda Civic wagon for our eldest child to learn to drive. With 174,000 miles on it, we replaced the struts, tires, belts, and hoses, gave it a tune-up and a recharge of freon. Three days after he passed his driving test, he totaled the car leaving the school parking lot!

"We replaced this car with a 1974 Chevrolet Caprice, pale yellow, purchased from a man in the neighborhood who had inherited it from the estate of his deceased mother, with 54,000 miles (the car, not his mom). Our son vowed not to drive the "banana boat," but it was amazing to see how well he adapted it to his needs."

Postscript on our own family's car saga: When our son headed off to college, our daughter inherited the Taurus wagon as well as the terms of operating it. Now Peter, our youngest, is driving it. We've just replaced the transmission, and we're not sure how much longer it will last. But the kids still think of it as "their" car. The older ones drive it when they're home from college, and none of them wants us to get rid of it. In fact, says Peter, it's so old it's "in" again—and much cooler than our minivan!

FIVE THINGS 16-YEAR-OLDS NEED TO KNOW

1. They will have to pay for their own gasoline and clothing out of separate allowances for gas and clothes—and earn extra money if they want to buy more.

2. They should have a reasonable idea of your family's finances and realistic expectations for college, so they know how much you can afford to pay and how much they will have to contribute.

3. They should know how to write a check and balance a checking account.

4. They should save half of everything they earn from a job for major high school expenses, such as a class ring or class trip, or for college.

5. They will not get everything they ask for.

For Parents: How to Cut the Cost

Because teen driving is such an expensive proposition, it's worth it for me to devote a few lines to telling you how to keep the costs under control. As I've said, adding your child to your own policy is your best bet (and even then your rates can more than double), because your child gets the benefit of your premium reductions, such as those for multiple policies and vehicles.

And there are other ways to cut the cost. For starters, shop around. Rates vary all over the lot, and you can't assume that your existing policy will give you the best quote. Check the largest companies, visit an online marketplace such as InsWeb.com, or shop with an independent agent. Insuring your cars with the same company that covers your house will probably earn you a break.

You may also be eligible for premium discounts if your child is a good student (with a B average or better); has completed a driver's ed course; or qualifies as a nonresident student (because he's at college or boarding school 100 or more miles from home without a car).

Rates are lower if your child is an occasional driver, driving the car on your policy less than half the time. You're probably stuck designating your child as the principal driver if he drives the car more than anyone else in the household. But if he's the principal driver of a clunker that doesn't require collision coverage, that would reduce the cost.

Of course, rates stay lowest for teens with a clean driving record. And the best way to insure that is to let your teens know what behavior is acceptable and what isn't. Have your kids sign a written agreement, such as the one at http://www.parentingteendrivers.com, which you can customize. Among the important tenets: no driving for at least 24 hours after alcohol consumption; no thrill-seeking behavior behind the wheel; a limit on the number of passengers; and a limit on cell phone and stereo use. Violating the contract leads to suspension of driving privileges.

If possible, you might also want to try delaying the day your child gets a license. Not only will you save money by putting off an increase in your insurance premium, you'll also save yourself some worry. A 16-year-old girl is three times more likely to have an accident than someone who is 25, and a 16-year-old boy is five times more likely to have a wreck. Even making children wait till age 17 to get a license can cut down considerably on the likelihood that they'll get into an accident. When his daughter turned 16, one dad went so far as to pay her $50 for every month she delayed getting her license.

Give Them Credit? Not So Fast

Not long ago, I was asked to appear on a TV show to discuss whether youngsters should carry credit cards. "What's to discuss?" I asked the producer. "That's the dumbest idea I've ever heard." Not so fast, I was told. Some people think that if kids use credit cards when they're still at home, they'll handle credit responsibly when they're on their own.

I repeat: It's the dumbest idea I've ever heard. Giving your kids credit cards is like letting them use drugs early so that they won't turn into addicts. I'm all for teens learning to use credit responsibly, but getting a card to practice on isn't the way to do it.

The best way to teach kids to manage credit is to have them start with cold, hard cash—*cold* and *hard* being the operative words. Spending money is more real to kids, even teenagers, when they have to count out the bills and look down into an empty wallet. As my 16-year-old son put it, "If I don't have cash, I can't buy stuff I don't need. If I have a credit card, I can buy anything." If they learn to manage money while they're at home, teens will be less likely to go crazy with credit when they're off at college (for more on credit cards and college students, see Chapter 14).

That's not to say you shouldn't discuss credit with high schoolers. As I mentioned at the beginning of this chapter, teens often don't understand that when they buy something with a credit card, they're taking out a loan on which they'll be charged a very high rate of interest. Instead of resorting to a lecture (and watching their eyes glaze over), use a quick, interactive example such as an online calculator (like the one at http://www.kiplinger.com/tools) to show them how long it can take to pay off a credit card bill. For example, if you owe $2,000 on a credit card charging 18 percent annual interest and you're making payments of $50 a month, it will take you more than five years to pay off the balance. Even more dramatic, if you're paying less than $30 a month, you'll *never* pay it off.

One gimmick to get plastic into the hands of children is the prepaid card, the best known of which is the Visa Buxx card. The idea is that parents can load (and reload) money onto the card, which youngsters can use to make purchases or get cash out of an ATM. Purchases can be tracked online, and promoters of this plastic bill it as a way to help kids learn to manage their money.

But kids won't get it. To them, any kind of plastic is magic money. Credit cards, debit cards, prepaid cards—you name it, they're all just a direct line to Mom and Dad's wallet. Referring to the Visa Buxx card, one young woman once e-mailed me to ask where she could get "the card that my parents can fill up when the money runs out." In one study, 35 percent of teens surveyed said having a prepaid cash card would make them "look cooler in front of their friends."

If there's anything more abstract and less real than shopping with plastic, it's shopping with plastic online. Not only does no money change hands, but you don't even have to sign for your purchase; you just click a button.

Despite their talk about helping kids manage money, what issuers of prepaid cards really want is to make it easier for youngsters to buy stuff, online and elsewhere. Particularly egregious is the Hello Kitty MasterCard (which calls itself the "cutest way to shop"), a prepaid card aimed at girls as young as 10.

To get parents to buy into the card, one of its creators told the *Washington Post* that parents can monitor where their daughters spend money: "You get a higher level of control than if you just gave your daughter $100 and said, 'Go to the mall.'"

But readers of this book know that you will have even more control if your children finance mall excursions out of their *own* earnings or allowance. I've got nothing against kids buying stuff, and I'm not interested in controlling their purchases (within reason and the law), so long as they don't hit up their parents for $20 or $100 every time they head out the door.

DEAR JANET

Q. In reference to your columns on teenagers and credit: I believe it makes a great deal of sense to give kids credit before they go off to college. My wife and I cosigned for a credit card (with a fairly low limit) for our daughter once she was in high school and was earning money of her own (mostly from babysitting, so it was not a lot). We made sure she knew that she would be responsible for paying off the credit card each month, not us. Today, at 23, our daughter has an impeccable credit record.

A. Every child is different, and some are ready to take on responsibilities—financial and otherwise—sooner than others. Parents need to know their kids, and you obviously knew that yours was ready for a credit card.

Nevertheless, I don't think you're typical of most families. Your situation was successful because your daughter had both maturity and money management skills, and you had the discipline to stay on top of things.

That's a rare combination. Many teens are hard-pressed to hand in their homework when it's due, much less pay a credit card bill on time. And parents have so much on their plates that they don't always follow up.

In addition, parents take on a big risk by cosigning for credit. If kids make late payments, it's a black mark on the parent's credit rating. If they don't pay at all, the card issuer can come after Mom or Dad.

Besides a mature daughter (and focused parents), you had a couple of other things going for you: Your daughter paid the bill with her own money, and to do that she must have had a checking account. So her credit transactions had a cash basis, which is more real to kids than plastic.

Given her background, I'll bet your daughter would still have an impeccable credit record if she had gone off to college with a checking account and a debit card, and waited until senior year to apply for credit.

Once teens have learned to handle cash, they can start to use plastic in ways that make sense. Think of it as a progression. When teens get a part-time job, they can open a checking account and start with an ATM or debit card so they can deposit, withdraw, and spend their own money.

That works just fine with college kids, too, because they don't need credit cards either. "I had a gasoline card for emergencies," one young man confessed, "and my roommate and I always used it to buy food at the gas station convenience store." Another young woman with an "emergency" card once told me that her father "used to ask me, 'Who's this Steve Madden guy whose name is all over your bill?'"

College students can always apply for credit during senior year, after they've had experience managing their own money for several years and can appreciate the distinctions among the various cards. That way, too, they'll have the convenience of a credit card after graduation without the burden of paying off pizzas they consumed during sophomore year.

What About a Prepaid Card?

Does it ever make sense for your kids to use a prepaid card, such as Visa Buxx? I can think of three possible situations in which it might be convenient:

1. You have a precocious teenager who has already proven himself to be a good cash manager but is too young for a checking account. In a situation like this, you could use the card to give your teen his allowance automatically. But you still have a responsibility to work with your child to set up a manageable allowance system (using the advice in Chapter 8) and not advance him money if his cash runs out early.

2. You want to keep more control over your college student's finances by giving him a monthly allowance instead of letting him use a checking account of his own.

3. Your child is going to be traveling for an extended time, and you want a convenient way of replenish-

ing his spending money (and tracking where he spends it).

Note: Visa Buxx cards are issued by a number of banks, each of which has its own schedule of fees that can include an annual fee, transfer fee, ATM fee, inactivity fee, replacement fee, or even a monthly service charge (http://www.visabuxx.com). So read the fine print carefully.

Who's Left Holding the Bag?

Aside from being bad from a money management point of view, lending teenagers your credit card and sending them off happily to the mall to buy a new pair of jeans can cause another problem you may not have bargained for. Suppose that instead of just buying the $50 jeans, your daughter spends several hundred dollars on clothes and DVDs, and you don't find out about the expenditure until you get the bill several weeks later. Do you have to pay the charges even though you didn't authorize them?

You sure do. In the eyes of the law, the fact that your daughter had your credit card was authorization enough. "If your child has your card, a store has the reasonable belief that it can approve almost any charges," said an official at the Federal Trade Commission. If your child were to take your card without your knowledge, you could take advantage of federal regulations to limit your liability to no more than $50 in charges. But to qualify, you would have to notify the issuer that the card had been stolen, which could lead to a criminal investigation of your child. And what parent would be willing to risk that?

In a situation like this, pay the charges, but make your daughter reimburse you—and next time, hold on to your credit card and make her pay cash for the jeans.

Here's another innocent scenario that can turn into a nightmare for parents. In a moment of weakness or expediency—which might occur, for example, when you're trying to run through a long list of errands quickly—you give your son your personal identification number and have him make a withdrawal from the ATM. Later he borrows your card to make a withdrawal of his own, which you don't discover until you get your bank statement. Can you get the bank to credit the money back to your account?

It could be a tough sell. You had disclosed your PIN to your son, so any transaction he makes can be considered authorized—and you can be held responsible for it. If your child were to get access to your card and PIN without your knowledge, you could limit your liability. But as in the case of credit cards, you would have to claim your card was stolen and be willing to let the bank prosecute your child.

In general, kids can be trusted not to clean out your account. But occasionally you do hear a horror story, as in the case of the 14-year-old boy who withdrew $600 from his parents' account before they caught on when their checks began bouncing. The boy had withdrawn the money in small increments and treated his buddies to video games and pizza.

The parents blamed the incident partly on youthful thoughtlessness and partly on themselves for divulging their PIN without explaining the connection between an automated teller machine and their checking account. They didn't throttle their son, but they did exact a stiff penalty: He had to get a job to repay the $600, along with an additional $600 (which his parents used to start a savings account for him). He was also grounded for several months, giving him plenty of time to sit down with his folks and watch them pay the household bills.

Checking Accounts for Kids

It should be obvious by now that I believe in making teenagers operate on a pay-as-you-go basis. Just as children need to walk before they run, they need to learn to manage cash before they can manage credit. My advice to parents has always been to help their teenagers open a checking account when they get their first real job, before they head off to college. But parents often report that they run into a brick wall when they try to open an account for a child under 18.

I didn't anticipate a problem when I went to my local bank branch to open a checking account for my daughter when she was 17. She had summer earnings to deposit, and I wanted her to get an ATM card so she could make further deposits and withdrawals. Two years before, I had opened an account for her brother when he was 17, and things had gone without a hitch.

But this time when I told the banker on duty what I wanted, his response was automatic: no checking account if you're under 18. I told him I knew my daughter couldn't have an account on her own, but I'd be happy to cosign. Would he please check the bank's policy with his manager? In a few minutes he was back: no checking account if you're under 18.

I asked to see the manager, who recited the rote response for a third time. When I told him I'd be willing to cosign, he replied that I'd have to open a custodial account instead. *Bingo.* That would be no problem, I said. Would Claire be able to have checks in her own name? Yes. Would she be able to get an ATM card? The card would have to be in my name, the manager explained, but she could choose the PIN. And when she turned 18, she could convert the account to her own name. Fine, I said. Let's do it.

For parents who want to help their teens open an account, the lessons are clear: Show up in person at your own bank branch. Ask the right questions and volunteer to open a joint or custodial account if necessary. No matter what the bank tells you, it isn't illegal to open a checking account for a minor. What bothers banks is that minors can't legally be held to a contract, so they need an adult's name on the account in case there's a problem.

FINDING A KID-FRIENDLY BANK. Let me hop up on my soapbox for a minute to say that parents shouldn't have to beg to get good service for their kids. Banks and other financial institutions that are quick to jump on

THAT'S LIFE

Consider a kid's eye view of the world. Food appears on the table. There's always (well, almost always) another clean shirt in your closet. A car and driver chauffeur you from place to place. Flick a switch and the computer turns on. Flick another and you're watching ESPN or MTV. Life is good. Life is cheap.

With so much taken care of for them, it's not surprising that children can't appreciate what it costs to keep a household running. To give them a glimpse into the real world (which might prove eye-opening for you too), try playing the following version of "Let's pretend," suitable for children of about 10 years old and up:

"Let's pretend that you're 18 and on your own. You work full-time at a fast-food restaurant making $8 an hour. That's $320 a week for 40 hours of work, or $1,280 a month.

"But you won't actually take home $1,280, of course; after taxes, your pay will be more like $1,120. And, remember, you're on your own now, so you'll have to rent an apartment. [Check market rents in your local newspaper. For hypothetical purposes we'll use $500 a month.] You'll have to pay for electricity and heat—but let's give you a break and assume that utilities are included in the rent.

"Now you're down to $620 a month, out of which you'll have to buy food. To keep things simple, figure that you'll spend about one-fourth of what we spend as a family of four, so your share is around $30 a week, or $120 a month. Remember, that's just groceries, not restaurant meals or pizzas!

"You'll want a phone to talk to your friends— and maybe, once in a while, your old Mom and Dad—so that's another $20 or so a month (double that if you want to go wireless). Can't do without the cable? Subtract another $40 a month. (And you thought it came with the TV!)

"Let's see, now we're down to $440. You already have a car—after all, we're just pretending—but gasoline sets you back at least $25 a week (we'll assume you learn how to change your own oil). There's also the not-so-small matter of car insurance, at $1,600-plus per year for someone who's still a teenager.

"That leaves you about $200 a month, or $50 a week, for all the good stuff, like pizza, movies, clothes, and DVDs. Of course, you could get a higher-paying job, which would require more education, so you may have to take out student loans. But that's life."

the financial literacy bandwagon would do us all a service if they were friendlier to kids on the front lines.

After my experience with my daughter, we at *Kiplinger's* conducted a survey of a half-dozen major banks to ask about their policy on setting up checking accounts for teens. The people we talked to didn't always know the answer. The most forthcoming spokesperson explained that although it isn't his bank's policy to routinely open checking accounts for minors, branch managers have discretion to make their own decisions based on several factors: Does the parent have an account at the bank? Is the child at least 16? Does he or she have a job? Is there a custodian?

Once again, the lessons are clear: Be persistent and ask the right questions. If you strike out at your own bank, try another. For example, KeyBank, which is headquartered in Cleveland and has branches in a dozen states across the northern United States, offers a student checking account for teens as young as 16 (http://www.key.com). Or, if you're eligible, try a credit union. In my experience, credit unions are often more kid-friendly than banks. When she was 16, Tiffany H. got her first checking account from the State Employees Credit Union in Michigan. As a result, "I was definitely way ahead when I got to college," said Tiffany. "I knew where my money was going better than many adults."

The closest thing to a nationally available checking account for kids is offered by Young Americans Bank (http://www.theyoungamericans.org; 303-321-2265), where the average checking account holder is about 16. The minimum deposit to open an account is $58 (including $8 for checks); the minimum to avoid service charges is $150. The bank offers debit cards with its accounts, which are available to customers throughout the country.

A Word about Daughters

When I began work on this book, a woman friend of mine who is single asked that I make a special pitch to parents to teach their daughters to be financially independent.

Don't worry, I told my friend, I'm way ahead of you. That point was brought home to me several years ago, when I noticed it was getting tougher to squeeze my Volkswagen between the behemoths in the parking lot of my daughter's all-girl high school. The *de rigueur* Jeep Cherokees had been joined by

Durangos and Tahoes and the occasional Mercedes SUV. Most of the cars were gifts from doting dads trying to shield their little girls with as much sheet metal as they could afford—and who, I suspect, got a kick out of showing off that they could afford a lot.

A study by Teenage Research Unlimited found that parents are more likely to buy cars and cell phones for their daughters than for their sons, possibly because the girls have persuaded them that they need them for safety. But in the name of safety, parents may be endangering the financial health of their daughters by leading them to expect that Daddy will always be there to bail them out.

I don't mean to be sexist. Parents can be just as adept at spoiling their sons, and there's no gene that makes men better money managers. All children learn about money from adults, and parents have a responsibility to teach both sons and daughters good money management skills.

But young women are particularly vulnerable because well-meaning parents in general, and dads in particular, have a tendency to want to make things easier for them. Showering a daughter with stuff because she's "our little princess" shortchanges her on financial responsibility.

Gender Gap

For the past decade, Oppenheimer Funds has been conducting a regular survey on women's attitudes toward money and investing. Over that time, women's confidence in their ability to manage their finances and invest has increased significantly, but they still express less confidence than men. Evidence indicates this gender gap may begin when kids are teens and boys have more financial independence than girls. For example, teenage boys spend more of their own money than girls—$59 per week versus $51 for girls, according to Teenage Research Unlimited—whereas girls spend more family money than boys—$43 versus $29. According to the Parents, Youth and Money Survey (sponsored by the American Savings Education Council), parents are more likely to require boys to save money than girls—possibly giving them a head start on investing. And that insidious Hello Kitty MasterCard aimed at young girls—the seeds of a *Sex and the City* shop-till-you-drop syndrome?

A survey by the Charles Schwab Foundation on teen attitudes toward money found that girls are more likely than boys to find financial topics "complicated and boring." But when they grow up, an overwhelming 80 percent of women told Oppenheimer they wish they had learned more about investing when they were younger.

In matters of money, young women need to learn to "think single"—a concept that has nothing to do with the state of matrimony. Rather, it's a state of mind in which they feel comfortable handling money and confident that they can manage their finances and support themselves. (See my book, *Think Single!*, available from Dearborn Trade Publishing.) Because women's lives are so bound up with others—parents, spouses, children—it's a lifelong challenge for them to build and maintain financial independence. And it's impossible if Dad (or Mom) is always standing there with an open wallet and a set of car keys.

Tough Love

Although young women aren't likely to look a gift car in the engine, they aren't always comfortable with parental handouts. "I am very scared about the day when I will have to keep my own budget," confided Chantal, a college student who relied on her parents to cover all her credit card bills and pay for her cell phone (she didn't even know how much she owed). "I am one of those college students who's likely to be in debt by the time I'm 25."

At 25, another young woman named Stephanie was already seeking credit counseling to pay off $7,000 she owed on three credit cards. "When I was a teenager, my dad was always one to take care of things," she told me. "If I was about to bounce a check, I'd call him and he'd say, 'Don't worry, I'll put some money in your account.' If I was going out, he'd say, 'I'll get you some gas and be right back.'" When she couldn't make the payments on her car, he helped with those too. And when she got into a credit mess, he offered to pay off one of the cards. "I know it's not good for me," Stephanie confessed, "but it's very easy to be dependent."

It's better for parents to practice a little tough love early on. When Paula, now in her 30s, was a teenager, she was grounded for a month because she borrowed $20 from a friend to buy something at the mall. "My parents might have been obsessive, but I have grown up to be a fabulous money manager," said Paula. She sized up prospective husbands based on two standards: Can he balance a checkbook? Is he free of credit card debt? That's thinking single.

My *Oprah* Experience

How might all this work in the real world? I had a chance to put it all together when I was a guest on the *Oprah Winfrey Show*. I was asked to give advice to a couple, Bob and Renae, who were trying to impose some fiscal discipline on their children, Danielle, 17, and Jason, 14. Bob was a high school graduate who had worked hard to become the successful vice president of a security company. Because he wanted to give Danielle and Jason everything he didn't have growing up, he was always "pulling out my wallet" when they asked for money. Danielle bought gas with a Speedpass (Dad paid the bill), and in one month Jason had run up a tab of almost $200 at McDonald's on his father's account.

Bob's freewheeling financial habits were causing friction with Renae, who wanted the family to "act more like a unit and be accountable for the money we spend." But she didn't like playing the role of bad cop.

What struck me was that in many ways they were a typical American family: financially comfortable, if not wealthy, and eager to spend money on their children—but worried about giving them too much of the good life. As in other families, the kids needed limits, and their parents needed a simple way to set them.

"Where's Our Stuff?"

We started by going through a hands-on exercise to show Danielle and Jason (and Bob and Renae too) how much money was coming in every month and where it was going. Sitting around their kitchen table, the kids got a stack of play money representing Bob's monthly take-home pay. Danielle, who had thought she knew her parents' income, wanted to know why there wasn't more cash. That got her father talking about tax withholding (the kids were suitably shocked by how much the federal government and state government take) and his monthly contributions to his retirement plan.

Bob and Renae, a stay-at-home mom, had a stack of their own—the family's actual monthly bills, which the kids proceeded to "pay" with the play money. The mortgage payment was far more than the "few hundred dollars" Danielle had expected, and Jason was floored by the credit card bills: "You bought all that stuff at Wal-Mart?" Jason liked the idea of making just the minimum credit card payment, but his parents explained that at that rate they'd never pay off the bill.

When all the bills were covered, Renae gathered up the $500 remaining on the table. "That's for groceries," she told the wide-eyed kids. "Where do we get money to buy *our* stuff?" Jason wanted to know.

Hidden Expenses

Because so many of their own expenses were buried in those credit card balances, the kids didn't have a clue about how much "their stuff" actually cost. "Danielle will buy two pairs of jeans online with her father's credit card and then complain that she has nothing to wear," said Renae. Instead of having unlimited access to credit cards and Speedpasses, I recommended that the kids learn to manage separate cash allowances for gas (in Danielle's case), clothing, and basic expenses.

Bob and Renae had already discussed giving the kids a clothing allowance but had abandoned the idea when they couldn't agree on a figure. Bob had proposed $1,000 a year per child, and Renae had countered with $200. I suggested $200 for each child twice a year, in the spring and fall, and they thought that sounded reasonable.

Another source of family tension was Renae's car, which Danielle was driving, although her parents paid for the gas. Danielle figured that was fair because she helped run errands. But a car isn't an entitlement; it's a convenience. If Mom and Dad are already paying for insurance and maintenance, the least that kids can do is cover their gas. And at 17, Danielle was old enough to earn money of her own. Until she did, her parents could replace the Speedpass with a weekly gas allowance of, say, the cost of a fill-up (or a little more if Danielle was indeed running family errands). Danielle didn't balk at the figure, but, her mother confided, "she's in for a surprise. She doesn't realize she's been spending twice that much."

Jason, meanwhile, was horrified at the prospect of getting a base allowance equal to half his age: $7 a week. "A movie and refreshments cost $14," he protested. I explained that his parents could use that as a guideline and adjust it upward, but they didn't have an obligation to cover everything he wanted to spend. Besides, he didn't have to go to a movie every week, and he could cut his food costs in half by sticking to a soft drink (with free refills). And he could always supplement his base allowance by working for pay, either at a regular job or around the house.

Making any system work requires a certain amount of discipline, something Bob and Renae had struggled with in the past. I suggested that they keep things simple by giving the allowance monthly, instead of weekly, and noting on the calendar when the money had been paid to avoid disputes—and advances.

With rules to fall back on, the whole family would know what was expected, and Bob and Renae could speak with one voice. "Now they'll know I'm not just being mean," said Renae. Bob "learned a lot" from our exercise, but admitted it would be tough for him to stop "sending a signal that Dad will take care of everything."

Light at the End of the Tunnel

Teaching your kids good money management skills will be for naught if, like the parents in the prom example that led this chapter, you're willing to buy into and finance all your kids' fantasies. (For advice on how to handle the prom issue in particular, see the question on page 232.) It's true that when your children reach their teen years, they—and you—will bear the full brunt of peer pressure. And they will want to buy things because their possessions will help them define who they'd like to be—a car for the man- or woman-about-town or a closetful of clothes for the glamour queen or hip king. Your job in meeting this irresistible force is to be, in a sense, the immovable object—not simply because *you* say no but because you give your *children* a reason to say no.

It can be tough to resist peer pressure when your kids are trying to fit in. Remember, though, that being part of a group doesn't have to mean spending a lot of money. Depending on their interests, encourage your kids to play sports, try out for the school play, work on the school newspaper, or join a service organization or church youth group.

Getting involved will not only keep them busy, but it will also expose them to a broader group of kids for whom money may not matter as much. In addition, they'll learn to shine in their own right instead of merely being a reflection of their friends.

Finding a comfortable niche can be tough for teens, but it's not impossible. One 20-something woman, the daughter of a teacher, recalls that when she was in high school she couldn't keep up with fellow students whose parents were wealthier. How did she cope? By throwing herself into music lessons. She performed a piano solo at her high school graduation, which conferred a status that money couldn't buy.

Turn page for Kids' Questions→

KIDS' QUESTIONS

Q. "I'd like to invite Andy/Andrea to the dance on Saturday night. Do I have to pay for both of us?"

A. Call me old-fashioned, but here's my first rule of dating etiquette: He or she who does the asking should pick up the tab. My second rule of dating etiquette: He or she who picks up the tab should do it with his or her own money.

In a dating situation, it's bad form to say, "I'd like to invite you to the movies on Saturday night, but I don't have any money so you'll have to pay." Kids (and adults) should wait till they have the money before issuing the invitation. Or they can go in a group where no one pairs off and everyone pays his own way.

If your child is on the receiving end of the invitation, it wouldn't hurt to bring along extra cash—just in case his or her date hasn't read my rules of dating etiquette.

Q. "The French Club is going to Quebec for spring break. Can I go (and will you pay for it)?"

A. If the trip in question is part of the academic curriculum, it would be reasonable for you to pick up at least part of the tab. But any kind of class trip should include class fundraising. Beyond that, your children will appreciate the experience more if they have to come up with some cash of their own, even if it's just in the form of spending money.

If the trip in question is purely social, there are less compelling reasons for you to pay for it. It's not unreasonable to expect teenagers to finance a trip like this from their allowance, savings, and money they earn from a part-time job.

Q. "The prom is going to be really expensive. You're going to help me pay for it, aren't you?"

A. Despite my rules of dating etiquette (see the first question), I can be flexible on occasion, and the prom is one of those occasions. It's such a big event in a teenager's life, and such a big expense, that it makes sense for you to help out. For instance, parents could certainly pay for the prom dress or tux, which, after all, counts as clothing (although kids who get a clothing allowance sometimes go it alone. One teen bought a dress two sizes too big on sale at Bloomingdale's for $35, and Mom paid for alterations).

But you should still make kids responsible for the bulk of the bill. That puts an automatic limit on expenses that have a tendency to get out of hand but can also inspire some creative alternatives. The preprom dinner moves from a splashy restaurant with attitude to a quieter one with atmosphere. Instead of one couple renting a limo, a number of couples can chip in to hire a van or bus. One PTA sponsored a successful used-dress sale. "When my friends were shopping for a dress, they always had in mind whether they'd be able to wear it again," said one practical teen, who has worn her own prom dress several times.

I also hear via the teen grapevine that it's cool for a couple to split the cost of a major event like this one. One senior who invited a boy to her prom paid for the tickets, and he picked up the tab for dinner.

In my opinion, neither parents nor children should be laying out money for a hotel room, and that's a matter of principle as much as price. To discourage the practice, one high school moved its prom venue from the hotel scene altogether, and class officers chose a local dance club instead. Tickets were a reasonable $15 per person, because the class covered much of the cost through fundraisers.

Perhaps the best way to keep expenses under control is for parents to take an active role in prom planning. They can host at-home preprom dinners or after-prom parties and breakfasts (supervised, of course) and have no trouble attracting kids. "I had 50 willing guests in my house after the prom," said one parent. "In my circle of friends, parents were always a part of things, so it was expected," said her daughter. At many schools, parents sponsor all-night parties, with movies in the auditorium, karaoke in the gym, and a breakfast buffet in the cafeteria—all with free admission.

In my experience, proms are exciting and memories pleasant, but the event is rarely socko enough to justify the kind of outlay that seems to be common nowadays. Parents have to keep their perspective lest kids expect more than one evening can deliver and end up both disappointed and broke.

One of the sanest observations about proms that I've run across was a newspaper quote attributed to a 15-year-old shopping for a gown. "I'm only a sophomore," she said, "and $250 is too much to spend on a dress."

Q. "What do you mean you can't afford to send me to a college that costs $20,000 a year? Haven't you been saving the money?"

A. Maybe you have been saving money, but if you have other priorities, you're not obliged to spend it all on college tuition. Even if you're willing to do that, your children should never take it for granted. Get them involved in college planning as soon as they become teenagers so they have an idea of how much you can afford and how much you expect them to contribute. Neither of you should be surprised later.

To Work or Not to Work?

Chapter Thirteen

A couple of years ago, when the son of a friend of mine turned 15, my friend made what she thought was an embarrassing confession. It seems that her son was bugging her to let him get a full-time job over the summer, but she wasn't crazy about the idea. "We go on lots of family outings during the summer, and this would really tie him down," my friend told me. "I don't want to give up that family time, and I don't think he really needs more money than the allowance he already gets. But I'm afraid I'm coddling him."

I reassured her that it sounded to me as if she just didn't want her son to grow up too fast. After all, once her son was in college, he'd probably have to work every summer to earn spending money for the school year. In my opinion, enjoying family time while all the family members are still in one place doesn't count as coddling.

I remember with gratitude that my own mother let me keep my summers free when I was in high school. One of my aunts frowned on such "coddling," and was always bugging Mom to make me get a job. But she held her ground, even though the extra money would have come in handy. "She'll have to start working soon enough," was Mom's rationale, "and once she starts she'll be working all her life." (Mom was right. I got my first job—working in a bakery for $1 an hour—the summer after I graduated from high school, and I've been working ever since.)

Don't get me wrong. I don't mean to say that teenagers shouldn't work. It's about time for them to start pulling some weight when it comes to paying for clothes, cosmetics, and concert tickets (not to mention gas and insurance for the car). Besides, you don't want to discourage their ambition or enthusiasm. Surveys by Teenage Research Unlimited show that once they hit 16, nearly half of teenagers are working.

The trouble is, even though a paying job can help teenagers sharpen their skills in the workplace, it can also be a two-edged sword. By encouraging kids to work, it's easy to create a generation of teenage were-wolves, obsessed with feeding their ravenous spending appetites for even more clothes, cosmetics, and concert tickets.

Two banker friends of mine have conducted seminars in money management for high school students. In one exercise, they asked kids to assume they worked 15 hours a week earning $5.50 an hour. Out of their pay, they had to cover transportation to and from work, entertainment, and food other than school lunches. The challenge: Work out a plan for buying a $700 stereo without charging it or laying it away. "Most of the kids opted for working more hours," my friends told me. "When we raised the question of how that would affect their homework, they said they hadn't thought about it." A few were willing to cut back their spending and save more money out of current income, in which case it would take them about six months to accumulate enough cash to buy the stereo. But that was rare; most kids wanted to buy it as quickly as possible.

The more hours kids put in on the job, the more likely they are to experience other not-so-desirable side effects. That's especially true of teens who work more than 20 hours per week, the national average among high school seniors who work. "When kids work a lot, they disengage from school," said Laurence Steinberg, a professor of psychology at Temple University who has done extensive research about teenagers in the workplace. Grades begin to suffer, children have less contact with their parents (who also have less authority over the kids), and drug and alcohol use go up, possibly because of exposure to older adolescents and stress on the job. Further, there's some evidence that all the real-world lessons picked up on the job aren't necessarily positive. "Our research finds kids more likely to become cynical," said Steinberg. "Over time, they're more likely to agree with such sentiments as, 'People who work harder than they have to must be crazy.'"

Less Is More

Does that mean you have to resign yourself to supporting your kids with precious little contribution from them? Do you have to put up with their planting themselves on the couch in front of the TV? Absolutely not. For one thing, studies showing the negative effects of working, although thought-provoking, aren't the last word. It's not clear, for example, whether working long hours caused the lower grades and other ill effects experienced by some students, or whether a lack of interest in school prompted the kids to work long hours in the first place. In fact, some research shows that working doesn't have an adverse effect on teens. It appears that getting a jump on a job, especially during senior year, gives students who don't go on to college a leg up in the labor market.

Steinberg himself found that teens who worked less than ten hours a week got better grades, on average, than kids who didn't work at all. And the kids said they learned other things as well: how the business world works, how to find and keep a job, how to manage both money and time, and how to get along with other people. Girls who worked had a greater sense of self-reliance.

So what's a parent to do? Remember that just because your kids are old enough to work doesn't mean they're grown-up. They still need your guidance in landing a job, setting their hours, and managing the money they earn. Have them start with a summer job as there's no conflict with school—which is, after all,

MAKE YOUR KID A MILLIONAIRE

As soon as kids have earned income from some type of job—mowing the neighbors' lawns, babysitting for the family down the street, or delivering newspapers, for example—they can start saving for retirement by opening a Roth IRA. Don't laugh. With a Roth, not only do contributions enjoy tax-deferred growth, but the money is tax free when it's withdrawn at retirement.

Suppose your 15-year-old daughter earned $2,000 at a summer job. If she contributed that amount to a Roth, it could grow to more than $140,000 of tax-free income (assuming 10 percent annualized growth) by the time she reaches age 59½. And if your kids need cash before retirement for expenses such as college, they can withdraw their *contributions* without paying tax or a penalty.

Age isn't a factor in setting up a Roth. What matters is that your child has *earned* income from a job; investment income or interest on a savings account doesn't count, nor does an allowance or sporadic payment for chores that kids typically do around the house. Delivering newspapers, babysitting, and mowing lawns for other people do count as paid employment. With a job like babysitting, however, it's unlikely kids would have a W-2 form reporting their income, so they should at least keep a careful written journal or a contemporaneous log of jobs completed. If your kids are working for you on a regular basis—as in the case of one young man who was being paid by his parents for specific chores to help with the upkeep of their two-acre property—it's even more important to keep careful records.

Your child may contribute a maximum of $4,000 in 2005 or 100 percent of earned income, whichever is less (the annual cap is scheduled to rise to $5,000 in 2008). Kids don't need to kick in the full $4,000 to get started. And, let's face it, you can't expect them to put in all their money and have nothing left to spend. Here's where you come in. To fund the Roth, you can give children cash equal to what they earn up to the $4,000 annual limit. Uncle Sam doesn't care where the money comes from, as long as it doesn't exceed a child's annual earnings.

The toughest thing about opening a Roth for a kid may be finding someone willing to take the money. Mutual fund companies and others may be reluctant to open an account for a child because minors can't legally enter into binding contracts. The firms' lawyers worry that if the investments go sour, a minor could complain about poor investment advice.

But a growing number of mutual fund families and many big brokerage firms are willing to open IRAs for kids—although some require an adult to cosign the paperwork. Among the firms happy to open IRAs for youngsters: Merrill Lynch, Charles Schwab, and T.D. Waterhouse brokerages; and the American Century, T. Rowe Price, Strong, and Vanguard mutual fund families. Note: This is one situation in which it's probably better to deal with the company by phone or in person rather than through its Web site.

Although many companies are reluctant to open Roth IRAs for minors, they'll be happy to open an account when your child turns 18. And that's when most kids start making real money from summer, part-time, or full-time jobs.

their primary responsibility. And because small doses of work seem to yield the biggest benefits, limit their hours if they want to continue working during the school year, at least until both you and they are satisfied that they can balance the job with schoolwork, family time, and extracurricular activities. Ten hours a week are sufficient for sophomores, or 15 for juniors and seniors—with the proviso that they cut back if grades suffer or be allowed to work more if they seem able to handle it. That should be plenty of time for your kids to learn the virtues of showing up on time, getting along with coworkers and customers, and not loafing on the job.

You're trying to strike a balance, as did the family who wrote me the following letter: "Several years ago our daughter volunteered at our local library during the summer. When she returned to high school, she was given the opportunity to work at the library 20 hours a week. We thought it would interfere with her studies, so we settled on 10 hours. She worked there for four years, through her second year of college.

"She developed a love for reading and became a history teacher for three years. Now she's an archivist at the National Archives in Washington."

Volunteering: An Alternative

If you don't need the money and you're more interested in having your teens learn such job skills as leadership and responsibility as well as how to take orders and work with people, you might look into volunteer positions—working at a hospital, a childcare facility, or a museum, for instance. Kids are often given more responsibility in these positions than in paying jobs, and they get exposure to a variety of careers and to slices of life that they might not normally come in contact with. If you would otherwise ask your children to divide their earnings among college savings, discretionary spending, and charitable giving, you might consider waiving the giving requirement if the kids are doing volunteer work. To encourage a son who wanted to be a doctor, one father offered to pay him what he would have earned flipping burgers if he volunteered at a hospital instead. The son volunteered throughout high school and eventually did enroll in medical school.

Don't underestimate the value of extracurricular activities. Stephen Hamilton, former director of the Youth and Work Program at Cornell University, points out that even more than school itself, extracurriculars give students a taste of life in the outside world because they often involve working with a group of people to accomplish a goal or task. In extracurricular activities, as in the workplace, teamwork can be so important that if you're late you let everyone down.

Extracurriculars can prove lucrative as well. A few years ago I interviewed Michelle Sippel, a high school student from Nebraska whose essay on financial literacy had won her an award from the National Endowment for Financial Education. During the summers Michelle worked for her father, a veterinarian. But during the school year she had set herself the task of finding scholarship money for college, a job in itself that required talking to school counselors, searching the Internet, and combing through guidebooks. She

---

WHAT THE LAW SAYS

Federal child labor laws limit the number of hours a 14- or 15-year-old may work: no more than 3 hours on a school day or 18 hours in a school week; and no more than 8 hours on a nonschool day or 40 hours in a nonschool week. (Also, work may not begin before 7 AM nor end after 7 PM, except from June 1 through Labor Day, when evening hours are extended to 9 PM.) The law doesn't restrict working hours for children 16 and older.

Teens aged 14 and 15 may work in offices, grocery and other retail stores, restaurants, movie theaters, amusement parks, baseball parks, or gasoline service stations. Older teens of 16 and 17 can work in any job that hasn't been declared hazardous (young workers under the age of 18 are prohibited from doing 17 hazardous jobs). Learn more at http://www.youthrules.dol.gov or call 866-4USWAGE.

set up a filing system so she knew which applications she had to submit each month. In the end, she amassed enough money to pay for her education—and then some. "Being involved in school activities helped me get scholarships," Michelle told me. "I earned a lot more than most kids earn from a job."

Lighting a Fire

Okay, but what if your kids aren't quite so ambitious and show no signs of getting up off the couch? Let's give them the benefit of the doubt and assume they don't want to be slugs: they just don't know how to find a job. That's certainly what I hear in many of my e-mails from teenagers: "Can you tell me where to go to get a job when I am 14? I start college in four years and I only have $80 saved." "I am 16 and I need to get a job. Can you help me?"

It's true that the adult labor force can be a forbidding place. My stomach still churns when I think about my own first job hunt, trudging from one temp agency to another, and taking typing tests on which I was invariably too slow. So prodding alone won't necessarily get your kids off the couch. They need your help to figure out what they can do and how to sell themselves to employers (and maybe to make a phone call or two on their behalf).

Start by getting them thinking about what kind of employment is best suited to their personality: working outdoors or in an office, being part of a team or on their own, or juggling lots of balls or focusing on one task at a time. The nature of the job has as much influence on kids as the number of hours they spend doing it. Who are they working with? Is the job interesting? Is it stressful? How much responsibility do they have? Will they get to make independent decisions?

All of my children were year-round swimmers, so it wasn't surprising that they gravitated to the water to take their first plunge into the labor pool. But each of them had a different comfort zone. John, my oldest,

DEAR JANET

Q. Last year my teenage daughter earned about $2,000 at a summer job, and money was withheld from her salary for income taxes even though she didn't end up owing any tax. Is there any way we can avoid withholding this year so she won't have to file a tax return to get her refund?

A. Possibly. Summer workers can block withholding if they didn't owe any tax the previous year and don't expect to owe any in the current year. And children claimed as dependents on their parents' returns can earn up to $5,000 at a job in 2005 before any federal income tax is due.

The fly in the ointment could be your daughter's "unearned income"—interest she's earned on a bank account or dividends paid by a mutual fund, for example. If your daughter's unearned income is $250 or less, the total of that and her wages can't exceed the same $5,000 threshold. However, when her investment income exceeds $250, she can't dodge income tax withholding if her total income will exceed $800.

Although some summer workers can avoid income tax withholding, there's no way around the 7.65 percent Social Security tax.

wanted to stick close to home, so he took a minimum-wage job as a lifeguard to work with his buddies at the community pool up the street. Middle daughter Claire preferred flexible hours, so she sought a job as the assistant coach of a swim team—with a lucrative side business giving private swim lessons on her own time. Youngest son Peter was motivated by money, pure and simple. He found out about a pool across town that was paying lifeguards more than $8 an hour, so, at 15, he hustled himself a job (and transportation to the pool).

Once kids turn 14, they can legally work in an office, retail store, restaurant, movie theater, or amusement park. If you have any contacts at such businesses, give them a call—not necessarily to get your child a job but at least to get him or her in the door. (I gratefully gave up typing when my uncle put in a good word for me with the owner of the bakery.) A good source of help for teenagers (and their parents) is http://www.teens4hire.org, which maintains a jobs database, along with job-hunting tips and other resources.

Stay in touch with your children's work life. On the job or not, they're still kids, and you're still their parents. Get the scoop on where they're working from other kids who are employed there, or "interview" the manager yourself and ask about policies on teen work schedules. Would your kids have to work a minimum number of hours a week? How many nights? Is the manager flexible enough to accommodate studying for a big exam, playing in a big game, or appearing in the school play? If the answers aren't satisfactory, steer your teens to another employer. And your children should know that if something goes wrong on the job, they can come to you.

Which Job Is Best?

Each child's personality and circumstances will be different. But in Steinberg's studies, two jobs stood out as being the most kid friendly overall:

1. **Retail sales in a small business.** One teen who worked for a small, family-run florist spent most of her time working side by side with the owner and got a unique perspective on the whole operation. Instead of just ringing up sales, she became experienced in ordering flowers, taking inventory, and setting prices.
2. **Babysitting.** Believe it or not, this job ranked high because sitters worked in relatively pleasant surroundings and were given a fair amount of responsibility for making decisions. In addition, babysitters tend to be independent contractors who can set their own work schedules and enjoy the benefits of self-employment.

It's probably unrealistic to expect most 16-year-olds to know what they want to do with their life. In fact, most kids that age have big gaps in their knowledge of how much education and training is required for a particular career and even how much they can expect to earn. So even if it's a low-paid (or unpaid) position or is temporary summer employment, any job in a field that might turn into a future career—being a copykid at the local newspaper, working in the mail room of a bank or other major corporation, helping out in an animal hospital, even working in a local T-shirt shop—can be an invaluable investment in the future. Linda Menzies, who at age 19 started her own graphic design business, began her working life at 16 as a graphic designer creating packaging for a man who invented kids' toys and other novelty items.

Teens should look for jobs that allow them to manage time, money, or people, advises one career consultant, and add new responsibilities each summer by building on their past experience. Students who do well in summer jobs establish good work habits that can last a lifetime and make contacts that could help them get a full-time job in the future.

For teens who don't plan to go on to college, the best jobs are those that exist in a school setting, such as vocational/cooperative education programs, so kids get the idea that work and school are related. Frank

DEAR JANET

Q. Last summer my 15-year-old cousin washed dishes in a restaurant and got paid only $4.25 an hour. His father said that was because he was considered seasonal part-time. Now he wants to get an after-school job and is considering going back to the restaurant. Shouldn't he be paid the minimum wage?

A. He should—as long as he goes back to the same restaurant.

When Congress increased the federal minimum wage to $5.15 per hour, it also created a special "opportunity wage" (or youth subminimum wage), which applies to employees under 20 years old. Employers are permitted to pay teenagers $4.25 an hour for the first 90 calendar days after their initial hire. Once the 90 days are up, teenagers must be paid the current minimum wage.

It doesn't matter whether the employee works only part-time or goes back to school in the interim. If your cousin started his job July 1, for instance, he would have been entitled to the minimum wage after September 28, and he still will be if he returns to the same employer.

If he works for someone new, however, the clock will be reset. The new employer could pay him the youth wage for the first 90 days.

Linnehan, who's on the faculty of Drexel University in Philadelphia, has done research showing that some key predictors of success on the job—measured in terms of both job attendance and performance—are grades and attendance while students are still in school. Employers who ask about grades and attendance often use them as positive signals of an applicant's job-related behavior. Linnehan studied the "career academy" model—a nationwide program of schools-within-a-school, in which high-risk kids get small-group attention in a specific field of study, such as business, law, or environmental science. In Philadelphia, which was the focus of Linnehan's study, students in career academies were given the opportunity to work after school during their junior and senior years. But they weren't permitted to interview for a job unless they had attended class regularly and maintained good grades—making the point in students' minds that the best way to succeed in the world of work is to succeed in school.

At Kentwood High School in suburban Seattle, students get a grade on their report card called the Employability and Life Skills Assessment. Teachers evaluate students on such characteristics as punctuality, attendance, teamwork, and pride in their work, which indicate whether they will be successful in the workplace. Students who achieve an average of 4 or 5 on a five-point scale earn a "hire me first" card they can present to potential employers.

When push comes to shove, many kids are going to end up—you guessed it—flipping burgers. That kind of work may not rank high on the list of stimulating, meaningful jobs, but it does have the advantage of being readily available and not too far from home.

And neither teens nor their parents should be job snobs. As a regular customer at fast-food joints, I certainly appreciate getting service with a smile from perky teenagers. Parents should be proud if their kids can survive, and even thrive, in what's perceived as a pressure-cooker atmosphere.

It's also true, however, that not all burger joints are alike. In one study, workers were more satisfied with management personnel in franchised stores owned by an individual or small corporation than they were in company-owned stores. And company policies make a difference. Burger King, for example, in conjunction with Communities in Schools, the nation's largest dropout prevention organization, runs a network of Burger King Academies, where at-risk kids get personal attention from teachers and counselors. A company spokesman said many store managers come up through the ranks. "This is not necessarily the place you go and stay for the rest of your life, but for many kids it's a first step."

How to Manage Part-Time Earnings

In a magazine article on teens who work, dozens of young people bared their souls—and their closets. One revealed a young man's back-to-school wardrobe: 2 leather jackets, 6 sweaters, 12 pairs of jeans, 4 pairs of shoes, 2 belts, and loads of shirts, including a half-dozen silk ones. One senior girl had 20 pairs of dress shoes with a purse to match each one plus 10 pairs of sneakers.

And it's all financed by those jobs that are supposed to teach teens the value of a dollar. It would seem, ironically, that they've learned the lesson: a buck will buy stuff, and lots of bucks will buy more. Teenagers have so much income for discretionary spending that they can often afford the designer clothes and electronic gizmos their parents can't.

Parents need to give their kids a more realistic vision of the world, yet like the parent who wrote me the following e-mail they are sometimes reluctant to intervene: "My teenage son has his first summer job, but the way he spends his money, I'm afraid he's not going to have much to show for it. He says he earned it, and I guess he has a point. But is there some way I can use this as a learning experience?"

Parents, don't be so shy about speaking up. Even though your children are earning money, you still have both a legal right and a parental obligation to have a say in what they do with it. Neither you nor they may be aware of this, but money they earn isn't automatically theirs. As long as you're supporting your children, you're entitled to at least a portion of their income unless you give them, either by formal agreement or practice, the right to spend and manage their own earnings. (In a number of states, the amount you can take is regulated. For example, in California the Coogan Law requires that a percentage of the wages earned by child performers be put in trust for them until they reach the age of majority.)

I certainly don't advise confiscating your kids' paychecks. But it's appropriate for you to sit down with them before they start working to hash out an agreement on how much you'd like them to save, and for what. Now that they have the opportunity to earn serious money, it wouldn't be unreasonable for kids to be socking away as much as half of their income for big-ticket senior year expenses or for college.

Now's also a good time to talk to your kids about how much you can afford to spend on college and how much you expect them to contribute. Is private school within your family's reach, or is a state school or community college more realistic? Will you expect them to earn their own spending money or help pay tuition as well?

One father agreed to foot the entire bill for college but required his daughter to save a big chunk of her earnings so that she'd be financially independent afterward, with money of her own to buy a car or put down a security deposit on an apartment.

DEAR JANET

Q. My 16-year-old son will probably earn about $3,000 this year. Is that the maximum he can contribute to a Roth IRA? Could I contribute an additional $3,000 on his behalf?
A. The dollar limit on annual contributions to a Roth IRA is $4,000 (scheduled to rise to $5,000 in 2008) or 100 percent of earned income, whichever is less. If your son earns $3,000, that's the most he can deposit. You can't match his contribution. And just in case you were wondering, you can't kick in an additional $1,000 to bring him up to the $4,000 maximum.

Before kids even get their first paycheck, take the opportunity to teach them a thing or two about taxes. First, the good thing. Many kids automatically claim zero withholding allowances on their Form W-4. But even if they are claimed as dependents on their parents' tax return, they're still permitted to claim one withholding allowance as a single person with one job. That will put a few extra bucks in their pocket each payday—not insignificant if they're making the minimum wage.

Now, the bad thing: Warn your teens that their paycheck will be smaller than they expect. Most kids don't realize that Uncle Sam will take a cut of their earnings. When my son Peter got his first check from that high-paying lifeguard job, he was taken aback to see that $39 had been withheld. And he was even more dismayed to learn that he would only get back about $17 in federal and state taxes as a refund. The $22 for Social Security and Medicare was gone for good. When your children cash that first paycheck, help them open a checking account so they can deposit and withdraw their own money and keep a rec-

---

DEAR JANET

Q. I'm self-employed, with both an outside and a home office. What would be required (paperwork, taxes, etc.) to have my two sons—an energetic 11-year-old and a lazier 13-year-old—work for me? Could they open a Roth IRA with their earnings?

A. Yes, your sons could open a Roth IRA if they worked for you—as long as they do real work and their earnings are legitimate.

To make sure you stay within the law, follow these guidelines:

- **Hire your sons** to do tasks that are suitable for their age and your business— cleaning the office, answering the phone,

opening mail, or entering computer data would all be acceptable.

- **Pay them a reasonable wage** and handle things in a businesslike manner by keeping records of the work done, the number of hours worked, and the hourly rate.

- **Pay with a check** drawn on a business account, and file a Form W-2 reporting the kids' earnings to the Social Security Administration.

A bonus for you: Social Security taxes aren't due on wages you pay to your own child under age 18, assuming your business is not incorporated.

ord of their transactions. As I've said in other chapters, learning to balance a checking account is a key financial skill teens need to learn before they leave home.

Finally, give your kids a head start on saving for retirement by helping them open a Roth IRA. A child can have his or her own Roth as soon as he or she has earnings from a job (investment income or interest from a savings account doesn't count). The dollar limit on annual contributions is the same for kids as it is for adults: a maximum of $4,000 a year (scheduled to rise to $5,000 in 2008), or 100 percent of earned income, whichever is less.

True, saving for retirement won't be at the top of your children's to-do list. But if they have already spent (or saved) their money for other things, you can provide the cash to open the account (as long as it doesn't exceed their total earnings for the year).

Even a kid appreciates the magic of compound interest. If your 16-year-old saves, say, $1,000 a year for the next five years, and that money grows at 10 percent a year, he'd have nearly half a million dollars at age 65. If he needed some of that cash in a few years—to help pay for college, for example—he could withdraw his contributions without paying a tax or a penalty (for more on Roth IRAs, see the box on page 238).

More about Taxes

One bit of real-world experience that goes along with holding a job is filing a tax return. Your children may not actually have to file, but it's a good idea to do it anyway—and not just because they're good citizens.

Let's say, for example, that your 16-year-old son earned $2,000 at a summer job. If that's his only income for the year, he doesn't have to file. But filing is the only way he can get back money withheld from his paychecks (except for Social Security taxes, which aren't refundable).

A dependent child can earn up to $5,000 from a job before a return is required. (That's the 2005 figure; it will continue to rise in the future.) But if any investment income—even interest on a savings account—is thrown into the mix, the rules change.

Because you'll claim your son as a dependent on your tax return, he can't claim a personal exemption on his own. Although he does get a standard deduction, it may not be a full-powered one. His deduction is either $5,000 (the regular 2005 amount for single taxpayers) or, if less, the total of the pay from his job plus up to $250 in investment income. If he had more than $250 in investment income, the excess would be taxed in the 10 percent bracket for savings interest, or 5 percent for dividends and capital gains.

(H&R Block offers an online tax education center, plus free online tax preparation for teens under the age of 18 who are filing their first tax return. Go to http://www.hrblock/com/goto/firstfilers.)

Tips on Finding a Job

For most teens, job hunting means keeping an eye out for stores with Help Wanted signs in the window, putting in an application, and waiting to be called. But they can improve their chances of getting a job—and, in particular, getting a job they want—if they approach their search more professionally. They should start looking early, presuming that it will take a couple of months to land a job, and be creative in their search. Don't assume, for example, that want ads are just for adults. Watching the classifieds could turn up a position as part-time receptionist in a doctor's office during after-school hours.

Other job-hunting tips for kids are reviewed in the following.

Prepare a Résumé

Children tend to downplay talents that adults appreciate, so they don't always give themselves enough credit for leadership skills and organizational ability that can translate into success in the workplace. Making the honor roll, being editor of the school paper, direct-

RISE AND SHINE

A question I received from a parent with a sleepyhead teenager spawned this fascinating exchange with readers.

Q. For the last year, our daughter, a senior in high school, has been working for a fast-food restaurant. The problem is that on the weekends the restaurant has scheduled her to work the opening shift. She has to be there at 5 AM, which means she has to get up at 4 AM.

My husband and I have no problem with her working that shift, except that she can't wake up on her own. I always have to go into her bedroom and shake her no matter how long the alarm has been going off. We have told her she will have to tell her employer that she can't work the opening shift any more, because this is robbing us of the only day we have to sleep in. But she complains that they will cut her hours and her pay if she doesn't open on the weekends. Her employer has been good to her and she doesn't want to change jobs.

She is saving for college, so she needs the money. And she rarely asks us for money now that she has been working. What is a good compromise or solution?

A. Have your daughter ask her employer about changing her hours so that she only has to work the opening shift every other weekend. Even high school students deserve one day to sleep in. If your daughter really is on good terms with her boss, it's likely that he or she would be receptive to her request.

If her employer is adamant and your daughter wants to keep the job, you'd be justified in telling her she's on her own when it comes to getting up. After all, when she heads off to college next year you won't be around to make sure she gets to class on time.

I can't help wondering, though, whether you're complaining a bit too much. If your daughter is willing to be at work at 5 AM, and if you're happy with the financial contribution she's making, getting up to awaken her is a small price to pay. After all, you can always crawl back into bed.

Dear Janet: I also had problems hearing the alarm when I was a young adult. It helps to set multiple alarms with varied times. I always used to set the alarms across the room so I had to get out of bed to turn them off.

Dear Janet: I saw myself in the letter from the parents whose daughter couldn't wake up for her job. Every day for years, I woke my son up or called to get him up. I didn't do him any favors.

When he bought his own home at age 20, his biggest worry was that he wouldn't be able to get up on time—not that he wouldn't be able to pay the bills, not that he wouldn't be able to handle working 50 hours a week while going to classes, but that he wouldn't be able to wake up.

Once he moved out of our house, he can and does manage to get out of bed on time. But the parents in your letter need to let their daughter do it on her own. Her parents are being a crutch, and in the long run their daughter will be grateful they backed off.

ing the school play, babysitting, or volunteering at a local hospital can all look impressive to employers (especially if most of the other kids they've interviewed haven't bothered to spell out their accomplishments).

Dress Appropriately

At a large corporation or small business, dress is conservative but not necessarily formal—jacket and slacks for a boy (a suit isn't necessary unless the company is super straitlaced), dress, or skirt and blouse for a girl. If kids are applying at a more laid-back operation, such as a summer camp or amusement park, they can afford to be more casual but never sloppy—shirt (with collar) and trousers for boys, skirt or slacks and blouse for girls (never jeans for anyone).

Observe the Niceties of Interview Etiquette

In one seminar on job skills for teenagers, participants are put through an exercise in which they are interviewed for hypothetical jobs ranging from astronaut to chef. Many kids "tend to be quite cavalier about it," the seminar director told me. "They will saunter up and slouch down in a chair." What they really need to do is look the interviewer in the eye, shake hands, address him or her as Mr. or Ms., sit up straight, and not be afraid to make small talk or ask questions.

Chalk it up to inexperience. But kids can be a quick study. To encourage her students to speak up, one seminar leader suggested a list of questions they could ask an interviewer. As instructed, one girl, who was being interviewed for a position as assistant zookeeper, asked the chief zookeeper why the previous assistant had left. "Oh, there was a terrible accident," deadpanned the zookeeper. "He was killed by a bear." "Then I think you need better training and safety procedures," the interviewee shot back at the surprised counselor. "I'm not interested in working at your zoo."

How to Succeed in Business

Much has been made of the fact that U.S. schools don't adequately prepare teens to succeed in the job market. Sometimes the skills that are lacking are academic ones in reading, writing, and math. But sometimes kids are handicapped by their unfamiliarity with the workplace and an inability to connect what they're learning in school with the jobs they will hold when they graduate. In that case, a part-time job can help, especially if the hours are manageable and the setting conducive to learning.

In the best of all worlds, your kids will be as fortunate as Danielle S. Danielle started working as a camp counselor when she was 15 and held several jobs in retail sales before finding her niche working 12 hours a week at a family-owned clothing and accessories store. The owners, she said, were "really good" about scheduling her work hours around school activities—she was a cheerleader, vice president of the student council, a member of the debating team, and an actor in school plays.

Danielle found that she thrived on the busy schedule and on the work itself: "I think I have a good sense of fashion, and I liked helping people pick out clothes." Her coworkers were "like a family," and the atmosphere was friendlier than in the big mall stores "where you are always selling, selling, selling." Sure, there were days when she'd rather have stayed home, but having to get up and go taught her "how to be responsible and budget my time, which you have to do when you go to college." If they could be as contented as she, said Danielle, "all kids should work."

Off to College and on Their Own (Sort Of)

Chapter Fourteen

Despite all the time families spend worrying about *how* to pay for college, they often neglect two issues that can produce even bigger headaches: *who* should pay and how much. Many parents will literally mortgage the roof over their heads to send their kids wherever they want to go (not necessarily a good idea if you are planning to live under that roof in retirement). On the other hand, one high school sophomore wrote to me to complain that although his parents were "extremely rich," they refused to pay for him to attend anything other than a state school. When I published his letter in my column, it prompted indignant responses from several parents. "Since when did paying for college become a parent's responsibility?" wrote one. "I paid my own way."

Just as important as opening college savings accounts is sitting down with your kids and leveling with them about how much you're able—and willing—to pay. Although we parents generally don't have a legal obligation to pay for college (unless there's a court agreement, such as a divorce decree), it's my view that we have a moral obligation to contribute. We aren't obliged, however, to pay full freight, nor should we.

"Paying for yourself makes you more responsible and gives you more motivation as a student," said Jessie O., a 20-something college graduate. "When I, instead of my father, was paying for my education, I was much less likely to drop courses." Jessie has no complaints about paying off her $30,000 in student loans.

Family Affair

Think of college as a joint venture, with kids pitching in to give themselves a stake in their own education. Even if you're financially able to pick up the whole tab, kids should at least be expected to earn their spending money.

Teens need to know your financial situation before they start applying to college, and they need your help to make some realistic financial decisions. "If your child wants to be a social worker making $45,000 a year, it's better to go to a less expensive school than to take on $120,000 in debt," said Gary Carpenter, executive director of the National Institute of Certified College Planners. That's not something your average 18-year-old is likely to think about.

You also owe it to your kids to give them some guidance on how to come up with the cash if you are not going to pay. For example, you still need to fill out federal financial aid forms (although if you are "extremely rich," your kids probably won't be eligible for aid, even if it's up to them to pay the bills). And forget about having your child qualify as an independent student. To do that, kids have to meet strict criteria: They must be at least 24, or be married, or have a legal dependent. "The only way I can get financial aid is to get pregnant or marry someone unable to support me," grumbled one student.

Covering the Costs

Actually, kids don't have to do anything that drastic. They can, for example, get a degree for a fraction of the cost by attending a community college for two years and then transferring to a four-year school. My daughter, God bless her, goes to school in Canada, where her expenses at McGill University in Montreal are equivalent to what she'd pay in state at the University of Maryland.

I've known students who graduated a year early by combining high school advanced placement credits, extra courses, and summer school. I've also known students who qualified for significant merit-based aid, as well as students who received full tuition ROTC scholarships in return for a commitment to military service.

For your children, figuring out a way to pay for their education is a lesson in itself. If the young man whose parents are "extremely rich" takes them up on their offer to foot the bill for an in-state college, he could graduate free of debt—and be in a great position to go elsewhere for graduate school.

School of Hard Knocks

Once you and your student have figured out how to pay that first semester's tuition bill, you may be tempted to breathe a sigh of relief that you have a firm grip on college expenses. But brace yourself. You're about to face the ultimate college financial crisis: sending an 18-year-old away from home with a book full of blank checks and independent access to credit.

When I interviewed a group of college students about their experience managing money away from home for the first time, here's what they had to say.

On who pays for what: "I assumed I'd pay for my computer and my parents would pay for my books," said Ryan C. "But they assumed I'd be responsible for both."

On keeping track of their money: "Don't tell my parents, but I haven't updated my checking account in months," said Maggie C. "Sometimes I go to the bank and I'm surprised by how much is gone," added Chantal A.

On setting up a bank account: "My bank at school had about four ATMs in the entire city," complained

---

DEAR JANET

Q. I'm a college senior. Instead of asking a question, I'd like to give new students and their parents a couple of tips that have helped me save money during my school years.

Students end up paying lots of money in ATM fees because it's not an easy battle to get the guy who's driving you to the party or the game to go to your bank when your bank is on the other side of campus and the rest of the guys are itching to go to the game. My advice is to plan ahead. Stop by the ATM on your way home from class on Friday and get enough money out for the weekend. This will also help with budgeting.

While it's a nice break to run out for a Coke, the convenience stores near campus are a rip-off. Encourage your students to make a weekly trip to a real grocery store for drinks and snack foods.

Lucy M. "When I came home I had to get money out of local ATMs, and I racked up huge fees."

On "emergency" expenses: "'Emergency' is a loosely defined word that usually includes new shoes and CDs," said Lucy.

What words of wisdom would the students offer new freshmen and their parents? "To save money buy books used or online," advised Jessica P. "Limit the amount of food you buy outside the dining hall," said Evan S., who figured he could have saved hundreds of dollars had he followed his own advice. Don't underestimate everyday expenses. "Laundry cost way more than I expected," said Martha C.

College Finance 101

If you want to avoid a flurry of "send cash" e-mails or that scary late-night phone call—"Help! I've fallen into credit card debt and I can't get out"— don't let your kids leave home without laying down a family financial aid policy.

KEEP CASH KING. If you haven't already helped your teenagers open a checking account, do so before they leave home so they can learn how to write checks, save their ATM receipts, record expenses, and maybe even balance the account once in a while. If they don't, they could get hit with a bounced check fee (see page 268). But once they know they're overdrawn, that at least limits the amount of trouble they can get into.

Ideally, you should choose a bank that will also have branches and ATMs where your child is attending school. If that's not possible, pay attention to the mailings you'll receive from financial institutions during the summer before your child enrolls so that you can choose a bank at school that has low fees and lots of convenient ATMs. (College students will invariably go to the closest ATM, even if they're charged a fee because the ATM doesn't belong to their own bank.) One family I know took advantage of an early summer orientation at their daughter's college to set up an account with a local bank—a great way to beat the crush of students when school starts in the fall.

GET A HANDLE ON MISCELLANEOUS EXPENSES. Figure on $3,000 or so in spending money for two semesters away from home, although that can vary widely depending on such variables as a school's location, transportation costs, and meal plans. Ask your child's school for its recommendation. If you think your student would be tempted to run through a semester's worth of money before Halloween, give him or her a monthly allowance instead. This is one situation in which a prepaid card, such as Visa Buxx (http://www.visabuxx.com), can come in handy. You can set up a regular deposit schedule to your child's account or add money to the card as needed. Your student can use the card to make purchases or get cash from an ATM.

Another tactic is to take care of as many expenses as you can in advance—by stocking up on shampoo and razor blades, for example. You probably don't need the most expensive campus meal plan. But look for a plan that offers some flexibility so that your child can grab a late-night snack if he or she skips dinner.

BE CLEAR FROM THE START ABOUT WHO'S GOING TO PAY FOR WHAT. When Ryan C. and his parents disagreed about who was going to pay for his books, they ended up in a last-minute argument instead of bidding each other a fond farewell. An argument is understandable when you consider that a year's worth of new textbooks can run close to $1,000. Urge your student to treat the campus used-book sale like a hot concert ticket or to hunt for dis-

---

DEAR JANET

Q. We have six children. When one of our sons went off to college, he had a prepaid meal plan from which money was deducted each time he ate. He ate a lot, and phoned home in a panic with a month left in the semester and only about $45 left in the account. Our response was to send him a five-pound jar of peanut butter and several boxes of cereal, with just enough cash to buy bread and an occasional chicken dinner. We never had a problem again.

A. Moral: Don't be afraid to cut off your kids cold turkey—or cold cereal.

counts at BestBookBuys.com, a Web site that compares prices charged by the most popular online booksellers.

When shopping for a computer, however, be sure to check your college's own online store. Thanks to bulk deals with computer makers, it could offer the best price. Often you may also find discounts on Apple computers and on software at Apple.com's education store (800-692-7753).

It's reasonable to expect your kids to use money from summer earnings or jobs during the school year to pay for their own day-to-day expenses. "If you're earning the money, you feel much more proprietary," said Joanne Y. "At school, my mother put money in my account, and I didn't keep track of spending. But over the summer I had a goal to earn $5,000, and I kept track of everything on a computer spreadsheet."

You'll probably want to pay for transportation home—but your kids should make reservations far enough in advance to get a discount fare. If they want to hit the beach over spring break, they should pay for the trip.

ENCOURAGE YOUR KIDS TO MONITOR THEIR EXPENSES, at least for the first month or two. "By setting monthly spending limits using Microsoft Money, I spent far less than $1,000 per semester," said Pat S. Not every student is so well organized. When Ryan C. blew through $3,000 of his summer earnings during his first semester—including nearly $500 for a space-age bed pad and pillow—he was "completely shocked and disgusted" with himself. During the spring semester, he jotted down his purchases and spent about one-third as much. "Keeping track of where you spend your money may not change how much you spend," he said, "but at least you'll know where it went."

DOWNPLAY CREDIT CARDS. As readers know by now, I don't recommend that college students have credit cards, not even for emergencies. A debit card attached to their checking account will do just fine. But once children turn 18 they can get a credit card on their own without a parent's signature—or even a parent's knowledge. And as soon as they hit campus, they'll be aggressively solicited by card issuers, who will tempt them with free phone time, free airfare, and trip giveaways. How can you guarantee they won't sign up?

You can't guarantee it, but you can certainly discourage it. And many young people have told me they steered clear of credit cards simply because they knew their parents didn't like the idea. After they've had experience managing cash for several years, they can always apply for a credit card shortly before they graduate so they can start building a credit history when they enter the "real" world. But there's no rush (read more about college students and credit below).

DECIDE HOW TO HANDLE TELEPHONE CHARGES. Campus phone service can be priced so high that many

---

DEAR JANET

Q. I'm a sophomore in college and I'm having trouble figuring out how to get my mom to give me money she promised me. We worked out in advance how much allowance I was supposed to get each semester at school and what it would go for. I keep track of the money flow, but she hasn't yet delivered. Luckily for me, she pays for school and most of my large expenses, so I feel very awkward asking her for the money she "owes" me. I save most of what I earn, so I never have to worry about my bank balance. But if I didn't have a healthy cushion for things like food, I would be in the red.

Recently I politely sent her a "bill," an action we both agreed upon, for more than $3,000. So it's not like it's just $20 in lunch money. As a parent yourself, what would you suggest I do?

A. I'm puzzled as to why your mother hasn't come across with the cash. If it's because of unexpected financial problems, she at least owes you an explanation. If she has simply neglected to live up to her end of the deal, she owes you the cash, as agreed upon—and you can tell her I said so, parent to parent.

Parents, when you make a bargain with your children regarding money, don't feel that you can back out just because your kid is a kid. Children deserve consideration and respect—especially when both of you have put time and thought into working out a sensible financial arrangement.

students don't use it except for local calls. For long distance, the most popular alternatives are cell phones or low-cost prepaid cards, which help keep chatty kids from talking themselves into a financial hole. When Marc C. started dating a girl at another college, he exceeded his quota of long-distance minutes for three months in a row and ran up a $300 bill on his cell phone—which his mother made him pay. After that, he said, "I learned to watch my minutes."

Another alternative: A prepaid cell phone plan, such as those available from Virgin Mobile (http://www.virginmobileusa.com) or TracFone (http://www.tracfone.com). Or consider a toll-free number for your home (compare rates at http://www.billsaver.com/tollfree.html).

ANTICIPATE SURPRISE OUTLAYS. What happens if your son comes home in December and announces that he wants to join a fraternity—at a cost of more than $1,500 in initiation fees and dues, not counting housing and meals? Or your daughter wants to take up an expensive extracurricular activity such as sailing or horseback riding? If expenses like these don't fit into your college budget or if you'd prefer they come out of your child's pocket, better say so early on in the semester before your student makes plans on the assumption that you're willing to pay.

Leaving the car at home can also save a bundle. Jessica S. paid $47 per semester for a parking permit, but it didn't guarantee a parking space—only the right to look for one. As a result, she racked up quite a few tickets at $20 apiece. What's more, it cost her parents about $2,000 a year to insure her car. On the other hand, if you send your child to a college more than 150 miles from home and persuade him or her to leave the car behind, your insurance premium will actually fall.

KNOW YOUR CHILD. Every child is different, and some will be able to take on more financial responsibility than others. I recommend erring on the side of caution so that you and your student are safe rather than sorry. Not every college student is a free-spender, however. Plenty of them are like the young woman who managed to live through a year of school in New York City on her summer savings, with a few hundred dollars to spare. "She's very frugal," explained her proud dad. "But then, she has frugal parents."

Insurance and Other Expenses

Your child's college will probably offer you health insurance for your student, but it's likely that you can avoid that expense if you already have family coverage. Most insurance plans cover adult children if they are full-time students, sometimes up to age 25. However, if your child is attending school out of town, he or she may have to get authorization before seeking medical care. Verify all the terms of your policy before your child signs up for coverage at school.

Also, the personal property coverage on your homeowners insurance will probably protect your child's possessions up to a certain amount as long as he or she lives in a dorm (again, confirm this with your agent). But a student who moves off campus may need to buy relatively inexpensive renter's insurance.

And go easy on outfitting a dorm room until you know how much space you're dealing with. If you feel your child must have a minirefrigerator or a microwave, it's probably cheaper to buy one than to rent one. But if your child's roommate is already bringing a fridge, there may not be room for two (or more, if your student is in a triple). It pays to confer with roommates in advance.

College Credit

Nellie Mae, the company that provides federal and private education loans for students, also conducts a regular study of college students and credit cards. Here are some results from its most recent survey:

- Of undergraduate students, 83 percent had at least one credit card. About 54 percent of freshmen carried a credit card, and that jumped to 92 percent in sophomore year.
- The average credit card balance was $2,327.
- Of undergraduates who have cards, 21 percent had balances between $3,000 and $7,000.
- Graduating students had an average of $20,402 in combined education loan and credit card balances.

To get a card, all college students usually have to do is prove that they're registered at a four-year school and don't have a bad credit history. If they have no credit history, which is highly likely, it won't necessarily count against them. Some cards stipulate that students have minimal income, but that requirement can generally be satisfied if the kids have a savings account, participate in a work-study program, or get an allowance from home.

Whatever possesses card issuers to extend credit to such potentially bad risks? For one thing, they get a golden opportunity to attract new customers who will stay on with them as adults. For another, they count on Mom and Dad's willingness to bail out their kids if they get in over their heads. "If a card issuer threatens to cause problems for a child, parents will sell the farm to come up with the money to pay off the bill," one college official told me.

But parents can't always ride to the rescue. Take the case of Ken W. When he was a college student in California and working as a part-time waiter, Ken ap-

DEAR JANET

Q. I'm a CPA, and when I sent my daughter off to college I thought I had explained everything she needed to know about her new checking account, which came with temporary checks. A couple of weeks (and a number of withdrawals) later, she called to tell me she had received her permanent checks. "Now do I start over with my original balance?" she wanted to know. Go figure.

A. Children aren't born knowing how to balance a checkbook or master any other financial skill; they have to be taught. Your experience just goes to show that parents should never assume any lesson is too basic.

plied for, and got, ten credit cards. You name it, Ken used his cards to buy it—and usually made only the minimum monthly payment. Then he started using one card to pay off another. "It became so easy that I kind of lost the idea of the true value of a dollar," said Ken. "I was just in my own little world."

When his debts hit $20,000 and he began to miss payments, he applied for a debt-consolidation loan from one of his card issuers but was turned down. Then he was laid off, and his house of cards collapsed. Faced with the prospect of coming up with more than $600 a month for three years just to pay off the principal, Ken filed for bankruptcy at the age of 23. That's hardly an easy way out, because a bankruptcy stays on your credit record for ten years and can affect your ability to get a job or to buy a car or a house. If he had it to do over, Ken would have stopped with two cards and never would have charged anything he couldn't pay off within two months. "People don't understand that 19 percent interest adds up really quick," he said.

Keeping Kids Clean

A number of colleges run programs for seniors or recent graduates in which they deal with the first year of transition from college to the real world. These programs are primarily career related, but credit overdose ranks high on the list of problems with which students and grads need help. One college administrator has said that use of credit cards is more of a problem on campus than sex and drugs. James A. Roberts, associate professor of marketing at Baylor University, has done extensive research on credit card use among adolescents. His conclusions back up my own gut feelings and anecdotal observations: Young people who use credit cards "are less price sensitive, spend more, and overestimate their available wealth compared to those who write checks or pay cash."

For all those reasons, I'm convinced that the best credit card deal for college students is none at all. Think of it: no interest rate, no annual fee, no late charges, no temptation to buy things you can't afford. I can't tell you how many times I've met 20-somethings who are laboring to pay off balances they ran up years before on dates with old boyfriends or girlfriends who are long since history. These young people tell me they wish they had never gotten a credit card in college. No one has ever told me they regretted *not* getting a card.

Ironically, sometimes it's easier for young people to apply for a major credit card such as MasterCard or Visa while they're students than it is after they graduate (in Chapter 19, I'll tell you how to get a card if you decide to wait). As I've said before, if students want the convenience of a credit card once they're out in the world—and the opportunity to build a credit history—they can always apply during senior year, once they've had several years to sharpen their money management skills (for a listing of banks that issue credit cards for students, go to http://www.cardweb.com or http://www.cardratings.org). And they also need a few lessons from you in smart ways to handle credit when they get it.

- **Pay attention to critical numbers:** the annual fee (look for a card that doesn't charge any); the interest rate (compare cards at their full rate rather than at "teaser," or introductory, rates that may not last long); the grace period (the amount of time you have to pay off the bill before interest is charged); and late payment or over-limit fees, which can be substantial.
- **Keep all receipts** and check off each purchase when the bill comes. One study by the Chubb Group of Insurance Companies showed that only 41 percent of college students regularly reconcile their credit card receipts with their monthly statements.
- **Don't charge anything you can't pay for in full when you get the bill,** except in emergencies, when you might allow yourself three months to repay.
- **Don't get into the habit of making only the minimum payment** each month.

- **Don't charge to the max.** Some cardholders assume that if an issuer gives them a limit of $1,000, they must be capable of repaying it. What counts is your cash flow, not the bank's high opinion of you.
- **Maintain a good credit history** by limiting the number of credit cards you have to one or two initially, keeping balances to less than half of your credit limit, and always making payments on time. In addition to lenders, prospective employers and landlords consult credit reports, and a record of delinquent payments can be read as irresponsible behavior—and cost you a job or the house you want to buy.

No Bailouts

If your kids do get into trouble, don't bail them out. Instead, give them an opportunity to dig themselves out of debt. To pay off several thousand dollars in credit card balances, one young woman took out a "consolidation loan" from her parents. They charged her 5 percent interest, compared with the 18 percent-plus she was paying to her card issuers. One dad simply pulled his son out of college and made him work off his debt before he could go back.

And don't cosign for your child's credit card (or any other kind of credit). If he or she doesn't live up to the terms of the agreement, not only can you be held responsible for the debt, but your credit rating will suffer from his or her bad behavior.

For a lecture on credit that doesn't come from Mom and Dad, your kids can listen to "Smart Credit Strategies for College Students," an audiotape available at http://www.goodadvicepress.com (800-255-0899).

If, despite my words of warning, you'd like your kids to have a credit card but you're not sure how they'd handle one, at least consider a "secured" card. To get one, your child will be required to open a savings account and deposit an amount that's equal to his or her credit line. As one example, Young Americans Bank in Denver (303-321-2265; http://www.theyoungamericans .org) issues a MasterCard with an annual fee of $15 and an annual percentage rate of 15 percent. The initial credit limit is $100, which can rise to $200 after six months. If kids secure the card by putting money in a savings account, the credit limit can go as high as the account balance. You'll find a listing of other banks that issue secured credit cards at http://www.cardweb.com or http://www.cardratings.org.

Secured cards have a couple of benefits. They guarantee that money will be available to bail out your child if necessary; and they emphasize the point that credit doesn't come without a cost.

Over the Limit

Even though I'm a big fan of debit cards attached to checking accounts as one of the best money management tools for college students, they're not without

---

DEAR JANET

Q. You once mentioned that your daughter attends McGill University in Montreal. I am considering applying to school in Canada and was wondering what financial issues I should consider.

A. Moneywise, Canadian colleges are generally a good deal for Americans. U.S. students at McGill pay considerably more than Quebec residents, but we figure costs for our daughter are roughly equivalent to what she'd pay as an in-state student at the University of Maryland.

Still, Canada *is* a foreign country, and we've encountered our share of financial challenges. For example, checks sent from home can take weeks to clear. So we opened a Canadian bank account for Claire and wired enough money to cover a semester's worth of costs, including tuition, which Claire pays herself. It's convenient—but it's a lot of responsibility for a student.

American students can use U.S. Stafford loans at Canadian schools, but we've found that McGill takes longer to process the paperwork than does our son's U.S. college.

When Claire moved off campus and wanted a cell phone, we couldn't find any plan that would work in both the United States and Canada for less than $80 a month. Like it or not, she got a landline that costs less than half as much, with bargain long distance as part of a package that includes cable and Internet service (she can also get discount long-distance minutes through OneSuite.com, a dial-around service that operates in the United States and Canada).

You can get more information about attending school in Canada from the Association of Universities and Colleges of Canada (http://www.aucc.ca) and the Canadian Embassy (http://www.canadianembassy.org/education).

problems of their own. Take this question I received from a reader: "My son in college lost track of his checking account balance (surprise!) and made three small purchases at local stores with his debit card when he didn't have any money in the account. All the purchases were honored, but his bank hit him with three overdraft charges of $30 each. Interestingly, when he tried to withdraw cash from an ATM, the machine rejected the withdrawals because of insufficient funds. Why didn't he get the same response when he used the card at a store?"

A cynic might suspect that this is one way for banks to collect fees from unsuspecting college students, but banks say they're actually doing customers a favor. As a convenience, bank check cards come with an automatic overlimit allowance that okays purchases even if you overdraw your account, up to a certain amount.

In this case, the bank in question said it allows purchasers to go as deep as $500 into the red. It isn't likely that a college student would rate an allowance that generous, but a caramel Frappuccino at Starbucks or a bottle of shampoo at the drugstore would be covered.

In return for sparing you the embarrassment and inconvenience of having the card rejected at the checkout counter, the bank extracts its pound of flesh in the form of a standard bounced-check charge; $30 is typical. The bank's overdraft allowance does not apply to ATM withdrawals, which is why this student's attempt to get cash was rejected.

If this should happen to your student, appeal the charges to the manager of your bank branch. "We may be able to be flexible, depending on the circumstances and your relationship with the bank," said a spokesperson. If fees aren't waived completely, they could be reduced.

If you can't convince your child to keep a closer eye on his or her bank balance, you have a couple of options to head off future penalties:

- Set up traditional overdraft protection, so money will be automatically transferred to your child's checking account any time he makes a charge for more than his balance. He'll pay a fee for the transfer, but it will be a lot less than $30.
- Ask the bank not to authorize point-of-sale overdrafts, so the card will be turned down if the account is empty. Your child's pride may be bruised at the checkout, but at least his pocketbook won't suffer any further damage.

Defusing Bombshells

The stickiest—and most costly—money conflicts you and your college student face could come as an unexpected bombshell. "We just found out our daughter is failing a course that she needs for her major, which means she'll have to take it again—costing us an extra $1,000," one of my friends once told me. What's more, said my indignant friend, her daughter would have to keep taking the class until she got at least a C. Who should pay for this expense, my friend wanted to know.

In this case, I told the parents that making their daughter foot the bill wouldn't guarantee that she'd make the grade. If she was doing poorly in other subjects as well, she might be in over her head. If that were the case, there would be no point in throwing good money after bad, no matter whose money it was. They should consider having her withdraw for a semester, or transfer to a junior college, until she was better able to handle the challenge.

But if their daughter was otherwise doing well and seemed to be struggling with just one course, there was no need to turn up the pressure even more by making her pay the whole bill (although they could make it clear that a voluntary contribution would be appreciated, even if it was turned down). I suggested they even try to cut future losses by paying for a tutor to help get their daughter through the class on the next go-round. If she failed again, it could be time to switch majors.

Some time after our meeting, my friend told me the rest of the story. When they got their daughter's first-semester grades, they found that she was, in fact, doing poorly in several courses and was on academic probation. "We were so shocked and upset when the letter arrived that we walked out of the room and told her we would need time to recover before we could even talk about it. When we finally did discuss things a couple of days later, it was our daughter who was upset. She said she had thought the money was the big issue, and it had never occurred to her that we would be disappointed in her.

"We told her we'd be willing to pay the $1,000 for retaking the course if she got her grade point average up to 3.0. She did even better than that, and she's considering changing her major so she may not have to make up the failed course."

In this case, although the failed course was the immediate financial crisis, there's a deeper moral: You can't depend on money to control your child's behavior as either a reward or a punishment. Timeout, grounding, loss of privileges, and financial penalties all have their place. But when you get right down to it, parents really have very little leverage over children of any age except the kids' desire to meet your high standards and not risk disappointing you. If kids have a healthy fear of letting you down, you'll still have influence over them when they're teenagers—and beyond.

A CREDIT CHECKUP

To impress on your kids that both good and bad credit habits are an open book, get your own credit report and examine it with your children. To request a copy, contact:

- **Equifax** (http://www.equifax.com), P.O. Box 740256, Atlanta, GA 30374; 800-685-1111.
- **Experian** (http://www.experian.com), P.O. Box 9563, Allen, TX 75013; 888-397-3742.
- **TransUnion** (http://www.transunion.com), P.O. Box 2000, Chester, PA 19022; 800-888-4213.

Giving and Getting with Grace and Gratitude

Money and gifts (and gifts of money) can make for some pretty tricky social situations, requiring the perfect balance of tact and common sense. Even if you get a grip on your own gift-giving impulses, what do you do about everyone else's? The dilemma begins at birth, as doting grandparents bring material offerings. It's aggravated throughout childhood by extravagant birthday celebrations. And it's altogether complicated in divorce situations. But take heart; in the following two chapters you'll find some commonsensical—and diplomatic—solutions.

Holiday Overload

Many parents feel overwhelmed by demands— from both kids and advertisers—during the holiday season. If you identify with that, consider that it's possible to cut back on holiday overload without your kids' even being aware of it.

You could, for example, give them as gifts what you would have bought anyway: a new backpack for school, ice-skating lessons, a family outing to the circus. Wrap everything in sight on the theory that to a kid, all gift-wrapped boxes are treasures. The boxes don't have to be physically large, and the gifts inside don't have to be expensive. But opening them prolongs the kids' pleasure without increasing your expense. When my children were younger, I even wrapped each Golden Book individually, although the kids eventually caught on to that gambit. In one family, parents who were planning a winter trip to

Walt Disney World stuffed the tickets into their kids' Christmas stockings along with guidebooks and other Disney paraphernalia. Planning the trip kept the kids happily occupied long after the postholiday blahs might ordinarily have set in.

If you're faced with an overabundance of gifts from generous relatives—especially for very young children, who quickly grow bored or enjoy the packaging more than the present—quietly put away some of the gifts to be opened on rainy days later in the year. Or set up a college savings fund with a bank or mutual fund and ask family members to contribute in lieu of buying presents.

If you want to make a clean break with commercial holidays past, take the money you would have spent on presents and spend it instead on a family getaway or some other nontraditional gift. Author and family counselor Eda LeShan recalls that when her daughter was about 8 years old, the child was part of a family conspiracy to surprise her grandparents by flying Aunt Lilly, one of their oldest friends, from California to New York for a visit. When Aunt Lilly,

---

WHAT DO KIDS WANT?

Think all children have holiday wish lists as long as your arm? Think again. When It's My Life, a Web site for children at http://www.pbskids.com, asked users, "What do you really want for the holidays this year?" these were some of the responses:

- "For the holidays, I would like my parents to stop fighting."
- "I want to see Santa for REAL."
- "I'd like our family to finally be on top of our money problems."
- "I want a boyfriend."
- "I want to give my mom the best gift ever because I love her a whole lot."

- "I want a nice family dinner."
- "I would like lots of video games, radio-controlled cars, money, movies, toys, and skateboards."
- "I want a few things, but I'm pretty happy with what I have."
- "This Christmas I would like a frog habitat. You can find them at Target."
- "For material things, I want a Walkman, a phone, a fuzzy sweater, and some Happy Bunny stuff. For real things, I really want to be accepted to the drama club at school. And I really, really, really want my mom's family to come for Christmas."

wrapped in tissue paper and a bow, appeared on the stairs, "it was a Christmas that all of us will remember more than any other," said LeShan.

One of the best gifts you can give your kids is time—presenting them with a certificate entitling them to an afternoon or evening of your undivided attention for an activity of their choosing.

In the end, the real test of a successful holiday isn't the number of gifts you buy or how much they cost, but how well suited they are to your children and how well they wear. It's only natural for kids to play with the glamour gifts first. But if, on December 26, they ask you to try the new board game, and on February 13 they build the model rocket, and on July 23 they start the third book in the complete *Anne of Green Gables* series, then you'll know you didn't go overboard. Once, when the power went out at our house during a hurricane, my son pulled out the game Stratego—a gift of several Christmases past—to play by candlelight with his teenage friends. For a mom, that's job satisfaction.

DEAR JANET

Q. After my daughter handed me a 14-item Christmas wish list, I asked her to add up all the prices and see how much it was going to cost me. Seven items—and a total of $159.95 later—she decided to stop and restart her selection in preference order. This exercise helped her practice her math by adding currency. It also helped her to set realistic expectations about holiday wishing in terms of U.S. dollars.

A. Let's see. If seven items cost roughly $160, then each item on your daughter's list cost an average of about $23. At that rate, the whole list would have set you back $320. That's not exactly peanuts, but things could have been a lot worse. You're fortunate in having a daughter who didn't go overboard in the first place and became even thriftier as a result of your exercise.

In Praise of Wish Lists

Even though wish lists often strike terror in the hearts of parents, I think they're a useful tool that can help the holidays run more smoothly. Here's why:

Lists are an outlet for some of the holiday "buy-me-that" pressure. Sometimes, just writing down all the things they'd like to have is satisfaction enough for kids. A toy that a child really, really wants in October may be totally forgotten by December. It's been my experience that children frequently make—and misplace—a number of different lists before settling

DEAR JANET

Q. What do you think about a holiday gift registry for kids? Stores say it's a convenience for parents and relatives who aren't sure what to buy.

A. I'm all for making a parent's life easier but not at the cost of removing whatever magic is left in the holiday season. It's one thing for a child to make a wish list and wait in agonizing anticipation to see what will materialize. It's quite another to put in your order and wait for Grandma to pony up. Besides, parents shouldn't need a gift registry to tell them what their children want. They can go straight to the source and ask the kids—and pass along the word to Aunt Martha.

on the one that goes to Santa. Older kids will be more discriminating, but they'll still push the envelope in hopes of stuffing it with as much as they can. They'll expect you to say no, so don't disappoint them. If they don't get what they want, they're not going to pack up and leave home.

Lists give you an opportunity to teach your kids how to set priorities. Take those lengthy lists your children have been compiling and have them rank their top ten items. (Tell them that the shorter the list, the more likely that Santa will remember what's on it.) Holiday catalogs can be a big help with older kids, who can appreciate how much everything costs. Ask the children what they'd keep on their list if they had, say, $200 to spend.

Lists are an organizing tool for your own holiday shopping. After all, you and other family members are going to be buying gifts for the kiddies anyway. You'll be less frantic and more focused, and get your shopping done more quickly, if you know what you're looking for.

One of the best bits of modern wisdom I ever heard on this point came from a great shopping mall Santa who didn't bat an eyelash when one youngster handed him a list of 28 toys. Santa patiently reviewed the items and told the child he'd plug it into his computer to see what came up as available. What he actually brought, said Santa, would depend on how much room he had in his sleigh.

At some point, of course, it's up to you to set a limit on how much stuff you buy. Here are some guidelines on when to call a halt:

- **You're embarrassed to tell your friends** how many presents you bought for your children.
- **You can't find enough hiding places** for all the gifts.
- **You can't remember what you hid.**
- **Your children resemble sharks on a feeding frenzy** when they open their gifts.
- **Your children get bored and wander away** in the middle of opening presents.

It's tough to put a number on just what that point is because every family has its own gift-giving tradition. Three gifts may be two too many for a toddler who can't appreciate them or for an older child who's getting an expensive new computer. But three gifts is probably too few if you like to surprise your family with inexpensive stocking stuffers. You could start with a nice round ten presents—three big ones and seven smaller gifts—and adjust that number up or down depending on how much you want to spend.

To parcel out gifts among their eight children, one family I know limits their children's wish lists to three presents each. Mom and Dad fill in with inexpensive but popular goodies the kids don't usually get, such as sweet cereal and snacks (every once in a while they slip in something practical, like a new toothbrush). Note: On average, U.S. families spend a little over $240 per child on toys, according to annual figures compiled by the International Council of Toy Industries.

What Role Does Santa Play?

Children find such pleasure in Santa Claus that they're happy to engage in what the poet Samuel Taylor Coleridge called "the willing suspension of disbelief." That gives you lots of room to maneuver when your kids cite Santa as the ultimate authority on gift-giving:

- **"If you won't buy it for me, I'll ask Santa for it."** Tell them that you and Santa are a team. He's not about to go against a parent's wishes—and jeopardize his job—by bringing a child a gift that is too dangerous, too expensive, or otherwise not in the cards.
- **"It can't be sold out; Santa's elves make it."** Santa is subject to the same supply glitches as everyone else. If a toy is a blockbuster hit, even the elves can't always keep up with demand. Sometimes Santa has to supplement the elves' output by going to toy companies (they're more than willing to help out because of all the great publicity), so when they're sold out, Santa is too.
- **"Why can't I put just one more thing on my list?"** Santa has to read so many lists that you're doing him a favor by keeping it short—and there's a better chance he'll remember what you asked for.

Don't back yourself into a corner by telling your children, "We can't get it for you, but maybe Santa will." If Santa is that generous, the kids will think that no request is too outlandish.

And some remarks strain even a child's credulity, as in, "If you don't behave, you'll get coal in your stocking." I suspect that there are precious few kids, no matter how mischievous, who actually suffer this dire fate. And no kid, no matter how mischievous, deserves it. A good friend of mine recalls vividly that when she was about 9 years old her parents put a small lump of coal (along with lots of real gifts) in her stocking as a joke. My friend failed to

---

DEAR JANET

Q. Our kids are great believers in Santa, but every year their questions get tougher. I don't have any trouble explaining how reindeer can fly (everyone knows it's magic). But what do I say when they ask why Santa doesn't bring as many presents to poor people as he does to them?

A. Tell them the truth—that you supplement Santa's largess with gifts of your own, something that poor parents can't always afford to do. Turn their concern into a positive by getting them to help you choose a toy to donate to a holiday collection drive.

see the humor and wondered what her parents were really trying to tell her. More than two decades later, her mom acknowledged that it wasn't a very nice thing to do, and the incident has taken its place in the family's Christmas lore.

The best way to avoid holiday disappointment is to be as honest with your children as possible, as early as possible. If there's a gift your children will never see under the tree, either because it's too expensive, too hard to find, or too extreme for your family's values, tell your kids. To track down something on my children's most-wanted list, I have shopped early, trekked from store to store (though I draw the line at three or four), and pored over catalogs. But I have never risen at dawn, stood in line, or paid an inflated price. When disappointment loomed, I tried to cushion the blow by warning them in advance and looking for other creative gifts to fill the gap. They always managed to shrug it off and move on.

Plausible answers forthrightly given will keep Santa alive in your household. By the time your children are no longer willing to suspend their disbelief, they'll be old enough to grow quietly out of the Santa myth. But for their sake, and yours, don't rush them into reality.

Should Kids Use Their Own Money?

When I was young, with no income of my own, my mother always gave me money to buy Christmas gifts for her and my father—along with hints on what to buy. One year she wanted a jewelry case, so I went out and bought her a zippered fabric pouch. As soon as she opened it I knew that I had goofed. What she really wanted was a box with compartments—which made me feel doubly bad because I had disappointed her with her money, not mine.

That childhood incident made such an impression on me that I always recommend that children use their own money to buy holiday gifts. Ideally, they have been saving for that purpose, or they at least have a general savings pot that they can dip into.

DEAR JANET

Q. My 13-year-old daughter hangs around with a group of about a dozen girls, and her popularity is hard on our pocketbook. It seems like we're always buying a birthday gift for someone, and CDs for 12 kids start to add up. With the holidays coming up, she'll want to buy a present for everyone. Am I the only one who thinks this has gotten out of hand?

A. I think that if this is the worst problem you have with your 13-year-old daughter, you're a lucky parent.

The holidays may be the most expensive time of year giftwise, but they also present the cheapest solution. Instead of buying presents for everyone, your daughter and her friends could each pick a name and play "secret Santa" for that person, giving small tokens and doing favors as the recipient tries to guess who her benefactor is. It's less expensive—and more fun—than buying everyone gifts.

There's no getting around birthdays, however. In a group like this, if you buy for one member you have to buy for them all. You could set a price limit per gift—but why are you doing the buying in the first place? At 13, your daughter is old enough to take on this responsibility and use her own money. If she's in charge, she'll be inclined to be less extravagant and more creative, and outlays will tend to regulate themselves.

If they're short on cash, give them an opportunity to do extra jobs around the house to earn more.

If your kids have been diligent about doing chores and schoolwork throughout the year, you could justify a holiday bonus to supplement their income. After all, even adults get bonuses for a job well done.

At our house, I have always given my children a monthly allowance, computed weekly based on a 4-week month, or 48 weeks throughout the year. That left us with 4 weeks unaccounted for, which the kids chose to take as a bonus month in December. They didn't mind forgoing the cash during the year in return for having forced savings when they needed it.

If your children are old enough to handle the money, you could increase their allowance year-round and turn over the responsibility for buying all gifts for birthdays and holidays. That way they'd have the wherewithal; they'd just have to be smarter about managing it.

If they're not old enough to take over all gift-buying responsibilities, you could spot them, say, $5 per holiday gift; anything above that they'd have to cover themselves. When one mom tried this tactic, her daughter was suddenly overcome with economy. "You'd be surprised at what you can buy for $6.19," said her mother.

Even under the best of circumstances, children probably won't have a lot of money to spend on gifts, so keep the task manageable. Give them advice along with (or instead of) cash:

- **Make a list.** What's good for Santa is even better for kids. Writing things down helps them get organized ahead of time, keep focused once they get to the store, and stay within their budget. Younger children in particular should buy gifts for just a couple of family members, such as parents or grandparents, rather than for every aunt, uncle, and cousin.
- **Check it twice.** Take the kids on a preshopping trip without cash in hand. Children tend to spend everything they have on the first thing they see. Scouting the stores in advance helps them find things they like and can afford, as well as learn how to tell the difference between something that's a bargain and something that's merely cheap.
- **Don't throw your catalogs away.** They're a great tool not only for helping your children find gift ideas but also for giving them a sense of how much things cost.
- **Remind children that gifts don't have to be store-bought.** Handmade crafts or thoughtful gestures can be even more memorable (hint to my kids: I'd love it if one of you would volunteer to put all of our family photos in order).
- **Next year, start a holiday club.** If the children begin putting aside gift money around Labor Day, they should have a tidy little fund to help them buy presents in December.

If children are still short on cash, they could chip in with siblings to buy a joint gift. Or choose one family member for whom they can play "secret Santa" with several small surprises. One more thing: No matter what your kids come up with, whether it's a zippered fabric jewel case or a tacky plastic trophy that says "Number-One Parent," never let them see that you are disappointed.

Emphasize the Meaning

One of the most sensitive gift-giving situations involves religious celebrations, such as first communions, confirmations, and bar/bat mitzvahs. "I'm afraid my daughter will get so carried away by the money she receives that she'll forget the religious significance of the occasion," one parent wrote to me.

When I put this concern to parents of different faiths whose children had celebrated religious milestones, they came up with a number of suggestions. The most extreme was simply to ask family members not to give any financial gifts. Another idea was for parents and children to agree to contribute any money to charity, perhaps using it to buy food baskets for poor families in their community. Still others thought it was fine for children to keep the money but recommended that they save most of it or put it in their college fund instead of spending it.

If you anticipate that everyone else in the family will be giving financial gifts, you should give one that has religious significance, such as a prayer book or Bible. Children take their cues from their parents. So long as you don't lose sight of the real meaning of the occasion, neither will they.

Get Birthdays under Control

When it comes to birthday parties, parents have been known to get more carried away than have their children, turning what should be fun into an exercise in one-upmanship. "First clowns, then ponies, and now my son has been invited to a party with a merry-go-round on the lawn," one father complained to me. "You feel obliged to buy expensive gifts, which the birthday child gets too many of. My kids are even starting to compare the size of the goody bags they bring home. Am I just a voice in the wilderness?"

Well, Dad, I'll join you to make a chorus of at least two. When things like goody bags get out of hand, parents have only themselves to blame. Perhaps what we need is a group called Birthdays Anonymous to support parents who want to withdraw from the party circuit. Some parents have made the break, and here's their advice on how to kick the habit:

■ **Don't get hooked in the first place.** You can solve lots of birthday problems (including too many gifts) by inviting fewer children. Young kids don't need a big blowout; asking the neighbor kids to drop by for cake and ice cream is excitement aplenty for both you and your child. One old rule of thumb is to invite a number of children equal to your child's age, with perhaps one more to grow on. My son was appalled to read a newspaper story about a birthday party to which 29 children had been invited—each of whom arrived bearing a gift. "If they don't want to get all those presents, they shouldn't invite 29 people," said Peter. "And who could have 29 friends anyway?" A variation on this is to have a big blowout every other year instead of annually, or perhaps for certain "milestone" birthdays—6, 10, and 13, for example. In the off years, you can invite Grandma, Aunt Sis, and all the cousins for cake and ice cream.

■ **Be creative.** If you must do something out of the ordinary, do it on the cheap. Take a group of kids fishing at a local pond; to a field for a pickup game of soccer or baseball; to a playground or a children's museum. Pack a picnic lunch.

■ **Be radical.** If you must have a crowd and don't want your children inundated with gifts, set a price limit of, say, $5 or $10 per gift. Or donate the presents to a local children's shelter. Another option: Ask guests not to bring any presents. "We did that once and our friends told us it was seditious," laughs one father. "But we told them their children's company was the best present they could give."

In most situations, of course, your kids wouldn't show up at a party empty-handed. But there's no need to go overboard, either. I think $10 to $20 is plenty to spend on a gift (according to the Toy Industry Association, the average retail price of a traditional toy is under $10). If the child in question is someone special—a best friend, a relative, or a godchild, for example—add $5 to those benchmarks. For older children or out-of-towners, gifts of money are appropriate (cash is better than a check as long as you're not sending a large amount).

A Good Time Was Had by All

Looking back on nearly two decades of planning birthday fun and games for my own children, I can say that I never hired a clown or a caterer. I never rented a limo to transport the guests to offsite entertainment. Our backyard never played host to pony rides, a merry-go-round, a moon bounce, or anything else that cost money to rent.

Yet judging by the reaction of my kids and their friends, I'd have to say (with some satisfaction) that my career as a party planner was a success. We started off with three rules: (1) no formal parties before the age of 5; (2) no more than 12 guests; and (3) until the kids hit middle school, no parties anywhere but home.

One year we set up an obstacle course in our yard. Another time we had a scavenger hunt. For my daughter's October birthday, we decorated pumpkins and played pin-the-nose-on-the-witch. I never baked a cake in any shape other than a circle or a rectangle, but once I used my meager creative and culinary skills to make spiders out of marshmallow Rice Krispies, with chow mein noodles for legs.

For goody bags, we used brown paper lunch sacks, filled and decorated (with stickers and markers) by my kids. (They loved doing it, and it was one less thing for me to worry about on party day.) My rule was to buy a couple of bags of a favorite candy and then head for the dollar store to buy multipacks of things like erasers or handheld games (the old-fashioned manual kind with pegs).

As the kids got older, sleepovers with pizza became a staple. When they outgrew party games, we headed for the movies, the bowling alley, and miniature golf. Probably our most expensive celebrations were taking my daughter and five friends to a play at the Kennedy Center in Washington, D.C., and taking my younger son and his crew to play laser tag.

All told, counting food and entertainment, we never spent more than about $150 on the whole shindig and usually much less. Even though that's not cheap, it wasn't extravagant—and it's proof that you can give kids a good time without breaking the bank.

Birthdays on Holidays

When a child's birthday coincides with a holiday, you have two options: You can play it up, or you can play it down.

For example, you can play up the Christmas connection by making a tradition of celebrating with a party that has a seasonal theme—going ice-skating or taking in a holiday movie or local performance of *The Nutcracker,* for example.

If you're too frazzled at that time of year or worried about gift overload from party guests and Santa, play down the occasion by holding the party a month

---

DEAR JANET

Q. A friend of mine bought my daughter a very expensive birthday gift. I don't like the idea of expensive presents, and my daughter was too young to appreciate it anyway. Now my friend's son has a birthday coming up, and I don't know what to do. Do I have to give him something of equal value, even though it's way over my usual limit of $20 per gift?

A. Stick to your limit. Your $20 budget is reasonable, so don't feel pressured to spend more. There's also a lesson here for your friend: Receiving an expensive gift doesn't necessarily make kids feel more grateful, and their parents may feel downright awkward if they can't afford to reciprocate or don't want to. Rather than spending a lot of money on a present, it's always better to buy something less expensive but more suitable to a child's interests.

TALES OF THE TOOTH FAIRY

Parents often ask me about the going rate for a tooth nowadays. Well, your kids can reasonably expect to get more than you did when you were a child. Depending on the rate of inflation in your household, anywhere from 25¢ to $1 a tooth would be appropriate.

Keep in mind, though, that the tooth fairy is an accommodating sprite who's happy to tailor her gifts to your wishes. Here's a selection of letters from readers who responded to a question I asked about whether the tooth fairy still makes nocturnal visits and how much she leaves behind:

■ **The tooth fairy at our house pays $1 a tooth.** Our 8-year-old tries to get the rest of his baby teeth to come out so he can collect!

■ **We pay $1 for each tooth**—as long as there are no cavities!

■ **The tooth fairy brings $5 a tooth** at our house. This seems to be more than she brings my son's friends.

■ **In our house the kids get $1 per tooth if it comes out during the week.** They'll get $2 per tooth if it comes out on the weekend. Both sets of grandparents "find" what the tooth fairy left at their house. So after all is said and done, if a tooth is lost on the weekend the child can reap up to $6 per tooth. Of course, all the money is deposited in their savings accounts and later transferred to their mutual funds for college.

■ **We just went through this for the first time.** We put the tooth into a box that goes under the pillow. Conveniently, when the tooth is removed the box holds four quarters. My son, to guarantee a return on his investment, suggested that the tooth fairy could place the money right in the box.

■ **One dollar per tooth is much more than I got as a child.** I should have saved all those teeth and converted them now instead of when I was young.

■ **No reply necessary:** What does the tooth fairy do with all those teeth?

■ **In Oakland, California, during the 1920s, there wasn't a tooth fairy.** During the 1940s, the going rate was 25¢. Now my great-grandson informed his mother that the going rate is $1. His mother's reply: "No way."

■ **The tooth fairy has visited my daughter, Elizabeth, for many years and always leaves her a very interesting coin.** She receives a coin with a picture of Queen Elizabeth on it. The value of the coin is not important to her, but the idea of a coin with her name on it makes her feel special. My husband and I collected the coins years ago while in England and never realized how special they would become.

■ **At our house the tooth fairy brings $1 per tooth, and the money goes into the kids' savings accounts.** My oldest daughter had to have nine teeth pulled within a few weeks for braces, so she got $10. P.S. It's harder to get the tooth fairy into the bedroom these days.

■ **Before my 6-year-old daughter lost her first tooth, I cross-stitched a** little "tooth fairy" pillow with a pocket on it, which is her special place for each lost tooth. She made a special request to the tooth fairy via letter to please leave her tooth behind because her daddy wanted to save it. Here is how the money added up on the last tooth:

First, my daughter charged her father $1 for each time he tried to pull it out. It took three tries, for $3. Then the tooth fairy left her $1 for the tooth—which she sold to Daddy for $1. Daddy owed her $4 (counting the three tries), but he didn't have change for a $5 bill and she got to keep the extra $1. So her last lost tooth cost the tooth fairy a total of $6.

The tooth fairy also leaves a little surprise such as a coloring book. As you can see, in our household the experience of losing a tooth is usually a big deal!

■ **I'm a pediatric dentist, so I collect lots of input from my little patients on what the tooth fairy left them for their lost teeth.** I've heard everything from 10¢ to $20 for the first lost tooth (that's a wealthy tooth fairy). Five dollars a tooth is pretty common, and that surprised me. I'd say the most typical amount is $2 per tooth.

■ **Almost without exception the children still put their teeth under their pillow at night** and still fear the tooth fairy won't come if the tooth got accidentally lost or swallowed. [Note to kids: For the tooth fairy, lost and swallowed teeth are all in a night's work. Just leave a note instead.]

■ **My daughter's bottom teeth were coming in, but her baby teeth had** not fallen out. The dentist was going to charge me $64 to remove the teeth. I told my daughter if she could wiggle the teeth out herself, the tooth fairy would pay her half of what I would have had to pay the dentist. It took her two weeks of wiggling, but the tooth fairy left $30 under her pillow. All the kids at school wanted to use that pillow!

■ **When our son was young, the tooth fairy would leave 50¢ under his pillow and steal the tooth away.** Many teeth later, the tooth fairy forgot to come one night. Our son came to us crying. We said to him, "You don't still believe in the tooth fairy, do you?" "No," he sobbed, "but I believe in money."

■ **Q. When did the tooth fairy first appear?** I always thought it was an American custom, but I have been told it was practiced in Italy in the 1940s.
A. It may have been, but the New York Public Library's reference desk tells me the custom most likely originated with the German tradition of placing a lost tooth into a mouse hole or rat hole.

According to the book *Curious Customs* by Ted Tuleja, people believed that when a new tooth grew in, it would possess the dental qualities of whatever creature found the old one—hence, the critters of choice were rodents, with their world-class pearly whites.

The principle of "fair exchange" was brought by German immigrants to America, where the tooth rat was replaced by the more acceptable fairy—and the desire for hard molars with the expectation of hard cash.

later to liven up the winter doldrums—or even six months later as a "half-birthday."

As for the appropriate number of presents to buy, I pass along this spontaneous exchange of sage advice between a 7-year-old and his 13-year-old brother:

Little brother: "I wish my birthday was on Christmas, so I would get lots more presents."

Big brother: "You wouldn't get any more presents than you do now. If you get 2 birthday presents and 10 Christmas presents now, you'd just get 12 presents if your birthday was on Christmas."

A Word of Thanks

I'm often approached by parents who confess guiltily that (like me, I confess guiltily) they have been lax in making their children send thank-you notes for gifts they have received. I detect in their mea culpas the desperation of harried parents seeking reassurance that with so much else on their plates, it's okay to skip the note, especially when a personal thank-you is only a convenient phone call away.

As an often-harried parent myself, I once would have been inclined to give that reassurance. But over the years I've changed my mind. Every gift deserves a thank-you in some form, and a written note is the most desirable. It's worth nagging your kids to sit down and write one. Their expenditure of time is small compared with the large amounts of money lavished on them. Your objective is to make them feel so guilty that they'll eventually remember to send a note on their own—and will one day nag their own children to write to you. One of my coworkers told me that when she sat down to write thank-you notes with her 4-year-old twins, the girls taught their mom an unexpected lesson. "Shouldn't we write a note to Santa too?" they asked.

Allowing for the fact that you are already stressed out, however, especially at holiday time, I'm willing to risk the ire of manners mavens and suggest a few rules of thank-you etiquette that will get the job done as painlessly as possible for you and your children:

■ **Thank-you notes should never be generic.** They should always include a specific mention of the gift plus a personal note on how the child liked it, or, if it's money, what he or she plans to do with it. But preprinted cards are acceptable. Giving your kids a nudge makes the job easier for them (and, by extension, for you). A tip of the pen to an editor friend of mine who tucks a pack of thank-you notes into the Christmas stocking of each of her kids. For young children, go ahead and address the envelopes.

■ **A computer-generated card is acceptable,** as long as it's personally designed, written, and signed.

■ **E-mail is fine** so long as the children do their own hunting and pecking on the keyboard.

It's probably unrealistic to expect that kids will sit down on Christmas afternoon to pen their thanks for a gift they got that morning. But do try to have them get the job done before they go back to school.

And a note to gift givers: Don't be miffed if the card is a little late. Give children (and their parents) the benefit of the doubt: They're probably not ungrateful; they're just running behind. Playing a game of beat-the-clock takes the joy out of both giving and receiving.

Make the most of the thanks you get. One grandmother framed a note from her grandson and hung it on the dining room wall—a painless yet effective reminder to him that such courtesies are appreciated.

Here's how one mom taught her 3-year-old to express her thanks: "We use construction

---

DEAR JANET

Q. What if your 11-year-old son wants to buy his "special" girl a Valentine's Day present—specifically, a necklace—but doesn't have enough money? Should you help out?

A. Call me old-fashioned, but I don't think an 11-year-old boy should be buying any gift for his "special" girl—certainly not something as expensive as a necklace he can't afford. One-on-one gifts should wait till at least eighth grade, if not high school, and then kids should spend their own money. If that automatically imposes a price limit, so much the better.

Have your son stick to a card, or, if you don't object, a small gift of candy or some other token that's within his budget.

paper and stickers to make thank-you cards. For example, I cut out an ice cream cone and our daughter is responsible for gluing it on to the paper and using stickers with the same theme to decorate it. I write something like, 'Thanks for the gift, it was really sweet!'

"It's corny, I know, but we've been doing this since she was 18 months old. Everyone loves receiving the cards since they are first and foremost a thank you. But they also show her progress in arranging items, coloring, and writing her name—not to mention being refrigerator art for the family."

Lessons in Giving

After the tsunami disaster in 2004, my friend Allison's daughter, Hannah, organized a group of her sixth-grade friends to raise money for the victims. "They talked and planned, then baked and baked," Allison told me. Then they stood outside a local supermarket in the freezing cold to sell their cookies and muffins. Hoping to raise a few hundred dollars, they pulled in a whopping $1,316—and ended up being featured on the evening news.

Because they made such a large sum, the children decided to divide the money among several relief agencies. Each of the kids chose an organization to research and made a pitch to the group. Then they put it to a vote and split the proceeds among the three winners.

Aside from the amount of money they raised, Hannah and her friends were "overwhelmed by the generosity of the supermarket patrons, many of whom gave $20 for a $1 treat," Allison told me. "It was quite an empowering experience for the kids." I would add that it was also a powerful lesson in the very human impulse to lend a hand to people in need.

I'm often asked how to encourage children to be philanthropic. My immediate response: Charity begins at home. Kids will follow your lead. Simple acts

DEAR JANET

Q. In our culture, it is the custom that at the age of 15 a girl gets to go to Europe or to have a huge party thrown in her honor. Our daughter, however, only wants money for clothes. The idea of turning 15 is to create a memory. What do you suggest?

A. This is a tough one. I could make the case that if your daughter regards her 15th birthday simply as an occasion on which to buy new clothes, then the day has lost any meaning it might have had for her as a rite of passage.

That being the case, you might as well save yourself some money and forget the trip to Europe and the huge party. That's an awfully expensive way to create a memory, especially when a new outfit or two will do the trick.

But your daughter's birthday apparently still has significance for you, so I'm reluctant to tell you to forget about tradition entirely. If you still want to take special note of the day, for yourselves as much as for your daughter, plan a celebration that preserves the spirit of the occasion without going overboard on a lavish blowout that your daughter won't appreciate anyway.

Remind your daughter of the significance this birthday has in your culture, and tell her it should be marked by something more than standard birthday gifts. Suggest that she invite a small group of friends to afternoon tea at a hotel, dinner at a nice restaurant, an evening at a concert or a sports event—something of her choosing that she would enjoy more, and therefore remember longer, than an expensive trip.

Here's a really radical idea: Suggest that she spend an afternoon volunteering at a local soup kitchen or some other charity as a sign of the new responsibilities she'll take on as she grows to adulthood.

such as supporting your kids' fundraising ideas or contributing to the collection at church won't go unnoticed by your children (nor will kicking in $20 for a $1 muffin).

To get your children involved, start small and make the experience as hands-on as possible—baking cookies or choosing a toy for a holiday toy drive, for instance. The more tangible the gift, the easier it is for children to appreciate the joy of giving.

One family, for example, required their children to contribute 10 percent of their allowance to a charity of their choice. One year the kids decided to "adopt" a single mother and her four children. "At Christmas, the gift giving was awesome; the kids used more than their allotted charity money to buy things for the family," said their proud dad. "On my son's Christmas card to us, he wrote that this year he had learned it was better to give than to receive."

Fed up with holiday overload, my friend Kathy suggested that her two children, ages 10 and 8, scratch off a toy from their list and use the money to buy gifts for needy children in another country (they used the World Vision catalog at http://www.worldvision.org). Samantha chose playground equipment for an orphanage in Romania, and Michael picked a

---

DEAR JANET

Q. My daughter was recently invited to a sweet-16 party. The girls met on a Saturday afternoon, had a lavish dinner at a hotel where they spent the night, and came home on Sunday afternoon. The host paid for dinner and the hotel, but I didn't realize that the "activity" for the weekend was shopping and going to a day spa for a manicure—which my daughter was expected to pay for.

As my daughter was leaving the house, she asked for money. I ended up giving her $80, but I'm still fuming. Why didn't the hosts tell us about the extra outlay? I don't mind buying a gift, but why should I be expected to pay for my daughter's entertainment?

A. Why, indeed. In my opinion, social niceties demand that whoever issues the invitation should pay for the party—the whole party, including food and entertainment. Guests should be treated at the host's expense, not theirs.

At the very least, the hosts should have told you ahead of time that your daughter would be expected to pay for her own weekend activities—and perhaps asked that she not bring a gift.

But it would have been even better if the hosts had planned a less lavish celebration and covered the cost themselves. Instead of the fancy dinner, they might have treated the guests to lunch and a manicure. Or they might have gone ahead with the dinner but brought the guests home afterward.

I've received other complaints from parents about birthday invitations that come with strings attached. One young woman was invited to a sports complex miles from home, with no offer of a carpool. The host covered admission, but her guests were told to bring money for food. Then there was the young man who was invited to go paintballing and asked to pony up $30 for his own ticket.

You know your child's birthday party has gotten out of hand when you can't afford to pay for it. Scale back the activities. Or organize a trip to the spa or paint-ball course at some time other than your child's birthday. Then you could offer to chauffeur the kids, but it wouldn't be ungracious to ask them to pay their own way.

brood of chickens for a family in Honduras (another charity that's appealing to kids is Heifer International, http://www.heiferproject.org, which provides livestock to needy families worldwide).

Although the impulse to give comes easily during the holiday season or after a natural disaster, don't neglect other opportunities throughout the year. One mother encouraged her 7-year-old daughter, Laura, to use her own money to buy Beanie Babies for the toy closet at the cancer treatment center of a local hospital and to deliver them herself. On one visit, the mother of a young patient came up to Laura and told her how much her daughter enjoyed going to the closet to select a toy. "Laura was a bit stunned and I was in tears," said her mom.

I once met a remarkable 10-year-old named Devon who had figured out a way to combine capitalism and altruism. Helped by her father, she had started her own recycling business, out of which she donated 30 percent of her profits to the humane society. Her parents matched all of her charitable contributions. "Bringing up this special young lady is an awesome responsibility," her dad told me.

Other tips for parents to keep in mind:

■ **Don't just send off a check** to your favorite charity. Talk with your children about what you're doing and why you chose that cause.

■ **Designate a special container for "found" money** that kids pick up under the sofa cushions or fish out of their jeans pockets. When the jar fills up, they can give the money to a charity or cause of their choosing.

■ **Have the kids pack up clothes they've outgrown** or toys they no longer play with. Bring the children with you when you give away the old stuff so that they feel they're part of the process.

■ **Remember that charity involves gifts of time** as well as money. If you have neighbors who are elderly or ill, encourage your children to offer their services to run errands, shovel snow, read, or just sit and talk.

**Turn page for
Kids' Questions→**

KIDS' QUESTIONS

Q. "Can I buy Jenny a new bike for her birthday? She really wants one."
A. To young children who don't yet understand the idea of relative value, one gift costs about as much as another. So they might as well get what their friends want most. Let your children down gently by telling them that a new bicycle is the kind of special present that Jenny's parents might like to buy for her. Then steer your kids toward smaller gifts with lower price tags.

If your children are older, tell them what you think is an appropriate price to pay for a birthday gift—in my opinion, $10 to $20. Kids may want to exceed that in the case of a special friend, but remind them that price isn't the only factor. The friend might be embarrassed by a gift that's too expensive—and the friend's parents might feel obliged to reciprocate, even if they can't afford it.

Older kids who are given the responsibility of buying birthday gifts with their own allowance money catch on quickly. "Instead of just going to the store and randomly selecting something, Luke thought a little more about the person he was buying for," one mother said of her 12-year-old. "In one case he remembered that his classmate was artistic, so he purchased drawing paper, colored pencils, and markers. It was the recipient's favorite gift."

Q. "Can I spend my birthday money?"
A. In general, children should be allowed to keep and spend the money they get as gifts. That's probably what the gift giver would want, along with a report on what the kids bought.

Nothing is less gratifying and more frustrating to a child than money that arrives in the mail and is promptly whisked away by Mom or Dad. But it's understandable if you don't want your 5-year-old dropping $50 at the toy store. So I offer the following guidelines as a compromise:

- Require the children to save a certain amount of their gift money—say, 10 percent, 50 percent, or some other portion that's easy to compute—and let them spend the rest. This works best if the kids are already accustomed to saving a portion of their allowance money or earnings.
- Deposit any gift *checks* in the bank, and let youngsters spend the *cash*. This works best if the kids get a workable combination of checks and currency.
- Set spending rules based on a child's age and the size of the gift. For example, preschoolers might be allowed to spend gifts of up to $20. Anything above that would be saved for another day.

Six- to 12-year-olds would get to spend gifts of up to $50. They have more expensive tastes and a better sense of how much things cost. Teens could have discretion over gifts of up to $100.

Regardless of a child's age, gifts over $100 require some parental input. One dad whose son occasionally gets gifts of $200 from his grandmother requires that his son spend $50 to $100 on something he needs—a new winter jacket, for example. With an amount that large, gift givers might consider consulting with you ahead of time to designate how the money should be spent.

Q. "I lost the $10 Aunt Barbara sent me. Can I do extra chores to make it up?"
A. Children have a responsibility to take care of their own money, so you're under no obligation to let them earn it back by doing extra chores. Nor should you require your kids to put an amount that small in the bank.

It's probably best to let them swallow the loss and count on them to be more careful the next time. Chances are they will be if it's a check that has been misplaced. Eventually Aunt Barbara will notice that the check hasn't been cashed, and the kids will have to 'fess up.

Lost Wallets and Other Sticky Situations

One day when my son Peter was a freshman in high school, he came home in a funk. He had left his wallet—with his school ID, a $20 bill, and several gift cards—on the bus. Over the next week, we called the bus company every day to see if anyone had turned it in. No such luck.

A couple of weeks later, Peter came home from school and announced that "the coolest thing" had happened. "Close your eyes and hold out your hands," he told me. When I did, he plunked down the wallet, with its contents intact. A woman had tracked Peter down through his ID and turned in the wallet to the school office.

"I wish I had met her so I could have given her a reward," Peter told me. He was so impressed that for days he would periodically stop, shake his head, and say in amazement, "I can't believe I got it back."

I don't know what impressed me more—that the wallet had turned up or that Peter was so shocked by its return. He had simply assumed no one would be honest enough to bring it back.

I found this incident particularly striking in light of the financial scandals and ethical breaches in corporate America that have made news in recent years. For all the ink and air time we have expended wondering what those lapses in ethics would mean to shareholders, employees, regulators, and markets, we've neglected to discuss the effect the scandals might have on children. And, believe me, they notice. In a poll of teenagers by Junior Achievement, nearly one-third of the 13- to-18-year-olds questioned agreed that you have to "bend the rules to succeed." That was up from 20 percent in the previous year's survey.

Corporations can be counted on to do whatever it takes to clean up their act. After all, financial markets must preserve the public's trust in order to be successful. When they go astray, public outrage inevitably pushes them back onto the straight and narrow.

As for children, it's up to parents to keep them on the right path. In the Junior Achievement survey, 68 percent of the teens interviewed said they turn to parents for help in making ethical decisions. A surprising 83 percent turn to their friends. But how are other youngsters to give good advice if they don't learn from their parents a well-developed sense of right and wrong, and a healthy fear of getting caught? At the peak of the bull market, a New Jersey teenager ran afoul of regulators by touting stocks on the Internet. The boy's parents seemed willing to look the other way—and enjoy his ill-gotten gains—when what they should have done was pull the plug on his PC.

DEAR JANET

Q. Recently my son was invited to the movies. I talked to the other parent ahead of time, and we agreed that he would pay for the tickets and my son, Josh, would pay for the popcorn. When they got to the popcorn counter, however, Josh announced, "I think I'd like to save my money." The other dad ended up buying the popcorn.

When Josh got home, I told him I was disappointed in him because he was supposed to buy the popcorn to share with Sean.
A. I hope (but somehow doubt) that Josh was equally economical about helping himself to Sean's popcorn.

To avoid creating a foxy freeloader, you're going to have to work a little harder to drive home your point. Assuming that you gave Josh the money for the popcorn in the first place, he shouldn't have been allowed to keep it. If the money he saved was his, he can use it to treat Sean to the movies.

The next time your son is invited out, emphasize that buying popcorn is a requirement, not an option. And tell him that if he keeps this up, he'll get precious few return invitations.

As Peter's experience showed, small lessons can make a big difference in developing ethical behavior in a youngster. If you don't want an inside trader in the family, don't look the other way when your children pilfer grapes in the produce department. Don't do their homework for them to get them better grades. Don't raid the supply closet at work to keep them in pens and Post-it notes. Don't cheat on your taxes (or theirs). When they find something that's been lost, whether it's a wallet on the bus or a beach towel at the pool, make sure they turn it in.

You can't peer over their shoulders all the time, but you can make them feel guilty when they stray—even when they've grown up. Shortly after Peter's experience, I went to a local stationery store to buy cards and a Christmas ornament. When I got home, I realized that the clerk had forgotten to ring up the $17 ornament. I could have been home free. The store hadn't noticed its mistake, and I didn't even have a child with me for whom to set a good example.

But I couldn't forget how "cool" Peter thought it was to find an honest person. The next day I went back to the store and paid up.

Fear of Fundraising

They may not be as serious as corporate scandals and lapses in ethics, but plenty of everyday situations result in financial faux pas and awkward moments. Anticipating these moments helps both you and your children avoid embarrassment and hurt feelings.

Take, for example, the annual school fundraising season. It traditionally starts with gift wrap in the fall, runs through Girl Scout cookies in winter, and winds up with candy bars or potted plants in the spring. It's tough to tell who dreads it more—the parents who have to sell all this stuff or their colleagues at work who see them coming. "You're a prime target, especially if you don't have kids," one of my coworkers once grumbled.

Let me say in defense of fundraising events that the schools, athletic groups, and other organizations that sponsor them really need the cash. Over the years, all those candy bars have sent thousands of students on class trips and bought enough band uniforms to outfit the Russian army. Sometimes schools depend on fundraisers to get money for their day-to-day operations. Lots of people actually like to buy high-quality gift wrap or fresh citrus fruit.

And some children are born salespeople who thrive on the challenge. In California, I once met a Girl Scout who was so good at selling cookies that she could sweet-talk Ron Popeil into buying a Veg-O-Matic. It's also true that with concerns about safety, kids (or their parents) often feel a lot more comfortable knocking on doors in office building corridors than they do along neighborhood streets.

But if colleagues in the workplace are tempting targets, they shouldn't be sitting ducks. I'd like to propose a truce in fundraising wars at the office, with a code of conduct for sellers and buyers.

First of all, don't bring your children to work. Sure, you'll be told that it's good for youngsters to participate in the effort so they can take on personal responsibility, gain self-confidence, and learn about

---

DEAR JANET

Q. My 19-year-old son lives with his mother some distance away from me. My ex-wife told me she had given our son $200 toward books for college, but when he came to visit me, he admitted he had spent the money on clothes and asked me for more. He had to have books, so I gave him another $200. I always feel pressured to give him money, but it's easy to get extravagant when I only see him once in a while and I have to compress years into days.

A. I sympathize with your situation, but letting your son manipulate you isn't going to improve it. It sounds like you and your ex-wife are on speaking terms, so next time talk to her in advance and tell her that you will pay for school books or other extra expenses. She'll probably appreciate the financial help, you'll get the satisfaction of spending money on your son, and he'll lose the opportunity to double-dip.

DEAR JANET

Q. My brother, who is single, loves to buy presents for my two daughters, ages 10 and 7. The trouble is, his gifts aren't always in the best of taste. He goes for novelties, such as "gross-out" powder that turns your teeth black and T-shirts with slogans that are slightly risqué. I won't let the girls wear the shirts, but I feel guilty about getting rid of them.

A. Off-color teeth are one thing. Off-color shirts are quite another.

Let your brother have his fun with the gross-out powder. It's just the kind of slightly-naughty-but-not-forbidden treat that kids love and uncles are supposed to buy. But let him know that suggestive shirts are out of bounds because they cross the line between good clean fun and a dirty joke. If he must be a merry prankster, tell him to stick to whoopee cushions.

---

business. But let's face it: The real purpose of fundraising is to raise money, not a child's self-esteem. Cute kids are just a convenient sales tool. Entrepreneurial kids (accompanied by their parents) can sharpen their skills without offending potential customers by setting up a table outside the local supermarket, for example.

As long as your employer doesn't frown on selling stuff at the office, it's okay to tap your coworkers on your kids' behalf. But follow these rules:

- **Avoid cyberclutter.** Don't annoy your colleagues with general e-mail telling everyone what you're peddling.
- **Target your sales.** Most effective are personal appeals to three groups of people: those who have expressed interest in what you're selling, those who have been customers in the past, and those who owe you because you've already bought something from them.
- **Let the rest come to you.** Post a signup sheet or notice in some central area. One mom set out a box of

candy bars that her saxophonist son was selling for his band, along with this note: "Don't feel obliged, but feel free (and don't forget to leave $1)."
- **Don't exploit your position.** The higher up you are in the office hierarchy, the less latitude you have. People who work for you shouldn't feel pressured to buy just because you're the boss.
- **Thank your colleagues for their support**—and have your checkbook ready when they pay you a return visit.

Coworkers shouldn't feel obliged to buy anything, and parents shouldn't take offense at a polite "No, thanks." In fact, Mom and Dad themselves should always have the option of saying "No, thanks" to sales efforts and fulfilling any money-raising obligations by simply writing a check.

On the Road

Fundraising is a classic "sticky situation," and there are plenty of others that often catch parents unawares. Vacations, for example. Children tend to want to overspend on everything from souvenirs to junk food, and parents' resistance is low. After all, they are on vacation, and they want to avoid grumbling in the back seat of the car. But there are ways to keep the peace without busting the budget.

First, let me put in a good word for long car trips. Although parents dread the sound of sibling squabbling and the "Are we there yet?" chorus, it seems that children actually like family vacations. In one survey, children ages 7 to 12 were asked about their worst vacation experience. Most agreed with the response of one 9-year-old: "I don't think there could be a vacation I wouldn't like."

Children enjoy being with family—"Your parents seem nicer and less likely to punish you"—said one 8-year-old. And kids appreciate having a say in planning the trip: "Mom is cool—she always asks us where to go."

Take advantage of your family's good feelings to deal with money matters before they become a source of friction on the trip:

- **Lay out your game plan.** Tell the kids what you're willing to buy in the way of souvenirs—maybe one T-shirt for each of them or postcards from each stop. They'll have to use their own money for anything else.
- **Collect inexpensive souvenirs** that are easy to find and will still bring back pleasant memories of the trip after it's over—key chains, pins, or snow domes are a few that come to mind.
- **Give the kids their regular allowance** ahead of time (something that's easy to forget in the rush of preparations). That way they have pocket money and won't have to bug you. To avoid wasting (or losing) money, they should bring only as much as seems reasonable to spend.
- **Buy off your kids with this "fine" solution** to backseat rowdiness: Give each child a roll of coins at the start of the trip. Each time one of the children gets out of

---

DEAR JANET

Q. My husband and I have no children, but we have four nieces and nephews. When the kids come to visit, they expect us to shell out for all kinds of goodies, and their parents (my sister and her husband) go along with it. For holidays and birthdays, they suggest gifts for the kids—usually expensive ones. We feel we're being taken advantage of.

A. Even if you love the kids dearly, you shouldn't have to pay dearly to keep them happy. Be specific about the limits of your generosity, as in, "Let's split the cost of this meal 50-50."

When your sister makes helpful suggestions about what the children want for their birthdays, tell her politely that you would rather choose your own gifts and surprise the kids.

hand, collect a coin. (Use the accumulated kitty to buy an occasional family treat.)

Before embarking on a 35-state road trip with their two children, ages 9 and 7, one mom and dad told the kids they'd pay for patches and postcards at stops along the way. The kids had to buy other souvenirs with their special vacation allowance of $1 per day. Another family makes it a point to include snacks and desserts in their children's travel budget. "We will buy no snacks or desserts unless it is our choice, not because someone has asked," said Mom. "It's amazing how this system has virtually eliminated whining for this or that souvenir or food item."

Guest Etiquette

You can't always buy peace among siblings when you're on the road. As kids get older they appreciate companions their own age, so you may want to invite a friend as a buffer if that's feasible.

But bringing along a friend (or accompanying someone else) brings up another financial issue: To what extent should the host finance the guest's visit, and how much spending money should the child bring? I'm puzzled by the reluctance of parents to discuss who's going to pay for what when their child is invited as a guest. Perhaps they think it isn't polite, or perhaps they take for granted that the whole excursion will be a freebie. Both assumptions are misguided, and parents who make them can put the host and their child in an awkward position.

So here, then, are my rules for invitation etiquette:

■ **If your child is invited to accompany another child** on a trip, assume that the invitation includes transportation by car (and accommodations, if it's an overnight stay), but that travel by air or rail is your responsibility. Ask the host parents how much your child will need for admission tickets or other costs.

Far from causing embarrassment, raising the subject will clear the air.

■ **If the host parents offer to pay for meals,** tickets, or other expenses, accept graciously. But your kids should still have their own pocket money for incidental expenses.

■ **If the guest's parents ignore the subject,** it's perfectly proper for the hosts to bring it up, as in, "We'll be paying for Joanie's activities here at the beach, but there's a nice souvenir shop, so she might want to bring some money just in case she sees something she likes."

■ **Even if your child is lucky enough to be invited** by someone who's footing all or most of the bill, send your child with enough money to treat the host family to ice cream cones or breakfast out. Children need to learn the art of reciprocation. (See Kids' Questions on page 315.)

■ **Remind children to abide by the host family's** rules, to be helpful while they're houseguests, and to keep an eye out for something appropriate that they can send as a thank-you gift later.

Splitting the Tab

As a veteran of dozens of soccer matches and other athletic activities, I can attest that the real competition often occurs after the game, when the entire team descends on some hapless restaurant, confusion reigns, and the grown-ups fight not to get stuck with more than their fair share of the bill. To win this contest, you have several options:

■ **Skip the after-game meal** (tempting but not always practical).

■ **Suggest that you all go to a restaurant where everyone orders and pays separately** (my personal favorite).

■ **Swallow the cost along with your food** on the theory that over time it will all even out.

■ **Volunteer to divvy up the tab** and collect what everyone owes. That's a pain-in-the-neck job, but you get to stick somebody else—er, make sure no one tries to beat the check.

On that last point, I'd like to add another request for parents: If you choose not to go along, it's only good manners to send your child with enough money to cover his or her portion of the check. In our neck of the woods, $5 won't cover it at a table-service restaurant.

"Our Daughter Is a Softie . . ."

I occasionally hear from parents who worry that their children are too willing to lend money to friends who never repay them. "How can we break our daughter of this habit without seeming to be mean?" one mother and father asked me.

In reply, I told them about interviewing a 20-something young woman who had to seek credit

---

DEAR JANET

Q. My kids and I are always fighting about their messy rooms. I don't want to resort to bribery to get them to clean up, but what else can I do?

A. You could simply shut their doors. If you get along well with your children otherwise, and if the chaos doesn't seem to interfere with their schoolwork, think twice before you fight this battle.

But if the mess really bugs you, try cooperation rather than confrontation. Take the kids with you to buy brightly colored storage bins, labels and markers, and anything else that will make the job more appealing. Then set a time when you and they can tackle the clutter together, deciding what to toss and what to keep.

Sometimes children just need help getting organized and breaking down the task. Tell them, for example, to line things up on a shelf in size order or put them in drawers by category. Or divide their room into quadrants and clean one square at a time. Introduce them to the vacuum cleaner and the washer. You can make the job fun, too, by letting them rearrange furniture or asking a friend to help (you provide the refreshments). Maybe they can even make a few bucks by selling castoffs at a yard sale.

counseling to help repay the $7,000 she owed on three credit cards—including a $2,000 cash advance she lent to a friend and never saw again. The lesson here is not to worry about being mean; children need to be tough to protect their self-interest and their pocketbooks.

It can be hard for kids to say no to their friends, but one way to do it is to put the blame on you. Your daughter could tell her friends that you give her an allowance, out of which she has to save a portion and come up with her own spending money, so she doesn't have any left over to lend. Once her friends realize she isn't an easy mark, they'll stop trying to hit her up.

In response to the worried parents above, one reader wrote to tell me that after "a few bad experiences" in his own youth, he had adopted a policy of never lending money to friends unless he would otherwise be willing to give them the cash outright. "This policy has been successful for me and now for my children."

Borrowing (or lending) is just one way money can come between kids. Problems also arise when some children have more money to spend than others. If your children are the ones with less, they should be honest and tell their friends that their allowance has run out or that they're saving for something special. Having control of their own money should be a badge of honor. If the amount is limited, that gives them an incentive to come up with activities that don't cost much or to find ways to earn more.

If your kids are the ones with more cash, perhaps you should consider cutting back on their spending money. It's a temptation for them to flaunt it, and certainly their classmates will be happy to reap any of the benefits. But in the end nobody likes a showoff, and throwing money around won't buy friends.

Dealing with Divorce

Take all the parent-child financial conflicts you can think of, multiply them by two, throw in a few more for good measure, and you have per-

DEAR JANET

Q. My daughter's friend, Diane, was taking pictures before playing in a school band concert. She asked if I would pick up the camera from the back of the auditorium when the performance started and hold it for her. I agreed—and then completely forgot to do it. When we looked for the camera after the concert, it was gone.

Even though the camera was inexpensive, I felt awful and replaced it with one that cost $20. But Diane's mother wouldn't let her keep it because she said it was Diane's fault the camera was lost. Did I handle this wrong?

A. Because you agreed to take charge of the camera, you were at least partly to blame for its loss. And the pictures are gone forever.

Your inclination to replace the camera was on target, and the price you paid was reasonable. Diane's mother obviously wants to teach her daughter to act responsibly. But it's also a valuable lesson for children to see adults admit that they goofed and make restitution. Call Diane's mother and try again.

haps the stickiest issue of them all: kids and divorce. A marriage may end, but kids and money form the glue that will bind parents together. "Children of divorce know more about their parents' finances than any other group of children I've worked with," a family counselor once told me.

Conflicts fall into several categories.

The Santa Claus Syndrome

This is a common complaint of custodial parents, usually mothers, who resent it when their children return from a weekend visit with Dad wearing expensive sneakers and new CD headphones, and chattering about their trip to the amusement park. Mom is sorely tempted to tell the kids that if their father is that well-off, he can darn well afford to pay more in child support.

Bite your tongue, take a deep breath, and remember that criticizing your ex-spouse isn't going to work. Whatever bitterness exists between the two of you, your children can be fiercely loyal to both parents and will resist taking sides (although they're not above trying to exploit the situation to their advantage). "In a way, putting down the other parent is like putting down the child," said one family counselor.

Instead of going off on a tirade against your ex-spouse, tell your children that since the divorce, your financial circumstances have changed and that paying for day-to-day expenses doesn't allow a lot of room for splurges. Kids sometimes have short memories and may need a gentle reminder of the little extras you have purchased recently.

Also explain that parents have different ways of showing their love, and the absent spouse may simply be trying to make up for time he or she doesn't get to spend with the kids. It may leave you gritting your teeth, but when talking to your children you can afford to be generous toward your ex-spouse. If you really have a beef with your ex, you should discuss it with him or her, not with the kids.

And if he or she really is trying to buy off the children, they'll eventually pick up on that themselves. Counselors agree that children learn that a "real" parent is one who makes sure they brush their teeth, helps with homework, and offers love and guidance—which can be both of you.

If you really think you deserve more money, take your former spouse to court and tell it to the judge. Better yet, couples can short-circuit future problems by addressing as many child-related financial issues as possible in the divorce agreement. Do your children have special needs or gifts that will require extra expenditures? Who's going to pay for piano lessons? Is summer camp still in the picture? If the kids are approaching driving

---

DEAR JANET

Q. I thought it was cute when my children, ages 7 and 5, decided to make money by selling their old toys at a yard sale. But I was horrified when some of the things they wanted to sell turned out to be gifts from relatives. Fortunately, they priced the stuff so high that no one bought anything. How should I handle this the next time?

A. Your kids are to be commended for their entrepreneurial instincts. But they also need to learn a thing or two about social graces, one of which is not to sell the gift they got last Christmas from Great-Aunt Sally (especially if there's any chance at all that Great-Aunt Sally will come for a visit).

Next time help them choose which items are okay to put on the block. And suggest a realistic selling price so they don't get too discouraged. If you suspect that deep down they don't want to get rid of their treasures, mention other ways they can make money—by selling artwork (of their own creation) or even those old standbys, lemonade and cookies.

age, who's going to pay for car insurance? Who's responsible for college tuition? Margorie Engel, an author and speaker on families and divorce, recommends building into the divorce agreement a procedure for reviewing the settlement periodically through your lawyers to allow for changes in your children's health, growth patterns, or emotional needs.

In the real world, rewriting divorce agreements often isn't an option, especially when child support payments are spotty or nonexistent. If that's the case, get your kids to help brainstorm ways in which they can cut back on expenses or can contribute money or sweat equity to the household. Said one divorced dad with custody of three children, "I don't hide the time and money pressures from my kids. We work together to do the household chores, and they no longer beg me for toys I can't possibly afford."

DEAR JANET

Q. How would you suggest handling finances for a 13-year-old who spends most of her time with her dad and me (the stepmom), but her mom has primary custody? Her dad is paying child support, but this child is constantly asking us for money. She also expects us to buy her clothes whenever she wants them, and the mom just comes unglued whenever we mention to this child that we are paying child support.

Should we give her extra money when she can't get it from her mother? Sometimes she won't even ask her mom because she sees us as doing better financially. For this reason, she feels that we owe her more than just the child support that we pay her mother.

A. Divorced parents still share an interest in raising financially responsible kids.

Whether divorced or married, parents should never hand out money, buy clothing on demand, or let kids think you owe them something just because you're well off financially.

All parents, even divorced ones, should speak to their children with one voice. In your case, Mom and Dad should decide what they are willing to buy for their daughter and what she should be expected to pay for on her own. If Mom is already buying clothes, Dad needs to know that. If Dad wishes to supplement those purchases, Mom needs to know that. And they both should agree on a fixed allowance for their daughter—possibly with each contributing a portion—that she has to use for agreed-upon expenses, such as entertainment.

For children, the financial effects of divorce aren't always negative. As long as they're not burdened with the family's financial problems, they can be creative and responsible in finding ways to earn money and save up for the things they want to buy.

The Ransom of Red Chief Syndrome

This is a complaint of noncustodial parents, mainly fathers, who feel that they are already giving enough in child support and resent the fact that their ex-spouse isn't accountable for how she or he is spending the money. They can't understand why the children always seem to be shabbily dressed and in need of money for some school or sports activity. They cough up more cash, but they feel like a chump.

> **DEAR JANET**
>
> **Q.** My husband and I are divorced. Our kids live with me, but he pays child support so he says he should get to claim the kids as dependents on his tax return. Is he right?
>
> **A.** The law generally gives the dependency exemption for children to the custodial parent named in the divorce decree. If the decree doesn't name either parent, the custodial parent is the one with whom the children live for the greater part of the year. It doesn't matter which parent actually provides the majority of support.
>
> It's possible for your ex-husband to claim the kids as his dependents if the court decree gives him that right or if you sign a waiver, Form 8332, to shift the exemption to him. Otherwise, you, not he, should claim the children on your return.

Remember, children aren't above manipulating a situation like this to their advantage. It may be that the $20 your daughter says she needs for the class trip was supposed to come out of her allowance, which she spent instead on DVDs. One woman recalls that when her parents divorced, her younger brother managed to collect an allowance from both Mom and Dad. When her parents found out what was going on, they put a stop to it but only after a major shouting match with each other.

You need to get together with your ex-spouse and discuss, in civilized tones, what's going on. Do the children need things that weren't budgeted for? If so, who's going to pay for them? Who should be responsible for taking the kids shopping for new clothes?

One of the most creative ways of handling child support that I've ever heard of is for both parents to draw up a budget for their children's expenses and

DEAR JANET

Q. My company is laying off workers and I expect to get a pink slip. We'll have to cut back on spending, but I'm afraid my kids won't understand. How much should I tell them?

A.. Enough to be straight with them but not so much that you burden them with problems they can't handle. Saying nothing doesn't necessarily shield your children from unpleasant situations. You're bound to be more worried or tense, and they'll pick up on your cues. Better to be honest than to have them imagine things are worse than they are.

Tell them you'll have to cut back on spending while you look for a new job, but that in the meantime you have resources to see the family through. Children don't want or need to know all the details of your balance sheet. Reassure them that, hard times or no, they will have a roof over their heads and food on the table—and that things will get better. For elementary-school students, a couple of good books that deal with the subject of a parent losing his or her job are *Tight Times,* by Barbara Shook Hazen, and *Ramona and Her Father,* by Beverly Cleary.

open a special checking account, funded proportionately based on both their incomes. The checkbook goes back and forth with the kids, so both parents are responsible for handling expenses—and each knows what the other has purchased.

All this assumes that the parents are still on speaking terms. In fact, family counselors recommend that parents make it a point to communicate regularly about their kids, even if it's just a phone conversation. "Make a list of the things you're going to talk about and stick to it," advises one counselor. "If one of you deviates, the other can hang up." If hang-ups become the rule, you might seek the services of a divorce mediator. (Contact the Academy of Family Mediators, 5 Militia Drive, Lexington, MA 02421; 781-674-2663; or the Association for Conflict Resolution, http://www.acrnet.org.)

As a result of mediation, one couple reached a written agreement that they and their teenage daughter would discuss extraordinary expenses. "The three of us would decide who could do what and whether the thing should be bought in the first place," said the father. "We paid the mediator $900 to settle something $75,000 in legal fees hadn't settled."

You and your spouse may have split up, but you're both still parents with a common interest in how money is spent on your children. Getting involved in a bidding war is a lose-lose-lose situation. Instead, ask yourselves how you'd handle things if you were still together.

The Cinderella Syndrome

This is a phenomenon of blended families in which one spouse shows financial favoritism toward his or her own children. (Members of the spouse's family, such as grandparents, can be guilty of this as well.) Parents who buy a toy or a shirt for their own kids but not their stepchildren risk creating a tremendous amount of ill will that could easily be avoided with a relatively small outlay of cash. When Margorie Engel remarried, her husband's mother "opened her arms to my two daughters," she recalls. "My kids got birthday cards and valentines just like her own grandkids did. They got checks too. The checks were smaller, but the kids were never forgotten. It's not the amount but the thought."

In most cases, said Engel, stepparents tend to step in and provide financial support even when they're not legally obligated to do so. But if at any time you feel that your children are getting short shrift, you need to raise the point with your new spouse, who presumably is easier to communicate with than your former one was. Rather than simply complaining about the unfairness, it might be better to put your case in writing, listing expenditures on each child and suggesting ways they might be equalized.

At the other extreme, don't be infected by the Fairy Godparent Syndrome, in which an overeager stepparent showers the children with stuff in an effort to buy their affection. "It isn't going to work," according to one family psychologist. "The new parent is auto-

DEAR JANET

Q. Here's a question I'll bet you've never been asked before: How do you deal with a situation in which your children accuse each other of stealing their money? We had this happen with our three children—in particular, our two daughters accusing their brother (or his friends). We could never prove it was true, and we finally told the girls to keep their money in a locked box. Could we have handled things differently?

A. You're right. I've never been asked that question before. But that doesn't mean I don't have an opinion.

My gut tells me that lots of families face this situation at one time or another, and that usually the accusations are groundless. I suspect that in many cases what we have here is a variation of the usual sibling rivalry—"Mom, she hit me." "Did not. He started it, Mom." More than likely, the child who brings the charge has misplaced his or her money (or forgotten how much he or she spent) and is looking for a convenient scapegoat.

In any case, suggesting that your daughters keep their money under lock and key was a good idea. Not only does it remove a temptation, but it also helps them keep better track of their cash. Children should get into the habit of storing their money in a fun savings bank, or in something as simple as an envelope or a glass jar, even if stealing isn't an issue.

As an extra safeguard—if you felt one was necessary—you could have kept the boxes in your room. And you might have instituted a rule that any loose change or crumpled bills found in the laundry, on the kitchen counter, or otherwise unaccounted for become the property of Mom and Dad.

matically seen as an interloper, and if that person comes on like gangbusters, it's going to look awfully crass." Give the children time, not money.

KIDS' QUESTIONS

Q. "Can we invite Kathleen to go to the movies with us this afternoon?"
(Asked with Kathleen staring longingly over your child's shoulder)
A. It's okay to extend a spur-of-the-moment invitation, but be prepared to pay for your guest. Neither Kathleen nor her parents have planned for the expense and might not have enough money on hand to cover it.

For future reference, tell your children that if they want to take a friend on an excursion that costs money, they should call the night before to extend the invitation. That way you can tell the other parents if the treat's on you or, if not, what the approximate cost will be. That gives them an opportunity either to decline gracefully or to send their kids prepared to pay.

Q. "When two grown-ups go out to eat, why does one of them offer to pay and the other say no? If someone wanted to buy lunch for me, I'd sure let them."
A. Plenty of grown-ups would love to accept an offer of a free lunch too. But more than money is at stake here. You might call it a matter of table manners. Picking-up-the-check etiquette is something kids need to learn just as much as they need to learn not to slurp their soup or eat peas with a knife.

Explain to your children that treating a friend to a meal is a great idea. Maybe you'd do it because it's your friend's birthday or as a way of saying thanks for something nice that he or she has done for you.

But it's always best to make clear ahead of time that you're going to pick up the tab. Making the offer on the spur of the moment often puts the other person on the spot. Your friend doesn't know if you really want to pay or if you're just trying to be polite. That's why lots of adults turn down the offer of a free meal. Unless you've agreed in advance that one of you is going to treat, assume that you'll each be paying your own way.

If the other person strenuously insists on picking up the check, it's better to say yes than to make a scene over the spaghetti.

Q. "You told me to pay for the amusement park, but Mr. Haynes wouldn't let me. What should I have done?"
A. Before you scold your child for accepting some other parent's generosity, think about this: In any showdown between an adult and a child, the child's natural inclination is to back off. Teach your kids the art of reciprocation. If their host pays for their admission, your children could offer to treat everyone to ice cream, for example. It may not be an even exchange, but making the gesture is what counts.

When your kids are invited on an excursion, assume that the other family is only going to furnish transportation and that your kids will be taking care of their own meals and other expenses. If there's any doubt, discuss it with the other parents ahead of time. If they are going to pick up the tab, make sure your children have their own pocket money to buy souvenirs or other extras—and to treat everyone to ice cream.

If you're the one who's issuing the invitation, you can avoid any misunderstandings by telling the parents what you intend to pay for. And when your guests offer to buy you an ice cream cone, don't turn them down.

Money Smart Grandparents

When I first started writing about kids and money more than a dozen years ago, grandparents were the subject of a question within a chapter. Now they get an entire chapter of their own, as befits their growing role in the financial life of their grandchildren. Today's grandparents are healthier, wealthier, and longer-lived, and they're notorious for their generosity. One survey found that in a typical month, about half of all grandparents buy gifts for their grandchildren. And the gifts are substantial—about $80 per grandchild for major holidays, about $40 for birthdays, and about $20 for lesser holidays such as Valentine's Day.

In my experience, grandparents are increasingly interested in longer-term largess, such as encouraging their grandchildren to invest in the stock market or helping to pay for their college education. In extreme cases, grandparents have taken on the role of surrogate parents in bringing up their grandchildren.

But there's far more to a grandparent's role in a child's financial life than giving the child money. When it comes to teaching about money, forget the generation gap—grandparents are right in sync with their grandkids.

Case in point: I once judged an essay contest in which fifth, sixth, and seventh graders were asked, "Who in your life has been most influential in helping you learn about money and investing, and what have you learned?" Of the nine winning entries, three from each grade, five cited a grandparent.

For instance, Caleb C. wrote that his Great-Grandma Mary "believes that a person should save money to buy what he wants rather than use credit." Hillary V. cited her grandpa's favorite expression: "Spend some, save some, give some." Steven M. said he plans to "carry on my grandma's reputation to save, invest, and love the earnings." Wrote Sara S.: "What I have learned from my grandmother is that money invested will grow into more money, while money under the mattress will grow mold."

Spoiling the Kids Rotten

Even though Grandma's help is often welcome and appreciated—and sometimes even taken for granted—it also presents plenty of opportunities for conflict, or at least some awkward moments, among grandparents, their adult children, and their grandchildren. Perhaps the two most common conflicts are polar opposites. On one side are parents who worry that grandparents are spoiling their grandchildren by showering them with too many

---

DEAR JANET

Q. During the summer my children are often invited to spend a week with their grandparents. Should I expect Grandma and Granddad to pay for meals out and other activities, or should I send the kids with money to pay for themselves?

A. In general, the closer your relationship is to hosts who extend an invitation, the more likely they are to want to pay your kids' way. So you could expect grandparents to cover more expenses than, say, a friend's parents.

In any case, you ought to feel free to broach the subject in advance with your parents or parents-in-law. Even if they insist on treating your kids, however, the children should still have their own pocket money for souvenirs and gifts (for more on financial etiquette for guests, see Chapter 16).

DEAR JANET

Q. After I had told my children they absolutely, positively could not have a new video game system, their doting grandparents arrived for a visit and presented them with one. I felt put on the spot and accepted the gift. But now I'm seething. I feel I should have stood my ground and turned it down. What do you think?

A. There are certain niceties that have to be observed in life, and accepting a gift graciously is one of them.

But don't let it end there. Stop seething and follow this three-step plan:

1. Set limits on the time your kids can spend playing video games.

2. Have a polite but firm talk with the doting grandparents (or aunt, uncle, or godparent, as the case may be) and ask that next time they consult you before springing for a big gift. Tell them you'd like an opportunity to discuss what the kids need, want, and are allowed to have.

3. Sit down and play a game or two with your kids, compliments of Grandma and Grandpa.

---

goodies. At the other extreme are parents who take all those goodies for granted and even ask for more.

In the first situation, grandparents and their adult children need to strike a balance between the satisfaction grandparents get from buying stuff for the kids, and the parents' right to say enough is enough. After all, grandparents have been known to go overboard. For example, there was the grandmother who bought her granddaughter 55—count 'em, 55—new outfits, or the grandparents who sent their 5-year-old grandson his own television set and DVD player.

Grandparents, feel free to be spontaneous with small gifts. Or if you're coming for a visit, arrive with plans to do something together—make a meal, bake a batch of cookies, have lunch at a burger restaurant. One grandma made a habit of picking up her grandchildren at school and taking them out for "front-seat fries" (so named because whoever sat in the front seat got first dibs).

But consult with your adult kids ahead of time about major purchases. To keep gift giving under control, one mom began sending her own parents toy catalogs, circling a selection of items with different prices and letting Grandma and Grandpa choose what they'd like to give. "We've been getting great presents ever since," said Mom. Or parents can have their children keep a running wish list of things they'd like but won't necessarily get. On birthdays and holidays, gift givers can take their pick.

Instead of trying to guess what her grandchildren wanted, one grandmother got into the habit of taking them shopping individually and letting them choose, setting a price limit of $100 for the teenage girls and $50 for the younger boy. "The girls shopped with an eye on price. I had to tell them that if it costs $5 or $10 more and they really love it, don't look at the price," she said. "My grandson, on the other hand, tried to talk me into everything. By the end of the day I was completely exhausted." But her shopping sprees had an ulterior motive: the kids spent money, but she spent time with the kids.

Taking Grandma for Granted

Whereas some parents wish that grandparents would cut back, others apparently expect them to produce on demand. At birthday time the grandkids (or their parents) call Grandma to put in their order—sometimes an expensive item that's out of Grandma's price range. But Grandma worries that if she doesn't produce, she'll be on the outs with her grandchildren.

Grandma, stop fretting. If this ever happens to you, tell the grandchildren you'd prefer to surprise them with a gift of your own choosing. If they ask for something expensive, tell them that even though you can't afford to buy it, you'll be happy to contribute to their own savings fund—or better yet, pay them for doing extra work around your house. You'll be giving them a lesson in deferred gratification—a gift that grandparents are uniquely qualified to give.

And don't worry about alienating your grandkids' affection. What children really love are grandparents who take an interest in their activities, joke with them, and create special occasions or share special interests that don't need to cost much money. One grandfather made a scrapbook of favorite comic strips he reads to the kids when they come to visit. A grandmother regularly sends her grandson newspaper clippings about her hometown football team, of which her grandson is a big fan.

One grandma started a tradition of sending her younger grandchildren storybooks with a homemade tape of her voice reading the story (the kids particularly liked her directives to "turn the page"). For her college-age granddaughter, she bought a computer, and the two began exchanging instant messages.

The Check Is in the Mail

Grandparents who live hundreds of miles from their grandchildren often send checks for birthday and holiday gifts, and then worry that money is too impersonal a gift. Are children disappointed when they don't get "real" presents?

Not on your life. I don't know many children above the age of 5 or so who turn up their noses at

---

DEAR JANET

Q. Our grandson is an avid rock collector. For his ninth birthday, our daughter suggested that we buy him a rock tumbling kit for polishing stones. We did, and it set us back $109. Several months have passed, and he still hasn't used the kit. We really feel taken—especially after we went into a toy store recently and saw a toy rock tumbler for $29.95.

A. Your daughter's gift suggestion sounds like a thoughtful one that was made in good faith. Just because your grandson hasn't used the kit yet doesn't mean that he never will. Maybe he just needs the right rainy afternoon with nothing else to do. Or maybe he needs help with what could be a complicated apparatus for a 9-year-old. Offer your services next time you visit.

There's a second lesson here. Grandparents understandably want to buy the best for their grandkids, but unless you can guarantee the children's interest, it sometimes pays to get a less expensive item with a price tag that's more in line with the kid's attention span.

money. In the words of one 6-year-old, "Money is importanter than toys. I can buy things with it."

For very young children, checks aren't so much impersonal as they are useless. The kids can't play with them, spend them, or cash them on their own. If you're giving a small amount of money—say, $5 or $10—consider sending cash, or at least enclose a couple of crisp dollar bills with your check. One set of grandparents customarily sends each of their grandkids a $20 birthday check along with cash equal to the child's age, up to a maximum of $10.

Depending on how much you send, make it clear that your grandchildren should spend all or part of the money on something they like. Parents have a tendency to confiscate their kids' cash and checks for safekeeping, but what fun is that? My own mother has always enclosed notes with money gifts for her grandchildren. A sample: "Dear Claire: This check is for your birthday. Have Mommy buy something for you, or you can save it to put in your billfold. Daddy can change it all into ones."

I'd also like to salute money smart grandparent Mary McEwen of Nashville, Tennessee, who won a contest with a wonderful suggestion for creating inexpensive yet memorable presents for her eight grandchildren. During the holidays, Mary makes a coupon book for each grandchild. Each book includes 14 coupons, 1 for every month plus bonuses for Valentine's Day and the child's birthday.

Each coupon is redeemable for $5—but that's not the most valuable part of the gift. The front of each coupon is imprinted with words of wisdom from Mary, and the back has space for a thank-you note. To redeem the coupon, a grandchild must present it to Mary each month, recite the advice, and tell her what it means. Then the kids have to complete the thank-you note on the back. When they're finished, they get the $5 gift. For $70, Mary gives her grandchildren a year full of fun, lots of great memories, and painless lessons in both money management and manners.

Leaving a Legacy

The ordinary routine of holiday and birthday gift giving is one thing. But many grandparents are also concerned about passing on a longer-lasting legacy to their grandchildren. "The older I get, the less important it is that my house be clean and ready for guests," said Jackie S. "You'll find me out in the mud with the kids instead." The kids are her seven grandchildren. Each summer Jackie and her husband, James, take two children at a time on boating and camping excursions and "mystery trips" on weekends. They keep in touch with their out-of-state grandchildren by e-mail.

Their grandparents, said Tommy and Tara, are "most definitely cool"—an assessment that will no doubt be reinforced when they get older and learn how their grandparents have given them a head start on their future. After discussions with their three

---

BROACHING A TOUCHY SUBJECT

Your adult children may find it difficult to bring up the subject of your finances; aside from not wanting to confront your death, they don't want to seem nosy or greedy. Yet they need to know the location of financial documents, provisions of your will, or plans for succession in a family business. In general, openness is better—things left unsaid or not confronted in your life can become bombshells to family members in your will.

Consider naming one of your adult children as executor of your estate (although you may want to choose a neutral third party if selecting one child would strain family relationships or if you have doubts about your child's ability to fill the role).

You should draft a living will, which specifies your wishes regarding what type of medical care you want in case of serious illness, and execute a durable power of attorney for both health and financial matters so that an adult child (or someone else) is authorized to manage your affairs if you can't.

Note to adult children: If grandparents are reluctant to talk about their finances, you can take a gentle stab at it to see if you get a response. For example, mention that you've recently drafted or updated your own will. Or talk about a health emergency experienced by a friend or neighbor of your parents. Or send your parents copies of topical books or articles. "My mom always saves clippings for me, so it's time to turn the tables," said one woman.

grown children, Jackie and James decided that their estate should be split equally among all the grandchildren and the money earmarked for paying college expenses. "It's not as if we're skipping over our children, because the grandchildren's needs are also their parents' needs," said Jackie. "We worked hard so that our kids could get a college education, so by relieving our children of that we are giving them something."

Grandma and Grandpa have also arranged for automatic deductions from James's paycheck to be deposited into seven savings accounts, one for each grandchild, at their credit union. "It will be a little cushion for when they get to college," perhaps to pay for books or maybe a computer, said Jackie. She and James hope that their grandchildren "will get the idea that this is how our family operates—each generation gives a boost to the next."

Gifts That Last a Lifetime

Giving a boost to the next generation can be as simple as buying shares of stock as a gift. Don't worry that the children will think you're old-fashioned. Kids like to make money just as much as grown-ups do. Behind many a budding Wall Street investor is a grandparent who took the time to talk about his or her own interest in the stock market. In the essay contest I judged, Amy A. wrote that her grandparents "have been a good example to me. They have an investment fund for each of their grandchildren. Instead of buying me an expensive toy for my birthday, they put money in my account. They then buy me something smaller for my birthday, but I know my future is growing bigger every year."

For grandparents who want to help out with college bills, the easiest route is to pay the college directly. Direct payments for tuition, no matter how large, aren't subject to the federal gift tax. So you don't have to worry about limiting gifts to stay within the federal gift tax exclusion, which is $11,000 per recipient per

2008 12,000
2009 13,000

year, or $22,000 if your spouse joins in the gift. <u>Because the money doesn't belong to your children or your grandchildren, you still control the assets and have the flexibility to change your mind about how you want to spend them.</u>

If you own appreciated assets, such as stocks, that you'd have to sell in order to raise money for college, you might consider making a gift of the assets to your grandchild. If your grandchild sold the assets, any capital gains would be taxed at his or her rate, not yours. <u>In the case of a child who's still years away from college, grandparents might consider opening a Coverdell education savings account or a state-sponsored 529 college savings plan.</u>

DEAR JANET

Q. A grandfather I know has set up custodial accounts for his grandchildren. The accounts have paid for such things as braces and private schools. Now the 16-year-old wants to take driving lessons, a reasonable desire. But this is causing problems with the child's parents, who are divorced. The mother is asking for money from the custodial account for one lesson. But it is the family's belief that that will require follow-up lessons plus insurance or a new car.

The father wants his daughter to wait until her grades improve, also a reasonable desire. Another consideration is that the father's main time with the children is in transporting them to and from school, as the divorce settlement requires only that he be allowed visits on weekends. These school ferries expand his time. Will that disappear if the older child drives?

A. Let's sort this out. Whether the grandfather pays for driving lessons is one thing.

He'd almost certainly have to pay for a series of lessons, not just one. But he doesn't have to extend his generosity to insurance or a new car.

The father's desire to spend drive time with his children is a separate consideration. Just because the 16-year-old gets a driver's license doesn't mean she has to be entrusted with driving younger siblings to school.

The father can't keep his daughter in the passenger seat forever, but there's no law that says a child has to start driving when he or she turns 16. Parents have every right to make their kids wait till age 17 or later, when insurance rates come down or grades improve.

All things considered, the grandfather should steer clear of family conflict and at least wait till his granddaughter is older before tapping the custodial account.

If you can't afford to foot the bill for tuition, don't worry. That's just one cost of college, and help is welcome on many fronts. You might buy your college-bound grandchildren a computer, pay for a trip home for the holidays, or even volunteer your time to travel with them to visit schools before they make their selection.

The Second Time Around

Increasingly, grandparents are playing a more permanent role in the financial support of their grandchildren, with millions of children under the age of 18 living with their grandparents. Sometimes the stay is temporary—at least, grandparents hope it will be—when adult children come home to recuperate and regroup after a divorce, for example.

But children, even grown ones, have a tendency to settle in. I once received a letter from a couple whose daughter and two grandchildren had come home for what was supposed to be a limited stay. "But as time goes on we find we are doing more and more to support our grandchildren, such as buying them clothes and paying for school expenses," the couple wrote. "We don't mind helping out, but we're not wealthy. How should we handle this?"

Once children have recovered their bearings emotionally, don't feel guilty about broaching the subject of their leaving. If you can't face that alone, have a third party, such as a financial planner, do it for you or at least be there to back you up. "You have to get it off an emotional plane and articulate what's best for the older people given their economic situation," said Robert Strom, who has developed a nationwide educational program for grandparents. "In my experience, adult children aren't insulted by this."

Grandparents who do end up raising their grandkids often face serious financial challenges, such as paying legal fees in custody battles or getting health insurance. In the case of health insurance, for instance, employers can set any policy they want as to

---

DEAR JANET

Q. Over the past five years I have given each of my three granddaughters common stock worth approximately $40,000 at today's prices. Because they were minors, I listed their father—my son—as custodian.

When I asked the girls, all of whom are now 21 or older, to change their accounts into their names only, I found they had no idea how much they had in their accounts. My son was very evasive when I asked him why the girls hadn't seen their shareholder statements.

Come to find out he has been selling the stock to pay expenses, and their accounts are down to approximately $2,000. I'm sure much of the money went for the girls' education, clothes, transportation, and other needs. But my son has not offered an explanation or financial report.

I would like your opinion as to what we could do about this while keeping the family together. I feel deceived and betrayed by my son.

A. Your son's behavior may have been illegal as well as deceitful if he used his daughters' assets to pay his own expenses or to fulfill his legal obligations to his children. In either case they could take legal action against him. But that would hardly keep the family together.

You—and other generous grandparents—might have avoided this situation by not being so trusting, even of a family member. Instead of naming your son as custodian, you could have chosen an institution, such as a bank or brokerage firm. If there were any question of misuse of funds by a bank employee, for example, the bank would be responsible.

Because you intended to give substantial gifts to your granddaughters, it would have paid to set up a formal trust agreement. In such a situation, "I generally try to have two people as cotrustees—typically the grandmother, if the grandfather is making the gift, and one parent," said Martin Shenkman, an estate planning lawyer and author of *The Complete Book of Trusts* (Wiley, 2002). "If two people have to sign off on the trust's tax return, it's a lot harder for one of them to skip off with the money."

It's too late to take your son over your knee, and you may have to accept the loss to keep the peace. But you can press for a better accounting and rethink giving any more money to your son as part of your estate plan.

---

who's eligible for family coverage, and often employers extend benefits to anyone who qualifies as a dependent under IRS rules—meaning, for one thing, that you provide more than half of your grandchildren's support for the year. Not every employer is so generous, however, and if you're retired, Medicare doesn't include dependents. For more information on grandparents raising grandkids, contact the AARP

DEAR JANET

Q. I am starting a money-saving and education club with my six grandchildren, ranging in age from 3 to 12. What is the best course outline to set up? I want to make this fun, too.

A. What a great way to bridge the generation gap! Not only will your grandchildren benefit from the financial knowledge they'll gain, but you and the kids will also have a special activity that you enjoy together.

With that in mind, I'd suggest that you put more emphasis on having fun, and less on setting up a formal course outline. That's especially true because there's such a big difference in the children's ages.

Twelve-year-olds are by nature far more sophisticated about money than 3-year-olds. Although you could include the youngest, don't expect much in the way of understanding until a child reaches age 4 or 5. For that reason, I'd set up different activities (rather than formal lessons) for each age group and keep them simple. For preschoolers, focus on hands-on activities. Buy each child a fun savings bank that they can play with. To encourage them to save, help them choose an item they'd like to buy—a toy, book, or collectible—and tape its picture to the bank (or even to a colorful money jar).

Show them what different coins look like and tell them that each has its own value. Let them use coins to buy juice from a vending machine so they learn that money can be exchanged for other things. Start a collection of state quarters.

Once your grandchildren are in grade school, take them to the bank and help them open a real savings account. Explain that they can earn interest in exchange for keeping their money on deposit. Encourage them to save for larger but still tangible goals—a new baseball glove, video game, or article of clothing—and perhaps offer to match a portion of what they put aside. Play financial board games with them, especially classics such as The Game of Life and Monopoly.

Because you want this to be an ongoing experience, consider giving each child a weekly or monthly allowance from Grandma that the children can choose to spend or save for a larger purchase.

Finally, take them to the store for a lesson in smart shopping. Dollar stores are great for the young ones; older kids can learn how to compare prices and shop for sales. And think of all the priceless together time!

Grandparent Information Center, 601 E St., N.W., Washington, DC 20049 (202-434-2296); Grandparents United for Children's Rights, 137 Larkin St., Madison, WI 53705 (608-238-8751); or Grandparents as Parents, P.O. Box 22801, Lakewood, CA 90714 (562- 924-3996).

KIDS' QUESTIONS

Q. "The sweaters Grandpa sends for our birthday every year are always too small. Can we ask for money this time?"
A. Asking for money is tacky, but suggesting that Grandpa send money in lieu of another gift is a reasonable request.

You can explain to him that as the kids get older, it's difficult to buy things that fit and meet with their approval. If you don't want to make an out-and-out request for cash, suggest instead a gift certificate for a book-, music, or clothing store. Or remind Grandpa to include a gift voucher or some other proof of purchase so you can exchange the item for another size if it doesn't fit.

Who knows? Grandpa may actually be relieved. It's possible that for all these years the kids have been getting too-small sweaters or fire-engine pajamas because Grandpa felt obligated to send a gift but didn't know what to buy—and thought that sending cash would seem tacky. It isn't fair to let him keep frittering away his money on presents that aren't being used.

Remember, though, that the kids should always thank Grandpa for his thoughtfulness, even if the sweater is too tight.

Q. Why does Grandma Pearl give bigger presents than Grandma Rose?
A. You might be tempted to say "Because Grandma Pearl has more money." Honesty is a good policy, but don't make too big a deal about any difference in wealth. You may be more sensitive about it than the children, who are probably just being curious and not passing judgment. Remind them that the size of a present has nothing to do with the amount of love that comes with it.

write thank yous even if you don't like the gift — in a timely manner

Mission Nearly Accomplished

Politicians and the media are obsessed with family values. Bookstore shelves are crammed with volumes advising families how to acquire them. Americans, it seems, are on a crusade to find stability and set standards.

Inevitably those standards are going to involve money, because many of the values and virtues we want to pass along to our children touch on finances either directly or indirectly—thrift, self-discipline, generosity, responsibility, planning for the future. If children acquire those traits in the context of managing money successfully, they'll be able to use them to manage other aspects of their lives as well.

But no one can give you a secret formula for achieving family harmony or financial balance. The answer is within the grasp of any family. It's a matter of commonsense principles effectively communicated to your children. In the case of money, those principles include living within your means and recognizing virtue as its own reward. That so many families struggle with principles that seem so obvious is a sign of modern times, when outside influences and affluence can upset the delicate balance of family life.

My contribution is to offer suggestions on how to counter those outside influences. Some parents are already doing a great job and just need a pat on the back and a word of encouragement. Others have lost sight of basic values and need guidance about how to get back on track. Still others know exactly what they want to teach their children but are looking for practical suggestions on how to discuss sensitive issues involving money or answer awkward questions.

Raising Money Smart Kids has tried to provide the pat on the back, the gentle reminder, the practical advice. Back in Chapter 1, I observed that when children ask their parents about money, parents are tempted to offer one of three responses: Yes, no, or maybe. Here, in a nutshell, is my prescription for answering those questions more effectively:

- **Never say no** unless you mean it.
- **Never say yes** unless you want to.
- **Never say maybe** if you can think of a better response—and, having read this book, you can.

No, money doesn't grow on trees. But if you can plant the seeds of good money management and watch your children blossom into responsible adults, you'll have reaped a priceless harvest.

The Big Payoff

As I said early on, all the advice in this book has been used successfully by some parent but not always by me. People often assume that my own children are financial whizzes who check their stock portfolios daily, or that I hold forth on fiscal policy at the dinner table, or that my poor deprived children never get a dime from dear old Mom. To which I respectfully reply: Humbug!

For the record, my children have thus far shown no interest in the stock market (although I hope someday they'll thank their father and me for opening IRAs with their summer earnings). If I even attempt to lecture them about money, their rolling eyeballs make me dizzy. As for buying stuff for my kids, I can (sometimes) be a real softie.

What I have learned after more than a decade of writing about children and money is to forget the finger-wagging and simply be tuned in to the subject when it comes up—as it inevitably does when my kids and I are shopping for clothes or groceries, buying holiday gifts, opening a bank account, or discussing who's going to pay for the class ring or gas for the car.

As my children have grown, they have taught me as much as I've taught them, and here are some of the things I've learned:

- Don't push too hard or too early.
- Keep things simple.
- Give your kids money of their own to manage.
- Use common sense, and trust your influence with your kids.

Now that my own children are speeding toward adulthood—and (almost) independence—I'm also learning they're never too old to need help from a parent. And here's the most satisfying lesson of all: There *is* a payoff.

Waiting for the Dough

I discovered this as a result of a saga involving my eldest child, John, when he was a junior in college. In the spring of his junior year, John's debit card was stolen at school. He discovered and reported the theft within 24 hours—just about the time the card issuer began calling him regarding $700 worth of suspicious purchases the issuer had flagged at Kmart, Athlete's Foot, and Wendy's, among other stores.

Because John had reported the theft so promptly, the student credit union, where he had his checking account, promised to credit back the withdrawals. But months went by, and the $700 did not reappear in his account.

John fretted about the missing money—a huge loss for a basically broke college kid. Over the summer I suggested that he call the credit union periodically to deliver a polite reminder. He became chummy with a guy named Kyle, who told him that the credit union had to wait for Visa to authorize the reimbursement.

John eventually decided on his own that he might be better off with a bigger financial institution, so he went online to open a new checking account with a major Philadelphia bank. Back at school, he e-mailed me that he had finally received his money from the credit union—but it was $50 short.

What's more, he had used his new check card for the first time and was charged a $1 fee when he bought a $5 sub at a convenience store—even though, he said, the terms of his account stated that there was no fee for check card purchases. "I don't have that kind of money," he wailed. "I can't win."

Lending a Hand

Time for Mom to lend a hand. First, I explained to John that when you report a stolen debit card promptly, your maximum liability by law is $50, which is why the credit union had elected to hold on to that amount. As for the $1 transaction fee, I offered to call the bank on his behalf to get an explanation.

A friendly young woman named Kathleen told me something that even I didn't know: When you pay with plastic, merchants sometimes run a $1 test transaction to see if the card is valid. The $1 charge showed up when John checked his account online, but Kathleen assured me it would disappear. She also confirmed that John's check card purchases were free.

And then came the payoff for me: "I'm impressed that your son realized what happened," Kathleen volunteered. "I get calls from college kids all the time who don't have a clue about the difference between credit and debit cards. They tell me, 'I have a Visa card, so how can I be overdrawn?' I ask them if the card says it's a check card. 'Yeah,' they say, 'but it's Visa.'"

Softie Mom surprised John with a check for the $50 he had lost. It was a reward for being *my* money smart kid.

They're Back. Now What?

Chapter Nineteen

When I'm asked by interviewers—as I often am—why parents should bother discussing financial issues with their children, I tick off a number of reasons. First, you want your kids to grow up with a healthy attitude toward money and the ability to manage it. Second, you want to teach your children not just the value of a dollar but the values that go along with it—thrift, self-discipline, generosity, personal responsibility, and planning for the future, to name a few. Third, at a time when there's so much emphasis on Americans taking charge of their own finances—from saving for retirement to choosing health coverage—it's critical that young adults be financially literate. And fourth, you want to turn out financially independent adults who will not land back on your doorstep after they've left the nest. If you follow the advice in this book, your young adults won't feel shaky when it's time for them to test their wings.

For better or worse, young adults are taking a longer time to achieve financial independence. More than half of college seniors consistently report that they plan to return home after graduation. Recent U.S. Census figures show that 56 percent of men and 43 percent of women ages 18 to 24 live at home. In fact, demographers say parents shouldn't expect to have an empty nest until their last child turns at least 24.

A lot of young adults boomerang home after college while waiting for a job to come through or attending graduate school. Many, especially those who live near big (and expensive) cities, don't earn enough in their first jobs to be able to live on their own (at least in the

DEAR JANET

Q. My 23-year-old son is moving home. I need to find an agreement as to rules, helping out, and paying rent. Is there some kind of document to print out and sign?

A. You can easily draw up your own agreement, using the following points as a guide:

1. Jim will live in his old room beginning July 1 and will have saved enough money to move out by _____ (date).

2. He will pay $100 a month for his room and $100 a month for food, beginning with his second monthly paycheck.

3. He will be responsible for buying and caring for his own clothing, doing his own laundry, and purchasing items for personal use.

4. He agrees to wash the car every Saturday.

5. He will alternate cooking and grocery shopping with Mom.

6. He will contribute half the cost of cable TV.

7. He may play music and the television set in his room but agrees to keep the volume low after midnight.

8. He may not have overnight guests except by prior arrangement with his parents.

style to which they've become accustomed in their parents' home). Others come back to regroup after a change in their life, such as getting a divorce or losing a job.

By and large, parents are happy to have them. It's only natural for moms and dads to lend a hand to their adult children. And parents and kids get along much better than they did a generation ago. "Young people today are much more approving of their parents, and parents are more comfortable with the culture of their children," said one economist who has studied generational issues.

Recently while I was waiting in the green room of a TV studio, one of the other guests announced she was "thrilled" that her 23-year-old daughter would be moving back home. "I've really missed her," said Mom. A good friend of mine fervently wishes her son had come back after college instead of struggling to make it as a writer in New York City. "He would be in much better shape financially if he could have worked for a year and saved money on rent," she told me.

In fact, it wasn't so long ago that living at home, or returning after college, was the norm, as it still is in many immigrant cultures, observes Florence Kaslow, a family psychologist. Kaslow said that the "extreme emphasis on independence" in recent years has often had the effect of breaking family bonds. "Maybe this is back to a good attachment."

That's the goal, anyway. But you don't want to end up in the predicament of this father, who wrote me a long and thoughtful e-mail:

"How do you stop being a doting dad? My 30-year-old daughter is a perpetual student, with two master's degrees, and I have been paying her bills all along. I have been thinking about putting her on a fixed allowance that would reduce over time to zero, but she is almost finished with her PhD and I don't want to pull the plug (although I think I have been using this excuse for quite a while). I have not wanted her to work as a waitress in order to pay for her schooling."

This doting parent should put into practice the sensible solutions he's already come up with. Notifying his daughter that her days of living off Dad are numbered lets her adjust without cutting her off cold turkey. And if she needs to supplement her income by working as a waitress, why not?

Come Up with *The Plan*

But how do you avoid getting into such a situation in the first place? Two words: *The Plan*. If college students want to come back home after graduation (or if young adults return home for some other reason or never move out in the first place), that's fine—as long as both you and your children work out in advance the terms under which they'll move back and what they'll do once they get there. The Plan should address three key points:

1. HOW LONG YOUR CHILD WILL STAY. It needn't be a brief interlude, but it shouldn't be forever. If your child is at home while looking for a job, give him or her, say, six months to find one, with an option to renew. For a graduate student, a year or two would make sense. Not being firm enough on this point is one of the biggest mistakes parents make. If your child's stay turns out to be open-ended, you're more likely to resent the drain on your financial resources or the interference with your own plans. And hanging around too long isn't good for young adults either, because it simply postpones the inevitable day when they have to leave for good.

2. WHAT THE HOUSE RULES WILL BE. Even though you can't control your adult child's behavior as you did when he or she was 15, it's still your house. Setting a curfew probably isn't reasonable, but asking your kids to call if they're going to be really late (or not coming home at all) certainly is. Establish your own policy on smoking or overnight guests. Will the kids be expected to show up for dinner every night—or even cook it once in a while? With two teenagers and two boomerang adults living at home, one family assigned each of the children one night of the week on which to plan and cook dinner and clean up afterward. "It turned into a fun thing," said their dad. "The kids were very creative."

DEAR JANET

Q. Our 27-year-old son makes about $40,000 a year. He's paying off student loans and a car loan, and rent costs him $1,000 a month. He doesn't have much left over to save for a down payment on a house.

I'd like to help him out by giving him $10,000, but my husband and I are close to retirement, and I'm not sure we can afford it. I've considered asking him to move home for a year so that he could save money, but he's been on his own since college and I don't know if that's a good idea. Any thoughts?

A. This is a switch. Usually I give parents advice on how to get their kids to move out. But in your case I wouldn't object if you asked your son to move back in temporarily.

Don't even think about giving your son money if that would jeopardize your own retirement. At your stage of life, your own financial security comes first.

It would be best if your son could come up with the money on his own, and saving the $1,000 he's paying in rent every month would be one way to do it. He has already taken the initiative to live independently, so there seems to be little danger that he would take permanent root on your couch, especially if he wants to buy a place of his own.

You could charge him rent and put the money into a savings account on his behalf. He would still feel that he's paying his own way, and at the end of a year he'd have a tidy sum for a down payment.

If your son nixes the idea, leave it up to him to come up with a way to get the money. He could move to cheaper digs, look for a higher-paying job, moonlight after work or on weekends, or set up an automatic savings plan to build a down-payment fund. If he wants to buy a house badly enough, he'll find a way.

Don't overlook minor irritants, such as loud music or crumbs on the kitchen counter. And don't let kids fall back into their old habits. John and Justin, two boomerang brothers showing no inclination to leave home, somehow got the idea that they were doing their mother a favor by letting her do their laundry: "If she's fed up," Justin said, "she hasn't mentioned it." Speak up, Mom!

One of the best ways to make sure your kids don't settle in for the long haul is not to make things too comfortable. "Kids want freedom," said Jeffrey Arnett, a developmental psychologist at the University of Maryland. "Nothing puts a damper on having a sex life more than moving back home with Mom and Dad."

3. HOW MUCH YOUR CHILD WILL PAY. When kids come back home, perhaps nothing is a bigger bone of contention between them and their parents than the touchy subject of room and board. In one survey of 125 families with at least one adult child living at home, the parents interviewed said they were surprised that their children didn't automatically offer to pay rent.

Several fathers were particularly bitter about the situation. Said one, "Not asking for room and board was the single biggest mistake I have made with my five grown children, who freely move in and out" and also feel free to ask him for extra money when they run short of cash.

So, parents, if your young adults have a job, work out an arrangement for them to pay some amount of room and board. They probably won't be able to afford a market rent, but a nominal amount each month is reasonable. One family didn't ask for rent while their kids were looking for work, but charged 10 percent of their salary once they found a job. Another mom started with $20 a week, then gradually increased the amount over time. "Once it got high enough, my daughter figured she might as well move out and rent her own place."

Justin and John, those boomerang brothers, didn't object when their dad asked them to write down what they thought would be a fair rent. But then Dad blew it by not actually making them pay.

Follow through. If you don't need the money, put it aside for the kids so they can pay off debt or save for a security deposit on an apartment.

If they're earning money, young adults should also be paying their own phone bills and contributing to the cost of food, cable TV, and other household expenses. Kids with no income can provide in-kind payment by cooking or taking over the yard work. One mother, whose son moved back home while he completed a management training program, settled on $150 a month in rent. But she also expected her son to treat her to an occasional dinner out, pick up extra groceries, and help out around the house with such heavy-duty chores as painting and putting up storm windows. (Mom was willing to do the laundry.)

Whatever you agree on, it helps to write down the terms in a contract so everyone is working from the same page (for a sample, see the box on page 336).

Financial Advice for Parents and Young Adults

Having adult children move back home also raises financial concerns of a different nature. You can't tell your kids what to do anymore, but they still need help with real-world financial situations they may not have dealt with on their own. Here's advice on dealing with two topical issues: health insurance and credit cards.

Getting Health Insurance

In general, your kids are covered by a family policy as long as they're full-time students, sometimes up to age 25 (check the terms of your policy to be sure). After that, they often go without coverage because they're temporarily unemployed or working at entry-level jobs that don't provide insurance. Or they choose

---

DEAR JANET

Q. My daughter is going to turn 18 next year. She wants to go to school, get a job, and live at home, so we are turning our upstairs into an apartment for her.

My husband—my daughter's stepdad— threw me a curve. He said he doesn't want her ever to have sex up there. My daughter will be 18 and a young adult. I can hope that she will wait till her wedding night, but I try to live in reality most of the time. I feel this is an unfair thing to make her promise, especially when she will be paying rent. What do you think?

A. Hooo boy, I think I shouldn't touch this with a ten-foot pole. It's not strictly a financial question but also an issue of values, standards, and family relationships. When a stepparent is involved, those relationships are even more sensitive.

Nevertheless, I'm going to make a couple of points.

First, parents can make whatever rules they wish regarding behavior in their own home. Regardless of their age, children should play by the rules.

It's true that charging your daughter rent can change the nature of your relationship.

But it's not clear from your letter how formal a landlord-tenant relationship you will have. Will your daughter have a separate apartment, with her own kitchen facilities and a separate entrance, or are you simply expanding her old bedroom? Will she be paying a market rent or a token amount?

Even if she qualifies as a tenant, landlords can always attach conditions to a rental agreement—no pets, no smoking, no loud parties. In this case, your husband's condition would be tough to enforce unless he banned overnight guests.

If this arrangement is causing friction in your family even before it gets off the ground, maybe you should rethink the whole idea. Perhaps your daughter should board at school or move in with friends. If she stays at home, stop the remodeling and let her continue to live in her old room, where the rules will be more clear-cut.

Wherever she lives, all you can do is make your values and wishes known, and pray like crazy that she abides by them— or at least feels guilty if she doesn't.

---

not to buy coverage when it's available, betting on their own good health.

That's a big financial risk (especially because parents could be left with the tab in case of an accident or unexpected illness). And your kids do have alternatives even if they're not covered at work. For instance, they (or you) could continue their coverage on your group policy by picking up the premiums—an attractive option if your child has a serious medical problem that makes it difficult for him or her to qualify for other coverage. But if your child is in good health, you may be able to find less expensive insurance elsewhere. Compare the costs of the following alternatives:

- **A student health plan** from an insurer such as eHealthInsurance.com or Assurant Health (http://www.assuranthealth.com). Only full-time students can apply, but once covered they can keep the policy for as long as necessary after graduation.
- **A short-term policy** that will provide coverage until your kids start working or while they're between jobs. The biggest providers are Assurant Health and Golden Rule (http://www.goldenrule.com). eHealthInsurance.com sells several companies' policies.
- **An individual policy with a high deductible** of $1,000 or more. Your kids would have to pay that much out of pocket before the insurance kicked in. But they'd be covered in case of a catastrophic accident or illness. And in return for the higher deductible, premiums would be considerably lower.

In addition, if they purchase a catastrophic policy with a high deductible, they can take advantage of a health savings account (HSA). With an HSA, you can put the amount of the deductible—up to $2,600 for singles—in an investment account, get a tax deduction for your contributions, accumulate tax-free earnings, and withdraw the money tax free to pay out-of-pocket medical expenses, such as the deductible and copayments. Individuals who are young, healthy, and single are ideal candidates for HSAs. For help finding an HSA-eligible policy, see http://www.hsainsider.com and http://www.hsadecisions.org. You can compare several companies' policies at eHealthInsurance.com or search for a local agent at the National Association of Health Underwriters Web site (http://www.nahu.org).

Another option: If your child plans to work part-time while waiting to start graduate school or searching for a "real" job, look for a company that offers health benefits to part-timers. Some candidates: UPS, Wegmans Food Markets, Starbucks, Whole Foods Market, Trader Joe's, REI, and The Container Store.

Solving Credit Problems

"My daughter has come home from college with $2,500 in credit card debt," one worried mother wrote to me. "Should I insist she pay it off right away with her earnings, or let her continue to rack up high interest charges while she pays and pays just to teach her a lesson?"

Such a lesson is way too costly. It's best to pay off credit card debt as soon as possible, even if it means taking your child's wages yourself to make sure the bill gets paid. One father I know who found himself

---

DEAR JANET

Q. Our 23-year-old son graduated from college a couple of years ago. Since then he has been working as an underwriting trainee in New York City and living at home. He doesn't have college loans, and we gave him a car when he graduated.

Our expenses are very high, so we asked him to pay $200 per month as a contribution toward room and board. He claims we are being unreasonable. Are we? What recourse do we have?

A. Unreasonable? You want to charge your 23-year-old employed son $200 a month for rent in the New York City area, and he thinks that's unreasonable? Not only are you being reasonable, you're being downright generous.

Tell your son that your expenses are high and that you need him to help cover the costs. Then get out the apartment-for-rent ads and show him what he'd be facing in the real world. Tell him he can either pay you $200 in rent or pay some other landlord on the open market. Just be prepared to show him the door.

in a similar situation came up with another solution. He paid off the balance for his daughter, and then made her pay him back plus interest (at a lower rate than the card issuer would have charged). She paid him $35 a week—in cash—until the debt was covered.

It's predicaments like these that make me strongly urge young people not to get a credit card while they're still in college. Ironically, it can be tougher for them to get a major credit card after they've graduated than when they were in school. But they can get a Visa or MasterCard in a matter of months by following one of these strategies:

- Start with the bank where they have their checking account. If that institution also issues credit cards, it may be more receptive to an application from a customer, especially if your child is employed and hasn't bounced any checks.
- Get a credit card from a retailer or department store. These cards generally aren't a good deal—even with the discounts they offer on initial purchases—because interest rates tend to be high. But they're easy to get, and kids can build a credit history in six months to a year by making purchases and paying for them on time. Pay the bill in full each month, and the high interest rate won't matter. After 6 to 12 months of prompt payments, they should apply again for a Visa or MasterCard.
- Apply for a secured card, which requires cardholders to make a savings deposit equal to their credit line (for a listing of secured cards, go to http://www.cardratings.org or http://www.cardweb.com).

Your child should ask the issuer if he or she can eventually be upgraded to unsecured status. That way, your child can qualify for a lower rate and an increased credit limit without adding to the savings account.

Worst-Case Scenarios

Do things right, and after a pleasant sojourn you'll eventually bid a fond farewell to your money smart young adult. Postgrads in particular are usually eager to go once they've got their financial sea legs.

But what if the worst case happens, and your kids turn into freeloaders who show no inclination to get up off the couch, much less pay for the cable TV? Judging by my e-mail, the worst case is more common than you think:

- "My almost-24-year-old son pays us monthly room and board, but how do we get him to be responsible and clean up after himself? His dirty clothes are thrown on the floor. He leaves his clothes in the dryer for someone else to remove. He never puts dirty dishes in the dishwasher. He does not believe in making a bed after having slept in it. What can I do to get him to understand that these actions are not acceptable in our home?"
- "My daughter just turned 25 and lives at home with us. All she does is go to work, come home, eat, and sleep. Is there something we can do to get her out on her own or to make her do some things around the house?"

Each of these situations probably could have been prevented if the parents had followed the advice outlined in this chapter—laying down the rules before the kids moved in and, most important, following through. It still may not be too late to draw up contracts outlining their responsibilities around the house.

DEAR JANET

Q. I am 20 years old and live at home with my parents. They gave me a verbal agreement that so long as I was in school, I could live at home for free. They won't pay tuition, insurance, or anything else. Recently they requested that I start paying rent. Do you think that's fair?

A. I don't know your family's financial situation, but it does seem that you're carrying a heavy financial burden for a 20-year-old student—and you can tell your parents I said so. If you are indeed covering all those other expenses, I'd be inclined to give you a pass on the rent.

But these young people are 24 and 25 years old, and each of them has a job. At this point it's probably time for them to move on—and out. Which leads to one of the toughest questions of all, put to me by a desperate dad: "What is the proper way to evict my daughter if she refuses to pay rent or have any respect for the home?"

Simply by asking that question, it's apparent that Dad is avoiding confronting a situation that only he can handle. In each of the cases above, parents need to tell their adult children that the arrangement isn't working and they'll have to leave. Give them a time-table—say, six months—and check weekly to see what progress the kids have made toward finding somewhere else to live.

Will young adults listen to such an ultimatum? Yes, if they know you mean it. If you have a history of caving in, you may face more resistance. But it isn't healthy for either of you if you continue to play the role of enabler, conspiring to keep your adult children from growing up. They need an identity of their own and so do you, apart from being child and parent. In addition, as you get older you can't afford the financial drain of continuing to support them.

DEAR JANET

Q. I have a 29-year-old son who is pursuing an acting career in Los Angeles. He works hard but in temporary positions that always leave him short of cash or without a job. Naturally, he turns to me, his 60-year-old Pop, for financial assistance. Although it's obvious that giving him money is simply a temporary fix, it's emotionally very difficult to withhold money for food and shelter. What's a parent to do?

A. As a parent, I can identify with your inclination to support your son. But Pop can't commit himself to backing a son's acting dream forever, and your son shouldn't expect you to.

At age 29, he should reassess whether his dream is still realistic. At the very least, he needs steadier employment of his own between acting gigs. Set a time limit on how long you're willing to continue subsidizing him, then gradually cut back. You don't want to be supporting your son in your own retirement.

The late Lee Salk, who was a clinical psychologist and author of many books on family-related issues, once told me that if adult children resist leaving by an agreed-upon deadline, parents should "help them find a place to live, even if it's at a Y and even if you have to pay for the room yourself. You have to make it sufficiently uncomfortable to motivate them to do something without being cruel."

In the case of John and Justin, the freeloading brothers, their father finally got their attention by threatening to deposit their belongings on the curb.

Striking a Balance

With luck, you'll never have to resort to such drastic action. One reason you've taken the trouble to read this book is to make sure you don't. Giving your kids an allowance when they're 8 years old is no guarantee that they'll grow into mature, self-reliant adults. But money is such a powerful symbol that being able to manage it is seen as a good indication of being able to manage life.

That's probably because both require self-discipline, something that's tough to teach your kids in today's world of instant gratification. Yet money offers teaching opportunities that are unique and concrete—not just managing an allowance but also distinguishing between needs and wants, saving for future purchases, juggling work with other responsibilities, resisting the temptations of TV advertising. In mastering these skills, your kids are mastering life—which is, after all, an exercise in setting priorities, working toward goals, and striking a balance.

Questions or comments? Contact Janet at moneysmartkids@kiplinger.com.

Index

Share the message!

Bulk discounts
Discounts start at only 10 copies and range from 30% to 55% off retail price based on quantity.

Custom publishing
Private label a cover with your organization's name and logo. Or, tailor information to your needs with a custom pamphlet that highlights specific chapters.

Ancillaries
Workshop outlines, videos, and other products are available on select titles.

Dynamic speakers
Engaging authors are available to share their expertise and insight at your event.

**Call Kaplan Publishing Corporate Sales at
1-800-621-9621, ext. 4444,
or e-mail kaplanpubsales@kaplan.com**

KAPLAN PUBLISHING